THE NEW
MAYO CLINIC
COOKBOOK

THE NEW
MAYO CLINIC
COOKBOOK

Eating Well for Better Health

FOREWORD

Donald Hensrud, M.D., and Jennifer Nelson, R.D., Mayo Clinic

RECIPES

Cheryl Forberg, R.D., and Maureen Callahan, R.D.

PHOTOGRAPHS

Sheri Giblin

WELDON
OWEN

CONTENTS

6   FOREWORD

9   Elegantly Simple Ideas for Healthy Eating
A NEW PHILOSOPHY OF COOKING • HOW TO USE THIS BOOK
VEGETABLES & FRUITS • CARBOHYDRATES • PROTEIN & DAIRY
FATS • ARE YOU EATING WELL? • HOW TO PLAN A MENU

28   Vegetables

72   Fruits

98   Salads

120   Soups

140   Pasta & Grains

180   Beans & Legumes

214   Fish & Shellfish

246   Poultry & Meat

266   Desserts & Drinks

292   GLOSSARY
298   GENERAL INDEX
300   RECIPE INDEX

FOREWORD

It's a common belief that what tastes good and what's good for you are two different things. "At home we try to eat only healthy foods," a friend said recently at a party, as the appetizers were passed. "You know what that means—less flavor."

But as this new cookbook elegantly demonstrates, that doesn't need to be the case. What you eat does directly affect your health, as research has shown and our own clinical experience has confirmed. At the same time, we've come to believe that eating well and eating healthfully can and should go hand in hand. Food that is deliciously rich in flavor doesn't have to be bad for you. Moreover, cooking with nutritious ingredients—such as vegetables, fruits, and whole grains—may actually lower your risk of developing many diseases, from heart disease to cancer. That's an important concept behind this remarkable new collection.

These recipes make up the first cookbook based on the Mayo Clinic Healthy Weight Pyramid. Although the pyramid was designed as a weight-control tool, it can easily be put to use by everyone interested in eating wisely for better health. This cookbook adheres to the pyramid's principles while showcasing the foods that provide an array of valuable nutrients. It also offers an abundance of great-tasting dishes that are low in "energy density"—that is, they're filling and satisfying but low in calories—so you can eat well without feeling either guilty or deprived. We know you'll enjoy cooking from this collection of versatile recipes, and we are excited to be able to offer them to you.

Donald Hensrud, M.D., and Jennifer Nelson, R.D., Mayo Clinic

ELEGANTLY SIMPLE IDEAS FOR HEALTHY EATING

Today we understand that good food is crucial to good health. People who regularly enjoy meals made with a variety of healthful ingredients may lower their chances of developing heart disease, diabetes, many kinds of cancer, osteoporosis, obesity, age-related vision loss, digestive disorders, and more.

But deciding to eat wisely doesn't mean having to seek out unusual "health foods" such as broccoli sprouts and wheatgrass. It doesn't mean denying yourself desserts and other delicacies you love. And it doesn't have to be complicated or expensive. After all, some of the world's most tempting dishes are built around the season's best produce, prepared simply to bring out the fullest flavors.

You'll find plenty of recipes here to match your tastes. Simple or fancy, familiar or adventurous, the 150 dishes in this book are designed to be as satisfying as they are good for you. In the following pages, you'll discover a whole new philosophy of cooking and eating, along with helpful suggestions on menu planning and practical insights on the ingredients themselves. To eat well, just help yourself.

Flavor comes first. The new approach to eating well is full of enjoyment and satisfaction.

Fava Beans with Garlic, page 186

A NEW PHILOSOPHY OF COOKING

We enjoy an abundance of food choices unparalleled in history—just take a look around in the aisles of a well-stocked supermarket. With so many great ingredients near at hand, it's easy to prepare dishes that not only are a pleasure to serve and eat but also benefit your health. The new kitchen philosophy, reflected in the recipes in this book, is to say yes to the extraordinary variety of foods that taste terrific and are terrific for you.

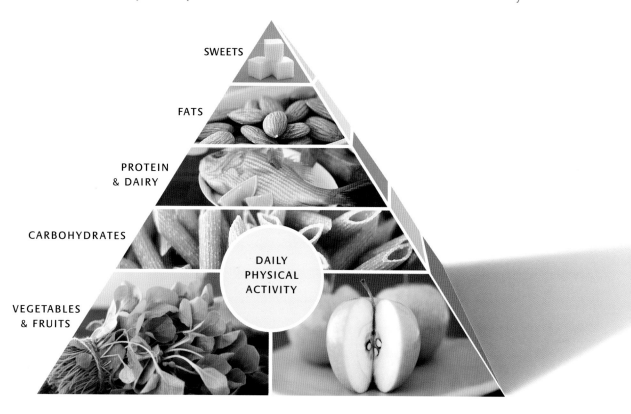

The Mayo Clinic Healthy Weight Pyramid

The Mayo Clinic Healthy Weight Pyramid depicts the nutritional principles of a regular pattern of healthy eating. The pyramid's sections represent six food groups. The bigger the block, the more servings of foods from that group you'll want in your meals.

To build everyday menus, start at the pyramid's wide base with ample vegetables and fruits. Include plenty of high-fiber carbohydrates, then add smaller portions of protein, dairy, and fats. Go easy on sweets, and remember to engage in daily physical activity.

Note that unlike some of the other healthy-eating pyramids you may have seen, this one rests on a broad foundation of vegetables and fruits, rather than grains and other carbohydrates, in recognition of the many scientific findings about their health benefits.

If you regularly enjoy a variety of colorful produce, from green broccoli and lettuce to red tomatoes and purple blackberries, you have already taken an important step toward choosing a full mix of health-promoting foods.

How the Pyramid Can Help

People who adopt the pyramid's principles may lower their risk of several major illnesses, including heart disease, diabetes, and some cancers. How?

Vegetables and fruits are endowed with fiber, vitamins, and antioxidants, which many experts believe work together to help fight disease. Fruits, in addition, can satisfy urges for sweets that are loaded with fat and sugar. Carbohydrates—and especially whole grains—are likewise abundant in disease-fighting nutrients, and there are many healthful protein sources.

Even the right kinds of fats can help fend off illness, although they're high in fattening calories—the reason they're given less space in the pyramid.

Why It's Called the Healthy Weight Pyramid

Without an eye to how much we eat, it's easy to take in too many calories, the food energy that fuels our bodies. Excess calories turn to excess weight, a health concern of its own.

To maintain a healthy weight, try to eat only as much food as your body can burn in a day—1,600 to 2,800 calories' worth for most adults. The servings goals in the chart at right and on the following pages are based on a daily average of 2,000 calories.

Within that calorie goal, it's easy to build daily meals using the pyramid's food groups. Aim for the targets at right—but don't worry if you don't always hit them. The ultimate goal is a long-term pattern of healthy eating.

Daily Servings Goals

VEGETABLES	5 or more per day
FRUITS	5 or more per day
CARBOHYDRATES	8 per day
PROTEIN & DAIRY	7 per day
FATS	5 per day

ABOVE LEFT **Baby Beets and Carrots with Dill,** page 30 ABOVE RIGHT **Yogurt-Almond Ice Cream, page 282**

HOW TO USE THIS BOOK

To help you cook, serve, and eat a well-balanced variety of healthy foods, each of the 150 recipes in this book is accompanied by two types of charts. The first includes a breakdown showing exactly how far one portion of a dish moves you toward reaching the Daily Servings Goals that accompany the Mayo Clinic Healthy Weight Pyramid. The second chart is a standard nutritional analysis that includes calories (kilojoules) and several other important nutrients (see the page opposite). Remember, it's not a single dish or menu but your overall eating pattern that matters most to your health.

THE SERVINGS DIAGRAM

Near the top of every recipe page in this cookbook, you will see Pyramid Servings, a graphic with several rows of shaded and unshaded circles that visually represent how the dish stacks up against the Daily Servings Goals listed in the chart at the bottom of page 11.

○ Unshaded circles show the total daily servings recommended.

● Shaded circles show how many servings are in each recipe portion.

◄ Left arrows with Vegetables and Fruits mean there's no daily limit.

Pyramid Servings	
VEGETABLES	◄ ○○○○○
FRUITS	◄ ○○○○●
CARBOHYDRATES	○○○○○○○○
PROTEIN & DAIRY	○○○○○○○
FATS	○○○○●

 SWEETS SMALL IS BEAUTIFUL

You won't find daily servings goals for sweets, even though they're at the pyramid's peak. That's because candies, cakes, and other goodies made with refined sugar or honey and usually lots of fat are high-calorie foods that are low in nutrients—what experts call empty calories. That's not to say they're off-limits. To satisfy your sweet tooth in moderation—up to an average of 125 calories a day—simply enjoy fresh fruit sometimes instead of prepared sweets or desserts. Here are some helpful calorie counts.

1 teaspoon sugar
16 calories (67 kilojoules)

1 homemade oatmeal-raisin cookie
65 calories (272 kilojoules)

4 ounces (125 g) sorbet
95 calories (398 kilojoules)

1 ounce (28 g) semisweet chocolate
135 calories (566 kilojoules)

THE NUTRITIONAL ANALYSIS

The recipes in this book incorporate a range of healthful ingredients and also meet widely accepted standards for heart-healthy menus. To present complete nutrition data, each recipe has been analyzed by a registered dietitian, enabling you to compare these dishes to those in other cookbooks and to packaged foods in the market. Nutrient measurements are in grams (g) and milligrams (mg). All measures have been rounded to the nearest whole number.

PER SERVING	
calories	101
kilojoules	423
protein	2 g
carbohydrate	13 g
total fat	5 g
saturated fat	1 g
monounsaturated fat	2 g
cholesterol	3 mg
sodium	184 mg
fiber	2 g

- Any ingredient labeled "optional" is counted in the nutritional analysis.

- Wine and other alcoholic beverages included as ingredients are optional.

- Where two or more ingredient choices are given, only the first is counted.

- Measurements reported as < 1 (less than one) fall between 0 and 1.

BELOW Photos, such as this pear and watercress salad, show one portion. The Pyramid Servings chart depicts how many standard servings each portion provides. The Per Serving box below it has full nutrition facts.

Grilled Pear and Watercress Salad

Its interesting, assertive flavor makes watercress a perfect partner for the richness of blue cheese and sweetness of spiced walnuts. This first-course salad can also be served as a main course for lunch.

SERVES 6

2 tablespoons firmly packed brown sugar

1 tablespoon water

¼ teaspoon freshly ground pepper

2 tablespoons chopped walnuts

2 firm yet ripe pears, cored and cut into 6 lengthwise wedges, peel intact

Lemon juice for brushing

FOR THE VINAIGRETTE

2 tablespoons fresh lemon juice, plus extra for brushing

1 tablespoon rice vinegar

1 teaspoon Dijon mustard

1 tablespoon minced shallot

¼ teaspoon salt

¼ teaspoon freshly ground pepper

1 tablespoon extra-virgin olive oil

6 cups (7 oz/220 g) watercress sprigs, tough stems removed

3 tablespoons crumbled blue cheese

Prepare a hot fire in a charcoal grill or preheat a gas grill or broiler (grill). Away from the heat source, lightly coat the grill rack or broiler pan with cooking spray. Position the cooking rack 4–6 inches (10–15 cm) from the heat source.

In a small frying pan over medium heat, combine the brown sugar, water, and pepper. Cook, stirring constantly, until the sugar dissolves. Stir in the walnuts, reduce the heat to low, and cook for 30 seconds. Remove from the heat and quickly spread the nuts on a sheet of parchment (baking) paper or a plate. Set aside and let cool.

Brush the pear wedges with lemon juice and arrange on the grill or broiler pan. Grill or broil, turning once, until the pears begin to brown, 3–4 minutes total. Set aside.

To make the vinaigrette, in a small bowl, whisk together the 2 tablespoons lemon juice, the rice vinegar, the mustard, and the shallot. Add the salt and the pepper and whisk to blend. While whisking, slowly add the olive oil in a thin stream until emulsified.

In a large bowl, combine the watercress and blue cheese. Pour the vinaigrette over the salad and toss gently to mix well and coat evenly.

To serve, divide the salad among individual plates. Place 2 pear wedges on each, then sprinkle with the walnuts.

Pyramid Servings

VEGETABLES

FRUITS

CARBOHYDRATES

PROTEIN & DAIRY

FATS

PER SERVING	
calories	101
kilojoules	423
protein	2 g
carbohydrate	13 g
total fat	5 g
saturated fat	1 g
monounsaturated fat	2 g
cholesterol	3 mg
sodium	184 mg
fiber	2 g

Salads 105

VEGETABLES & FRUITS

To enjoy a full mix of foods that help fight disease, pick a variety of colors from the produce bin.

It's hardly news that vegetables and fruits are good for you. The real news is why. More and more is being learned about how fresh produce, beyond its rich stores of vitamins, can supply us with substances that help ward off many illnesses.

Strong evidence is stacking up that people who regularly eat generous helpings of vegetables—a *variety* of vegetables—run a lower risk of developing heart disease, a leading killer of American adults.

Most vegetables are loaded with the antioxidants beta-carotene and vitamin C. Antioxidants can be important because these substances play a role in inhibiting molecules called oxygen free radicals, which can damage healthy cells in the body. Vegetables are also key sources of essential minerals, including potassium and magnesium. Many are rich in health-enhancing fiber, and some even have calcium. In addition, researchers have identified another class of substances in these plants—called phytochemicals—that appear to offer some protection against cancer.

Tomatoes, for instance, get their red color from lycopene. Studies suggest that getting plenty of this phytochemical may lower prostate cancer risk.

Fruits, like many vegetables, have an abundance of fiber—not to mention a long list of healthful antioxidants, including vitamin C.

Researchers have also discovered that many fruits contain generous amounts of flavonoids, substances that apparently work together to lower the risk of cancer and heart disease. Some fruits and vegetables contain the antioxidants lutein and zeaxanthin, which may help guard against certain conditions related to aging, such as the eye disease macular degeneration. Oranges, for instance, are rich in a little-known compound called beta-sitosterol, which is believed to help lower blood cholesterol.

These many benefits are the reason why under the pyramid there's no limit on the daily servings of fresh and frozen vegetables and fruits. The exceptions are dried fruits and fruit juices, which measure for measure are much higher in calories than the fresh fruits from which they're made.

ABOVE LEFT Red grapes are an abundant source of a phytochemical called resveratrol, thought to help shield against cardiovascular disease and cancer.

ABOVE RIGHT Cruciferous vegetables such as broccoli and cauliflower are rich in compounds that are believed to help fend off certain forms of cancer.

THE GOAL

5 OR MORE VEGETABLE AND 5 OR MORE FRUIT SERVINGS A DAY

A vegetable serving is about 25 calories; a fruit serving, 60 calories.

GETTING THERE

A DAY'S MENU MIGHT INCLUDE (EACH ITEM IS 1 SERVING)

1 tomato or 8 cherry tomatoes   1 orange, apple, or banana

2 cups (2 oz/60 g) salad greens   ½ grapefruit

½ cup (2 oz/60 g) carrot sticks   ½ cup (3 oz/90 g) grapes

1 cup (2 oz/60 g) broccoli florets   1 cup (4 oz/125 g) berries

IN THE KITCHEN

A FEW RECIPES TO TRY

105 Grilled Pear and Watercress Salad

127 Fresh Tomato Soup with Crispy Herb Toasts

63 Steamed Summer Squash with Warm Leek Vinaigrette

90 Ambrosia with Coconut and Toasted Almonds

75 Mixed Fresh Berries with Ginger Sauce

LEFT Each ½ cup (2 oz/60 g) of Mixed Fresh Berries with Ginger Sauce, made with fresh blackberries, raspberries, and red currants, equals 1 fruit serving.

 DAILY ACTIVITY BE A MOVER AND A SHAKER

Staying active is just as important as nutritious food for a healthy life. Physical activity burns calories, making it easier to maintain your weight. It's also just plain good for you, strengthening your heart and lungs. Inactivity, on the other hand, is clearly dangerous—perhaps as bad for you as smoking. As little as 30 minutes to an hour of brisk walking most days of the week can help reduce your risk of heart disease and stroke as well as several forms of cancer.

- Take a brisk walk around the neighborhood in the morning or in the evening after work.

- Find activities you enjoy, such as hiking, swimming, tennis, throwing a Frisbee, playing catch with the kids, or hitting the trail with the dog.

- Do errands on foot when you don't have to drive.

CARBOHYDRATES

The message is nearly this simple: the less refined a high-carbohydrate food, the better it is for you.

Think of every kind of food containing carbohydrates laid out in a line. At one end are whole wheat, oats, and brown rice. In the middle sit white flour, white rice, potatoes, and pastas. And at the far end are cookies, candies, and soft drinks.

The foods in that spectrum incorporate all three kinds of carbohydrates: fiber, starch, and sugar. It's not hard to point to the healthy and less healthy ends—unrefined whole grains on one hand, refined sugar on the other.

But the health pros and cons of many items in the middle aren't so clear. Rice, pasta, bread, and potatoes can all shift depending on how they're produced and served.

Consider, for example, white and whole-wheat (wholemeal) breads. Both begin as whole grains, as do both white and brown rice. That whole, or unrefined, grain consists of outer layers, known as the bran and germ, surrounding a starchy interior, called the endosperm.

Whole grains abound with nutrients. Some are rich in vitamin E, an antioxidant that has many health benefits. Others contain estrogenlike substances that may help protect against some forms of cancer.

During processing, however, the bran and germ are refined away, and by the time the wheat has become a loaf of white bread or the rice is a steaming white side dish, they've lost many of their vitamins and almost all of their fiber. That's why it's wise to choose whole-grain breads, pastas, and cereals, and to serve brown rice instead of white.

Similarly, the edible skins so often removed from potatoes and sweet potatoes are full of nutrients and fiber. (For more information, see Fiber: The Two Types and Their Benefits, opposite.)

Of course, many foods not always thought of as carbohydrates contain amounts of fiber, starch, and sugar—not only vegetables and fruits but also sweets, chips, and other processed products. The key word is *whole*. Generally, the message is that simple: The less refined a carbohydrate food, the better it is for you.

ABOVE LEFT Bulgur, a type of cracked wheat, is a quick-cooking grain with a mild, nutty flavor and a respectable amount of fiber. It's good in side dishes and salads.

ABOVE RIGHT Whole-wheat (wholemeal) pastas are made from wheat grains with their germ intact. They contain more vitamins and fiber than standard pastas.

THE GOAL

8 CARBOHYDRATE SERVINGS A DAY, MOSTLY WHOLE GRAINS

A carbohydrate serving is about 70 calories.

GETTING THERE

A DAY'S MENU MIGHT INCLUDE (EACH ITEM IS 1 SERVING)

½ cup (1½ oz/45 g) dry cereal

½ whole-grain English muffin

1 slice whole-grain bread

½ cup (3 oz/90 g) cooked bulgur

2 cups (½ oz/15 g) fat-free popcorn

½ cup (3 oz/90 g) cooked pasta

½ medium baked sweet potato

1 oatmeal cookie

IN THE KITCHEN

A FEW RECIPES TO TRY

173 Three-Grain Raspberry Muffins

158 Savory Buckwheat Pilaf with Toasted Spices

170 Whole-Grain Buttermilk Biscuits

159 Barley and Roasted Tomato Risotto

162 Double-Corn Spoon Bread

LEFT Made with wheat bran, oats, and corn-meal, each Three-Grain Raspberry Muffin equals 1 carbohydrate serving, plus 1 fruit serving from the fresh berries.

FIBER THE TWO TYPES AND THEIR BENEFITS

Grains, fruits, and vegetables all contain a kind of carbohydrate, called fiber, that resists digestive enzymes and cannot be absorbed by your body. There are two main types—insoluble and soluble—both of which are found in varying amounts in most plants. Fiber-rich foods slow the uptake of glucose, thus helping to keep blood sugar steady. Research suggests that the more fiber people get from grains, the lower their risk of type 2 diabetes. Experts recommend consuming 20 to 35 grams of fiber a day.

- Insoluble fiber—called roughage—is coarse, indigestible plant material best known for promoting healthy digestion. Many common vegetables and whole grains contain significant amounts.

- Soluble fiber—vegetable matter that turns goopy in water—helps lower blood cholesterol levels. Barley, oats, and beans contain notable amounts.

PROTEIN & DAIRY

Many beans and legumes have so much protein that when they're on the menu, meat can step aside.

Protein is essential to human life. Your skin, bone, muscle, and organ tissues are made up of protein, and it's present in your blood, too. Protein is also found in foods, many of animal origin.

But despite what you may have heard, it's not necessary or even desirable to eat meat every day.

Although rich in protein, many cuts of chicken, turkey, beef, lamb, and pork are too high in saturated fat and cholesterol to include regularly for good health (see Healthful and Harmful Fats, page 21). Remember, other everyday ingredients, including low-fat dairy products, seafoods, and many plant foods, furnish protein, too.

Legumes—namely beans, lentils, and peas—are also an excellent source. And because they have no cholesterol and very little fat, they're great for fill-ing out or replacing dishes made with poultry or meat.

Unlike meat, beans actually help lower the "bad" form of cholesterol, and the minerals they contain help control blood pressure.

You may also have heard that beans' protein is "incomplete," meaning it lacks essential amino acids that meats provide. That's true; among legumes, only soybeans have protein containing all the amino acids. However, the missing nutrients are plentiful in other plant foods, so people who lighten up on meat can easily get all they need.

Likewise, nonfat and low-fat dairy products, especially milk and yogurt, can help supply you with protein. On top of that, milk is rich in calcium and is fortified with vitamin D, which helps bodies absorb that important bone-building mineral.

And don't neglect fish and shellfish. Not only are they fine protein sources, but some supply omega-3 fatty acids. Research suggests that most people would benefit by eating at least two servings of fish a week.

The omega-3 fats in fish help lower triglycerides, fat particles in the blood that appear to raise heart disease risk, and may also help prevent dangerous heartbeat disturbances known as arrhythmias, improve immune function, and help regulate blood pressure.

ABOVE LEFT Yogurt, like milk and other dairy products, delivers protein and calcium, a bone-building mineral that may also help protect against high blood pressure, stroke, and kidney stones.

ABOVE RIGHT Lentils—including the French green variety here—are legumes, plants whose seeds develop in pods. Legumes are a source of folate, or folic acid, a B-vitamin that helps prevent some birth defects.

THE GOAL

7 LOW-FAT PROTEIN AND DAIRY SERVINGS A DAY

A protein serving is about 110 calories.

GETTING THERE

A DAY'S MENU MIGHT INCLUDE (EACH ITEM IS 1 SERVING)

1 cup (8 fl oz/250 ml) low-fat milk	2 ounces (60 g) lean beef
1 cup (8 oz/250 g) nonfat yogurt	3 ounces (90 g) fish or shellfish
¼ cup (1¼ oz/40 g) feta cheese	½ cup (3 oz/90 g) cooked beans
½ cup (4 oz/125 g) tofu	1½–2 oz (45–60 g) skinless chicken

IN THE KITCHEN

A FEW RECIPES TO TRY

213 Classic Boston Baked Beans

254 Braised Chicken with Mushrooms and Pearl Onions

201 Sesame-Crusted Tofu

243 Pan-Braised Swordfish with Feta

282 Yogurt-Almond Ice Cream

LEFT Each helping of Pan-Braised Swordfish with Feta provides 2 protein and dairy servings and contains enough golden raisins (sultanas) to provide 1 fruit serving.

SODIUM A LIGHT HAND WITH SALT

Sodium occurs in many foods, from milk and cheeses to crackers and pie. It also makes up about 40 percent of table salt. For some people, consuming too much sodium raises blood pressure, and elevated blood pressure increases the risk of heart disease and stroke.

Nutrition experts suggest aiming for no more than 2,400 milligrams of sodium a day—about what's in a teaspoon of salt—from processed foods and from what you add at the stove and table.

- Keep an eye out for the hidden sodium in breakfast cereals, dairy products, chips, and breads.

- Instead of heavily salted canned and processed foods, choose fresh or frozen fish, poultry, or meat, and make your own soups.

- Go easy with the salt shaker. Your tastes buds will adjust.

FATS

Avocados, olives, nuts, seeds, and vegetable oils, used wisely, can actually help prevent heart disease.

The idea that all fat is bad is so widespread that many people are surprised to hear health experts say some kinds can be beneficial. Studies over the past two decades have confirmed that people who replace much of the animal fat in their meals with liquid vegetable oils stand a good chance of bringing down their blood cholesterol levels, thereby lowering their risk of cardiovascular disease.

Other findings suggest that people who favor foods made with liquid oils, such as canola and olive oils, over ones with solid shortenings and margarines may derive similar health benefits.

Meats, seafoods, and many dairy products can be fatty, of course, which is to say that some foods traditionally considered proteins can add significant fat to a day's meals. Fats from all sources—including those listed in the pyramid's sweets and protein and dairy sections—are best held to 9 to 13 servings a day, with 5 of those from foods in the pyramid's fats section.

Keep in mind, however, that the pyramid's fats section addresses only the high-fat ingredients that are typically *added* to a day's meals. These include salad dressings, cooking oils, butter, and high-fat plant foods, such as avocado, olives, seeds, and nuts.

Most of these foods are good for you. Nuts, for instance, contain a type of oil that helps keep hearts and arteries free of harmful deposits. They also deliver many other key nutrients, including protein, thiamin, niacin, folate, selenium, and vitamin E.

But while nuts and vegetable oils may be beneficial, they're best used in moderation. A tablespoon of peanut butter weighs in at nearly 100 calories; a tablespoon of olive oil, 140. In other words, the goal is to use *just enough* of these naturally high-fat ingredients.

On the other hand, some fats are best kept to a minimum. Saturated fat, largely from foods of animal origin, has long been known to raise LDL ("bad") cholesterol. Now research has shown that foods high in trans fats, common in processed foods, also raise LDL cholesterol in addition to lowering HDL ("good") cholesterol (see Healthful and Harmful Fats, opposite).

ABOVE LEFT Almonds, like other nuts, have abundant protein, making them a fine companion for vegetables in stir-fries, casseroles, and other dishes.

ABOVE RIGHT Avocados are a rich source of beta-sitosterol, a compound that may help lower blood cholesterol.

THE GOAL

5 ADDED FAT SERVINGS A DAY, MOSTLY MONOUNSATURATED

A fat serving is about 45 calories.

GETTING THERE

A DAY'S MENU MIGHT INCLUDE (EACH ITEM IS 1 SERVING)

7 almonds

4 walnut or pecan halves

1½ teaspoons peanut butter

1 tablespoon sunflower seeds

9 large olives

3 slices avocado

2 teaspoons mayonnaise

1 teaspoon canola or olive oil

IN THE KITCHEN

A FEW RECIPES TO TRY

177 Nutty Berry Granola

114 Avocado Salad with Ginger-Miso Dressing

118 Fennel and Leeks with Roasted Onion Vinaigrette

279 Almond and Apricot Biscotti

188 Chickpea Polenta with Olives

LEFT Chopped Niçoise olives give Chickpea Polenta with Olives its 1 serving of added fat. Chickpea (garbanzo bean) flour contributes 1 serving of fat-free protein.

HEALTHFUL AND HARMFUL FATS EASY DOES IT

Eating wisely used to mean cutting back on all fat, but health experts now believe that some varieties of fat, used lightly, can actually be beneficial.

- Monounsaturates, in nuts, avocados, canola oil, and olive oil, help lower blood levels of LDL cholesterol, a cause of heart attacks and strokes. They also help keep arteries clear by maintaining levels of helpful HDL cholesterol.

- Polyunsaturates, including corn and soy oils, also keep harmful LDL cholesterol levels down. Among them are the heart-healthy omega-3 fats in fish, flaxseed, soybeans, tofu, walnuts, and walnut oil.

- Saturated fats, from meats, full-fat dairy products, and tropical oils, raise blood levels of LDL cholesterol. Limit these fats by choosing low-fat dairy products and by combining lean meats with vegetables and grains.

- Trans fats, found in hydrogenated vegetable oils in cookies, crackers, and deep-fried foods, may be even more harmful than saturated fats.

ARE YOU EATING WELL?

To see how your current food choices match up with the new philosophy of cooking and eating, answer the ten questions below and note your responses. Instead of an exact rating or score, you'll receive a broad view of the way you cook and eat—a view that can guide you toward making some basic choices for better health.

1 How many servings of vegetables do you eat in a typical day? (A serving is 2 cups [2 oz/60 g] of leafy greens, 1 cup [2 oz/60 g] of broccoli florets.)

   A four or more
   B two or three
   C one or none

2 How many servings of fruit do you eat in a typical day? (A serving is usually one small piece.)

   A three or more
   B two
   C one

3 How often does fish appear on your weekly menu?

   A two or more times
   B once
   C rarely or never

4 When you shop for bread, pasta, and rice, how often do you buy the whole-grain versions?

   A always
   B sometimes
   C rarely or never

5 Which of the following are you most likely to use?

   A canola or olive oil
   B corn oil
   C butter or margarine

6 How often during a typical week do you eat out and order hamburgers, cheese-rich pizzas, or sandwiches layered with meat and cheese?

   A not more than once
   B two or three times
   C four or more times

7 A dinner of 2 cups (12 oz/375 g) of cooked pasta in a tomato sauce is how many servings?

   A four
   B not sure
   C one

8 What kind of milk do you usually drink?

   A fat-free milk or soy milk
   B 1 or 2 percent
   C whole milk or none

9 What are you most likely to reach for when you're thirsty?

   A water
   B fruit juice
   C regular sweetened soda

10 What's your usual snack?

   A nuts, fruit, or carrot or celery sticks
   B energy bars or other "healthy" sweets
   C potato chips, pretzels, or cookies

A **IF YOU COUNT MOSTLY A'S** among your answers, congratulations. You're well on your way to healthy eating.

B **IF YOU COUNT MOSTLY B'S AND C'S,** your menu could use a tune-up. You'll find plenty of tips and great-tasting recipes in the following pages.

C **IF YOU ANSWERED WITH MOSTLY C'S AND FEW A'S,** it's time for some fresh ideas about good food. See Ten Easy Steps to Healthier Eating, opposite.

TEN EASY STEPS TO HEALTHIER EATING

You don't need to turn your life upside down to eat for better health. A few simple changes can make a big difference in the nutrition profile of your daily meals.

1 Have at least one serving of fruit at each meal and another as snacks during the day.

2 Switch from low-fiber breakfast cereal to lower-sugar, higher-fiber alternatives.

3 Lighten your milk by moving down one step in fat content—from whole to 2 percent, for instance, or from 1 percent to fat-free.

4 Cook with olive, canola, or other vegetable oil instead of butter or margarine whenever you can.

5 Choose coarse whole-grain breads, switch to brown rice, and experiment with whole-wheat (wholemeal) flour when baking.

6 Include at least two servings of vegetables at lunch.

7 Have at least two servings of vegetables at dinner.

8 Have fish as a main course at least twice a week.

9 Serve fresh fruit for dessert.

10 Replace high-calorie sweetened beverages with water, iced tea, or unsweetened fruit juices.

ABOVE LEFT **HAVE FISH AS A MAIN COURSE AT LEAST TWICE A WEEK.** Seafood dishes such as Mahimahi with Macadamia Nut Crust, page 219, not only provide protein but also furnish omega-3 fatty acids, polyunsaturated oils that appear to help prevent heart ailments.

LEFT **SERVE FRESH FRUIT FOR DESSERT.** Colorful desserts such as Tropical Fruits with Mint and Spices, page 80, make it a pleasure to add servings of fruit to your daily menu. Fruits are rich with compounds that help fend off cancer and heart disease.

HOW TO PLAN A MENU

This book is designed to make it easy to put balanced meals on the table. Not only does every dish meet sound nutrition guidelines, but the recipes are also arranged to correspond generally to the Mayo Clinic Healthy Weight Pyramid. You'll find nine different dinner menus in the next few pages, each showing its pyramid servings of vegetables and fruits, carbohydrates, protein and dairy, and fats. Use the following principles to plan your own weeknight dinners and weekend celebrations.

REMEMBER THE PYRAMID

As a way to approach nutrition goals, try to include more than one serving from most food groups in most menus. In thinking about fruits, for instance, aim for at least one serving at breakfast, lunch, and dinner, plus two more as snacks during the day. To get plenty of vegetables every day, build lunches and dinners that incorporate two or three servings each. Getting there is actually easier than it sounds, because many dishes contain more than one vegetable serving (for examples, see page 15).

ABOVE Each helping of Salade Niçoise with Tapenade, page 226, balances protein-rich grilled tuna with plenty of steamed fresh green beans and roasted new potatoes.

CHANGE WITH THE SEASONS

Although it's possible to find bell peppers (capsicums) in January and summer squash in March, they may not be truly fresh. Whenever you can, look for recently harvested produce—asparagus, peas, and cherries in spring; peaches, sweet corn, and tomatoes in midsummer; apples, pears, and beets in fall—and you'll enjoy the freshest and most nutritious foods available. Even in winter months you can shop for freshness by seeking out winter squash, red cabbage, and root vegetables such as carrots, turnips, and sweet potatoes.

PLAN BY THE WEEK

Don't get hung up on hitting exact daily servings goals. If on Monday you don't reach your fruits target, add an extra serving or two on Tuesday. Boost your weekly greens and whole grains totals by making some lunches and dinners vegetarian—a strategy that will also help you move toward healthful proteins, such as beans and lentils, tofu, and low-fat dairy products.

MAKE PLEASURE A PRIORITY

While it's gratifying to know you're reaching nutrition targets, number crunching can become a chore. Good food is one of life's great pleasures, which is to say that eating well is not about deprivation. It's about enjoying superb ingredients with remarkable health benefits. So when cooking, take advantage of flavors, colors, and textures to present pleasing dishes.

BE ADVENTUROUS

Discovering new foods and flavors is part of the joy of cooking, so don't be afraid to explore unfamiliar recipes. Some of the world's most intriguing ingredients—quinoa, edamame, bok choy, bulgur—are as healthful as they are delicious. Bear in mind that the best way to get the full range of health benefits is to plan menus with a wide variety of nutritious foods.

FLAVORS OF ITALY

Fennel and Leeks with
Roasted Onion Vinaigrette
118

Barley and Roasted
Tomato Risotto
159

Artichokes alla Romana
55

Almond and Apricot Biscotti
279

ABOVE A make-ahead salad of fennel and
leeks anchors a grain- and vegetable-rich
dinner with a traditional Italian flair.

Pyramid Servings per Menu

VEGETABLES ● ● ● ● ●
FRUITS ○ ○ ○ ○ ○
CARBOHYDRATES ○ ○ ○ ○ ○ ● ● ●
PROTEIN & DAIRY ○ ○ ○ ○ ○ ○ ●
FATS ○ ○ ● ● ●

SPRING CELEBRATION

Asparagus with
Hazelnut Gremolata
50

Sea Bass en Papillote
224

Fava Beans with Garlic
186

Strawberry Balsamic
Sorbet
284

ABOVE Fresh asparagus, which appears
in markets in early spring, sets the mood
for a relaxed dinner.

Pyramid Servings per Menu

VEGETABLES ○ ○ ○ ○ ●
FRUITS ○ ○ ○ ● ●
CARBOHYDRATES ○ ○ ○ ○ ○ ○ ○
PROTEIN & DAIRY ○ ○ ○ ○ ● ● ●
FATS ○ ○ ○ ● ●

ASIAN SAMPLER

Fresh Spring Rolls
with Shrimp
229

Sesame-Crusted Tofu
201

Yellow Lentils with Spinach
and Ginger
203

Sweet Ginger Tisane
289

ABOVE Tofu and yellow lentils, both
sources of protein, star in this menu.
Shrimp (prawns) play a supporting role.

Pyramid Servings per Menu

VEGETABLES ● ● ● ● ●
FRUITS ○ ○ ○ ○ ●
CARBOHYDRATES ○ ○ ○ ○ ○ ○ ●
PROTEIN & DAIRY ○ ○ ○ ● ● ● ●
FATS ○ ○ ○ ● ●

SUMMER SUPPER

Yellow Pear and Cherry
Tomato Salad
112

Warm Potato Salad
39

Grilled Flank Steak Salad
with Roasted Corn
Vinaigrette
117

Yogurt-Almond Ice Cream
282

ABOVE Vine-ripe tomatoes and sweet corn
are some of the season's finest offerings.
They add fresh flavor to this menu.

Pyramid Servings per Menu

VEGETABLES   ◀○○●●●
FRUITS   ◀○○○○○
CARBOHYDRATES   ○○○○○●●●
PROTEIN & DAIRY ○○○○○●●
FATS   ●●●●●

MIDDLE EASTERN FLAVORS

Fattoush
115

Spicy Beef Kabobs
252

Bulgur and Chickpeas
with Preserved-Lemon
Vinaigrette
156

Tropical Fruits
with Mint and Spices
80

ABOVE This menu is rich in grains and
spices. The simple bulgur and chickpea
(garbanzo bean) dish is boldly flavored.

Pyramid Servings per Menu

VEGETABLES   ◀○○○○○●
FRUITS   ◀○○○●●
CARBOHYDRATES   ○○○○○●●●
PROTEIN & DAIRY ○○○○●●●
FATS   ○○○○○●

WARM WEATHER FARE

Watermelon-Cranberry
Agua Fresca
291

Steamed Summer Squash
with Warm Leek Vinaigrette
63

Swordfish Tacos with Lime
and Cilantro
241

Mixed Fresh Berries
with Ginger Sauce
75

ABOVE This casual menu is easy to prepare. The agua fresca makes a refreshing
change from iced tea or lemonade.

Pyramid Servings per Menu

VEGETABLES   ◀○○●●●
FRUITS   ◀○○●●●
CARBOHYDRATES   ○○○○○●●
PROTEIN & DAIRY ○○○○○○●
FATS   ○○●●●

WINTRY WEEKEND SUPPER

Beef Stew
with Fennel and Shallots
264

Baby Beets
and Carrots with Dill
30

Two-Potato Gratin
64

Baked Apples with Cherries
and Almonds
96

ABOVE Serve Baby Beets and Carrots with
Dill to put a dash of color into a cold-
weather dinner centered on a beef stew.

Pyramid Servings per Menu

VEGETABLES	◀ ○ ●●●●
FRUITS	◀ ○○○ ●●
CARBOHYDRATES	○○○○○ ●●●
PROTEIN & DAIRY	○○○○○○ ●
FATS	○○ ●●●●

TASTE OF THE MEDITERRANEAN

Pita Wedges with Green
Olive Tapenade
52

Cannellini Beans
with Wilted Greens
193

Ratatouille with Roasted
Tomato Vinaigrette
109

Fresh Figs with Walnuts
and Mascarpone
92

ABOVE Crisp whole-grain pita wedges
topped with green olives and herbs start
this dinner full of colorful vegetables.

Pyramid Servings per Menu

VEGETABLES	◀ ○○ ●●●
FRUITS	◀ ○○○ ●●
CARBOHYDRATES	○○○○○○○ ●
PROTEIN & DAIRY	○○○○○○ ●
FATS	○ ●●●●

ENTERTAINING EVENING

Fresh Tomato Soup
with Crispy Herb Toasts
127

Roasted Rack of Lamb
with Parsley Crust
262

Sugar Snap Peas
with Fresh Marjoram
61

Orange Slices
with Citrus Syrup
76

ABOVE Lean lamb chops make an elegant
dinner when paired with tender vegetables
such as sugar snap peas or asparagus.

Pyramid Servings per Menu

VEGETABLES	◀ ○○ ●●●
FRUITS	◀ ○○ ●●●
CARBOHYDRATES	○○○○○○○ ●
PROTEIN & DAIRY	○○○○ ●●●
FATS	○○○○○

Vegetables

In their pleasing variety of flavors, colors, and textures, vegetables are the foundation of healthy eating.

30 Baby Beets and Carrots with Dill

33 Green Beans with Red Pepper and Garlic

34 Wilted Greens with Warm Balsamic Vinegar

36 Eggplant with Toasted Spices

37 Creamed Swiss Chard

39 Warm Potato Salad

40 Grilled Portobello Mushrooms with Thyme and Garlic

42 Sichuan Broccoli and Cauliflower

45 Butternut Squash and Plantain Mash

47 Roasted Root Vegetables with Cumin and Coriander

48 Grilled Radicchio

50 Asparagus with Hazelnut Gremolata

52 Pita Wedges with Green Olive Tapenade

54 Braised Kale with Cherry Tomatoes

55 Artichokes alla Romana

57 Garden Peas with Fresh Mint

58 Baked Acorn Squash with Pine Nuts and Garlic

61 Sugar Snap Peas with Fresh Marjoram

63 Steamed Summer Squash with Warm Leek Vinaigrette

64 Two-Potato Gratin

66 Brussels Sprouts with Shallots and Lemon

67 Braised Celery Root

69 Pan-Braised Onions with Rosemary

70 Broccoli Rabe with Toasted Garlic

Baby Beets and Carrots with Dill

Red and yellow baby beets, particularly those varieties with striped flesh, make this dish special. If you can't find them, full-grown beets and carrots will also work. Simply cut them into small pieces.

Pyramid Servings

VEGETABLES	◀○○○○●
FRUITS	◀○○○○○
CARBOHYDRATES	○○○○○○○○
PROTEIN & DAIRY	○○○○○○○
FATS	○○○○●

PER SERVING	
calories	68
kilojoules	285
protein	1 g
carbohydrate	8 g
total fat	4 g
saturated fat	1 g
monounsaturated fat	2 g
cholesterol	3 mg
sodium	261 mg
fiber	2 g

If the beet greens are still attached, cut them off, leaving about 1 inch (2.5 cm) of the stem intact. In a large pot fitted with a steamer basket, bring 1 inch water to a boil. Add the unpeeled beets, cover, and steam until tender, 20–25 minutes. Remove from the pot and let stand until cool enough to handle, then peel and cut into quarters. Set aside and keep warm.

Check the pot, add water to a depth of 1 inch if necessary, and return to a boil. Add the baby carrots, cover, and steam until tender, 5–7 minutes. (If the carrots are varied sizes, cut the larger ones into halves or thirds for even cooking.) Remove from the pot.

In a large bowl, toss the carrots with the butter, olive oil, lemon juice, and chopped dill. Add the beets, toss gently to combine, and transfer to a serving dish. Serve immediately, garnished with the dill sprigs.

1 lb (500 g) red and yellow baby beets, about 1½ inches (4 cm) in diameter

½ lb (250 g) baby carrots, peeled

2 teaspoons butter

1 tablespoon extra-virgin olive oil

1½ teaspoons fresh lemon juice

2 teaspoons chopped fresh dill, plus sprigs for garnish

Green Beans
with Red Pepper and Garlic

Green beans, also known as string beans or snap beans, are available year-round. To preserve their fresh flavor and texture, parboil the beans, immerse them in ice water to set their color, then sauté briefly.

SERVES 6

- 1 lb (500 g) green beans, stems trimmed
- 2 teaspoons olive oil
- 1 red bell pepper (capsicum), seeded and cut into julienne
- ½ teaspoon chile paste or red pepper flakes
- 1 clove garlic, finely chopped
- 1 teaspoon sesame oil
- ½ teaspoon salt
- ¼ teaspoon freshly ground black pepper

Cut the beans into 2-inch (5-cm) pieces. Bring a large saucepan three-fourths full of water to a boil. Add the beans and cook until they turn bright green and are tender-crisp, 1–3 minutes. Drain the beans, then plunge them into a bowl of ice water to stop the cooking. Drain again and set aside.

In a large frying pan, heat the olive oil over medium heat. Add the bell pepper and toss and stir for about 1 minute. Add the beans and sauté for 1 minute longer. Add the chile paste and garlic and toss and stir for 1 minute longer. The beans will be tender and bright green. Drizzle with the sesame oil and season with the salt and black pepper. Serve immediately.

Pyramid Servings

VEGETABLES	◀○○○●●
FRUITS	◀○○○○○
CARBOHYDRATES	○○○○○○○○
PROTEIN & DAIRY	○○○○○○○
FATS	○○○○○

PER SERVING	
calories	50
kilojoules	210
protein	2 g
carbohydrate	7 g
total fat	2 g
saturated fat	<1 g
monounsaturated fat	1 g
cholesterol	0 mg
sodium	201 mg
fiber	3 g

Wilted Greens with Warm Balsamic Vinegar

SERVES 4

Look for greens in bunches or, to save time, buy prewashed, chopped greens. A quick blanch tames the greens' pungent flavor. Serve with Braised Chicken with Mushrooms and Pearl Onions (page 254).

Pyramid Servings

VEGETABLES	◀○○○○●
FRUITS	◀○○○○○
CARBOHYDRATES	○○○○○○○○
PROTEIN & DAIRY	○○○○○○○
FATS	○○○○●

PER SERVING

calories	67
kilojoules	280
protein	3 g
carbohydrate	7 g
total fat	4 g
saturated fat	<1 g
monounsaturated fat	3 g
cholesterol	0 mg
sodium	239 mg
fiber	4 g

Bring a large saucepan three-fourths full of water to a boil. Add the salt and greens; stir until wilted, about 30 seconds. Drain and rinse immediately with cold water to stop the cooking. Squeeze the greens to remove excess water. Chop the greens coarsely and set aside.

In a large frying pan, heat the olive oil over medium heat. Add the onion and sauté until soft and lightly golden, about 6 minutes. Add the garlic and sauté for 1 minute; do not let the garlic brown. Add the chopped greens and the stock and sauté, stirring occasionally, until the greens are tender and most of the stock has evaporated, about 5 minutes. Add the vinegar, stir well, and season with the pepper. Serve hot.

¼ teaspoon salt

2 pounds (1 kg) collard, mustard, or turnip greens, stemmed, or 1 lb (500 g) cleaned, chopped cooking greens

1 tablespoon olive oil

½ yellow onion, chopped

1 clove garlic, minced

½ cup (4 fl oz/125 ml) chicken stock (page 138) or vegetable stock (page 139), or broth

1 tablespoon balsamic vinegar

¼ teaspoon freshly ground pepper

Eggplant with Toasted Spices

SERVES 4

In this recipe, toasted mustard seed and other spices often used in India infuse olive oil with pungent flavor. The oil is then used to make a fresh cherry tomato sauce for smoky slices of grilled eggplant.

Pyramid Servings

VEGETABLES	◀○○●●●
FRUITS	◀○○○○○
CARBOHYDRATES	○○○○○○○○
PROTEIN & DAIRY	○○○○○○○
FATS	○○○○●

PER SERVING	
calories	117
kilojoules	490
protein	3 g
carbohydrate	19 g
total fat	4 g
saturated fat	<1 g
monounsaturated fat	3 g
cholesterol	0 mg
sodium	163 mg
fiber	6 g

Prepare a hot fire in a charcoal grill or preheat a gas grill or broiler (grill). Away from the heat source, lightly coat the grill rack or broiler pan with cooking spray. Position the cooking rack 4–6 inches (10–15 cm) from the heat source.

Trim the eggplant and cut lengthwise into slices about ¼ inch (6 mm) thick. Arrange the slices on the rack or broiler pan and grill or broil, turning once, until the eggplant is tender and browned, about 5 minutes on each side. Set aside and keep warm.

In a small bowl, combine the spices. In a large frying pan, heat the olive oil over medium heat until hot but not smoking. Add the spice mixture and cook, stirring constantly, for about 30 seconds. Quickly add the onion and sauté until soft and translucent, about 4 minutes. Add the tomatoes, molasses, garlic, and vinegar. Cook the sauce, stirring occasionally, until thickened, about 4 minutes. Season with the salt and pepper.

Transfer the eggplant to a warmed serving dish or individual plates, pour the sauce over, and garnish with the cilantro.

1 large eggplant (aubergine), about 1½ lb (750 g)

1 teaspoon mustard seed

½ teaspoon ground cumin

½ teaspoon ground coriander

½ teaspoon curry powder

Pinch of ground ginger

Pinch of ground nutmeg

Pinch of ground cloves

1 tablespoon olive oil

½ yellow onion, finely chopped

2 cups (12 oz/375 g) cherry tomatoes, halved, or 1 cup (8 fl oz/250 ml) tomato sauce

1 tablespoon light molasses

1 clove garlic, minced

1 teaspoon red wine vinegar

¼ teaspoon salt

¼ teaspoon freshly ground pepper

1 tablespoon chopped fresh cilantro (fresh coriander)

Creamed Swiss Chard

Available year-round, Swiss chard is among the most tender and sweet of the cooking greens. Like all dark leafy greens, it is high in nutrients. Here, soy milk contributes richness but virtually no fat.

SERVES 6

2 tablespoons olive oil

1½ tablespoons unbleached all-purpose (plain) flour

3 cloves garlic, finely chopped

1¼ cups (10 fl oz/310 ml) low-fat plain soy milk (soya milk)

2 lb (1 kg) Swiss chard, washed, stemmed, and cut crosswise into strips ½ inch (12 mm) wide

¼ teaspoon salt

½ teaspoon freshly ground pepper

1 tablespoon grated Parmesan cheese

In a large frying pan, heat the olive oil over medium heat. Whisk in the flour to make a smooth paste. Continue whisking and add the garlic; cook for 30 seconds longer. Whisk in the soy milk and cook until the mixture thickens slightly.

Add the chard and stir to coat well. Cover and cook just until tender, about 2 minutes. Season with the salt and pepper. Sprinkle with the Parmesan and serve hot.

Pyramid Servings

VEGETABLES	◀○○○●●
FRUITS	◀○○○○○
CARBOHYDRATES	○○○○○○○
PROTEIN & DAIRY	○○○○○○○
FATS	○○○○●

PER SERVING	
calories	101
kilojoules	423
protein	4 g
carbohydrate	11 g
total fat	5 g
saturated fat	<1 g
monounsaturated fat	4 g
cholesterol	1 mg
sodium	297 mg
fiber	3 g

Swiss Chard

Related to beets, Swiss chard is a large-leaved, mild-flavored green that, like spinach, goes well in dishes from salads to stir-fries. Standard chard has a wide, white midrib, while red, or rhubarb, chard has darker leaves and a crimson rib and veins. To cook chard, cut off the greens and slice the ribs thinly crosswise. Steam or sauté the rib pieces for a few minutes, then add the greens and cook until soft.

Warm Potato Salad

A mixture of smooth and whole-grain mustards forms the base for a vinaigrette much lighter than traditional mayonnaise dressings. This salad is most flavorful when served warm or at room temperature.

1 lb (500 g) small red or white new potatoes (about 1½ inches/4 cm in diameter)

1 tablespoon Dijon mustard

1 tablespoon whole-grain mustard

2 tablespoons rice vinegar

2 teaspoons red wine vinegar or sherry vinegar

2 tablespoons minced shallot

4 teaspoons extra-virgin olive oil

2 tablespoons chopped fresh flat-leaf (Italian) parsley

¼ teaspoon salt

¼ teaspoon freshly ground pepper

Put the potatoes in a saucepan, add water to cover, and bring to a boil over high heat. Reduce the heat to medium and cook, uncovered, until the potatoes are tender, 15–20 minutes. Drain and let stand until just cool enough to handle. Cut each potato in half (or quarters, if the potatoes are large) and place in a warmed serving dish.

In a small bowl, whisk together the mustards, the vinegars, and the shallot until well blended. While whisking, slowly drizzle in the olive oil to make a thick dressing. Stir in the parsley, salt, and pepper. Pour the dressing over the warm potatoes, mix gently, and serve immediately.

Pyramid Servings

VEGETABLES	◀○○○○○
FRUITS	◀○○○○○
CARBOHYDRATES	○○○○○○●
PROTEIN & DAIRY	○○○○○○
FATS	○○○○●

PER SERVING

calories	89
kilojoules	372
protein	3 g
carbohydrate	15 g
total fat	3 g
saturated fat	0 g
monounsaturated fat	2 g
cholesterol	0 mg
sodium	202 mg
fiber	2 g

Grilled Portobello Mushrooms with Thyme and Garlic

SERVES 4

A splash of olive oil with thyme and garlic brings out the mushrooms' smoky flavor and meaty texture. Serve them on toasted whole-grain bread or with Creamy Polenta with Roasted Red Pepper Coulis (page 165).

Pyramid Servings

VEGETABLES	◀○○○○●
FRUITS	◀○○○○○
CARBOHYDRATES	○○○○○○○○
PROTEIN & DAIRY	○○○○○○○
FATS	○○○○●

PER SERVING	
calories	68
kilojoules	285
protein	3 g
carbohydrate	7 g
total fat	4 g
saturated fat	<1 g
monounsaturated fat	2 g
cholesterol	0 mg
sodium	297 mg
fiber	1 g

Combine the stock, olive oil, vinegar, garlic, thyme, and salt in a large lock-top plastic bag. Arrange the mushroom caps in one layer in the marinade, turning once to coat. Seal the bag, pressing out excess air. Marinate the mushrooms at room temperature, turning occasionally, for about 1 hour.

Prepare a hot fire in a charcoal grill or preheat a gas grill or broiler (grill). Away from the heat source, lightly coat the grill rack or broiler pan with cooking spray. Position the cooking rack 4 inches (10 cm) from the heat source.

Arrange the mushrooms on the rack or broiler pan and grill or broil, turning often, until tender, about 7 minutes.

Using tongs, transfer the mushrooms to a cutting board. Slice thinly and serve warm.

2 tablespoons vegetable stock (page 139) or broth

1 tablespoon extra-virgin olive oil

1 tablespoon balsamic vinegar

3 cloves garlic, minced

1 tablespoon chopped fresh thyme leaves or 1 teaspoon dried thyme

¼ teaspoon salt

4 large portobello mushrooms, brushed clean and stemmed

Sichuan Broccoli and Cauliflower

SERVES 6

Equal measures of green beans, bell peppers (capsicums), or other favorite vegetables can be substituted in this quick and easy recipe. Serve with Grilled Miso Salmon (page 234) and steamed brown rice.

Pyramid Servings

VEGETABLES	◀○○○○●
FRUITS	◀○○○○○
CARBOHYDRATES	○○○○○○○○
PROTEIN & DAIRY	○○○○○○○
FATS	○○○○●

PER SERVING

calories	58
kilojoules	243
protein	3 g
carbohydrate	8 g
total fat	3 g
saturated fat	0 g
monounsaturated fat	2 g
cholesterol	0 mg
sodium	87 mg
fiber	3 g

Bring a large saucepan three-fourths full of water to a boil. Add the cauliflower and broccoli and return to a boil. Cook until the vegetables are tender-crisp, about 1 minute. Drain the vegetables and then plunge them into a bowl of ice water to stop the cooking. Drain again and set aside.

In a small bowl, stir together the oyster sauce, water, and chile paste; set aside.

In a large, heavy nonstick frying pan, heat the olive oil over medium-high heat. Add the ginger and garlic and sauté for 30 seconds; do not let the garlic brown. Add the carrot and sauté for 1 minute. Add the cauliflower and broccoli and toss and stir until just tender, about 2 minutes. Add the oyster sauce mixture and toss and stir until the sauce is evenly distributed and the mixture is heated through, about 1 minute.

Transfer to a warmed serving dish and garnish with the green onion. Serve immediately.

3 cups (8 oz/250 g) ½-inch (12-mm) cauliflower florets

3 cups (6 oz/185 g) ½-inch (12-mm) broccoli florets

3 tablespoons oyster sauce

1 tablespoon water

¼ teaspoon chile paste or red pepper flakes

1 tablespoon olive oil

1 tablespoon peeled and minced fresh ginger

3 cloves garlic, minced

1 carrot, peeled and thinly sliced on the diagonal

1 green (spring) onion, green top only, thinly sliced on the diagonal

Butternut Squash and Plantain Mash

This recipe, a variation on a dish that's traditional in the Dominican Republic, merges starchy banana-like plantains with winter squash and garlic. Pair with Jamaican Barbecued Pork Tenderloin (page 259).

SERVES 6

1 butternut squash, about 1½ lb (750 g)

1 large firm yet ripe plantain

4 cloves garlic, unpeeled

¼ cup (2 fl oz/60 ml) vegetable stock (page 139), chicken stock (page 138), or broth

1 teaspoon extra-virgin olive oil

½ teaspoon salt

¼ teaspoon freshly ground pepper

Preheat the oven to 375°F (190°C). Lightly coat a baking sheet with cooking spray.

Halve the squash and scoop out the seeds and fibers. Peel the halves and cut into 1-inch (2.5-cm) pieces.

Trim the ends of the plantain. Cut a slit lengthwise through the inner curve of the skin, pry off the skin, and cut the plantain crosswise into 1-inch (2.5-cm) segments.

Place the squash, plantain, and garlic cloves on the prepared baking sheet. Roast until very tender, about 25 minutes. Let cool slightly and peel the garlic cloves.

In a saucepan, heat the vegetable stock over high heat until simmering. Remove from the heat and add the garlic, squash, plantain, and olive oil. Mash with a potato masher until almost smooth. Season with the salt and pepper. Serve immediately.

Pyramid Servings

VEGETABLES	◖○○○○
FRUITS	◖○○○○
CARBOHYDRATES	○○○○○○●
PROTEIN & DAIRY	○○○○○○
FATS	○○○○○

PER SERVING	
calories	79
kilojoules	331
protein	1 g
carbohydrate	19 g
total fat	1 g
saturated fat	0 g
monounsaturated fat	1 g
cholesterol	0 mg
sodium	219 mg
fiber	3 g

Roasted Root Vegetables with Cumin and Coriander

The secret to perfect roasting is a hot oven and a pan large enough to eliminate crowding. This ensures a crisp, evenly browned exterior. Be sure to cut the vegetables to an uniform size for even cooking.

SERVES 8

½ lb (250 g) sweet potatoes, peeled and cut into 1-inch (2.5-cm) pieces

½ lb (250 g) parsnips, peeled and cut into 1-inch (2.5-cm) pieces

½ lb (250 g) rutabagas, peeled and cut into 1-inch (2.5-cm) pieces

½ lb (250 g) turnips, peeled and cut into 1-inch (2.5-cm) pieces

2 tablespoons olive oil

1 teaspoon ground cumin

1 teaspoon ground coriander

½ teaspoon salt

¼ teaspoon freshly ground pepper

2 tablespoons chopped fresh cilantro (fresh coriander)

Position a rack in the lower third of the oven and preheat to 400°F (200°C).

In a large bowl, combine the vegetables, olive oil, cumin, ground coriander, and salt. Toss well to coat. Arrange the vegetables in a single layer on a large baking sheet.

Roast, stirring or shaking the vegetables every 15 minutes, until tender and evenly browned, about 45 minutes. Sprinkle with the pepper; taste and adjust the seasoning.

Transfer to a serving dish and sprinkle with the cilantro. Serve hot or at room temperature.

Pyramid Servings

VEGETABLES	◖○○○○○
FRUITS	◖○○○○○
CARBOHYDRATES	○○○○○○●
PROTEIN & DAIRY	○○○○○○○
FATS	○○○○●

PER SERVING	
calories	101
kilojoules	423
protein	2 g
carbohydrate	16 g
total fat	4 g
saturated fat	1 g
monounsaturated fat	3 g
cholesterol	0 mg
sodium	179 mg
fiber	4 g

Grilled Radicchio

SERVES 8

Radicchio, with its distinctive burgundy leaves, is commonly used in fancy salads. But in its native Italy, it is often served grilled. Brushing it first with orange juice and olive oil releases a profusion of flavors.

Pyramid Servings

VEGETABLES	◀○○○○●
FRUITS	◀○○○○○
CARBOHYDRATES	○○○○○○○○
PROTEIN & DAIRY	○○○○○○○
FATS	○○○○●

PER SERVING	
calories	54
kilojoules	226
protein	1 g
carbohydrate	4 g
total fat	4 g
saturated fat	1 g
monounsaturated fat	3 g
cholesterol	0 mg
sodium	188 mg
fiber	1 g

Prepare a hot fire in a charcoal grill or preheat a gas grill or broiler (grill). Position the cooking rack 4–6 inches (10–15 cm) from the heat source.

Pull off any wilted outer leaves from the radicchio. Cut each head into quarters through the stem end, leaving the core portions intact so the quarters hold together.

In a small bowl, stir together the orange juice, olive oil, and orange zest. Brush the olive oil mixture onto the cut sides of the radicchio quarters. Sprinkle with the pepper and arrange the radicchio on the grill rack or broiler pan. Grill or broil, turning frequently, until tender, 8–10 minutes.

Transfer the radicchio quarters to individual plates and sprinkle evenly with the salt. Place an orange wedge on each plate and serve immediately.

2 large heads radicchio

3 tablespoons fresh orange juice

2½ tablespoons extra-virgin olive oil

½ teaspoon grated orange zest

¼ teaspoon freshly ground pepper

¾ teaspoon coarse salt

1 orange, cut into 8 wedges

Asparagus with Hazelnut Gremolata

SERVES 4

Gremolata, a mixture of chopped parsley, lemon zest, and garlic, here includes freshly toasted hazelnuts as well. This aromatic blend also complements steamed green beans, broccoli, and brussels sprouts.

In a large pot fitted with a steamer basket, bring about 1 inch (2.5 cm) water to a boil. Add the asparagus, cover, and steam until tender-crisp, about 4 minutes. Remove from the pot.

In a large bowl, combine the asparagus, garlic, chopped parsley, hazelnuts, the ¼ teaspoon lemon zest, the lemon juice, the olive oil, and the salt. Toss well to mix and coat.

Arrange the asparagus neatly on a serving platter and garnish with parsley sprigs and lemon zest. Serve immediately.

Pyramid Servings

VEGETABLES	◀ ○○○○●
FRUITS	◀ ○○○○○
CARBOHYDRATES	○○○○○○○○
PROTEIN & DAIRY	○○○○○○○
FATS	○○○○○

PER SERVING

calories	37
kilojoules	155
protein	2 g
carbohydrate	3 g
total fat	2 g
saturated fat	0 g
monounsaturated fat	2 g
cholesterol	0 mg
sodium	154 mg
fiber	1 g

1 lb (500 g) asparagus, tough ends removed, then peeled if skin seems thick

1 clove garlic, minced

1 tablespoon chopped fresh flat-leaf (Italian) parsley, plus sprigs for garnish

1 tablespoon finely chopped toasted hazelnuts (filberts)

¼ teaspoon finely grated lemon zest, plus extra for garnish

2 teaspoons fresh lemon juice

1 teaspoon extra-virgin olive oil

¼ teaspoon salt

Pita Wedges with Green Olive Tapenade

SERVES 6

The secret to this Mediterranean-inspired appetizer is to use good-quality green olives. Look for a brine-cured version such as Cerignola, Lucque, Manzanillo, Picholine, Provençal, Sevillano, or Sicilian.

Pyramid Servings

VEGETABLES	◀○○○○●
FRUITS	◀○○○○○
CARBOHYDRATES	○○○○○○○●
PROTEIN & DAIRY	○○○○○○○
FATS	○○○○●

PER SERVING

calories	143
kilojoules	598
protein	3 g
carbohydrate	21 g
total fat	5 g
saturated fat	<1 g
monounsaturated fat	3 g
cholesterol	0 mg
sodium	293 mg
fiber	3 g

Preheat the oven to 400°F (200°C). Arrange the pita bread wedges in a single layer on a baking sheet. Bake until crisp and lightly golden, about 8 minutes. Set aside to cool.

In a small frying pan, heat the olive oil over medium-high heat. Add the shallot and sauté until softened, about 3 minutes. Add the tomatoes, garlic, oregano, and the red pepper flakes, if using, and sauté until the tomatoes are tender, about 2 minutes. Add the wine and slowly bring to a boil. Reduce the heat to low and simmer, stirring often, until the liquid has evaporated, about 6 minutes. (The mixture will be thick.) Remove from the heat, spoon the mixture into a small bowl, and let cool completely.

When the tomato mixture has cooled to room temperature, add the olives and lemon zest. Stir to combine. (The tapenade may be made ahead, covered, and refrigerated for up to 2 days. Bring to room temperature before using.)

Spoon 2 teaspoons of the tapenade onto each pita wedge, sprinkle evenly with the parsley, and divide among individual plates. Serve immediately.

3 whole-wheat (wholemeal) pita breads, 6 inches (15 cm) in diameter, each cut into 8 wedges

1 teaspoon extra-virgin olive oil

1 shallot, finely chopped

2 plum (Roma) tomatoes, peeled and seeded (page 127), then finely chopped

1 clove garlic, minced

1 teaspoon finely chopped fresh oregano or ½ teaspoon dried oregano

½ teaspoon red pepper flakes (optional)

½ cup (4 fl oz/125 ml) dry white wine

¾ cup pitted (4 oz/125 g) green olives, rinsed, drained, and roughly chopped

Grated zest of 1 lemon

2 tablespoons chopped fresh flat-leaf (Italian) parsley

Braised Kale with Cherry Tomatoes

SERVES 4

Kale holds its texture well in cooking. Although any variety will work in this dish, curly, dark green dinosaur kale looks spectacular, especially alongside a mix of red, yellow, and orange cherry tomatoes.

Pyramid Servings

VEGETABLES	◀○○○●●
FRUITS	◀○○○○○
CARBOHYDRATES	○○○○○○○○
PROTEIN & DAIRY	○○○○○○○
FATS	○○○○●

PER SERVING	
calories	93
kilojoules	389
protein	4 g
carbohydrate	15 g
total fat	3 g
saturated fat	0 g
monounsaturated fat	2 g
cholesterol	0 mg
sodium	206 mg
fiber	3 g

In a large frying pan, heat the olive oil over medium heat. Add the garlic and sauté until lightly golden, 1–2 minutes. Stir in the kale and vegetable stock. Cover, reduce the heat to medium-low, and cook until the kale is wilted and some of the liquid has evaporated, about 5 minutes.

Stir in the tomatoes and cook uncovered until the kale is tender, 5–7 minutes longer. Remove from the heat and stir in the lemon juice, salt, and pepper. Serve immediately.

2 teaspoons extra-virgin olive oil

4 cloves garlic, thinly sliced

1 lb (500 g) kale, tough stems removed and leaves coarsely chopped

½ cup (4 fl oz/125 ml) vegetable stock (page 139) or broth

1 cup (6 oz/185 g) cherry tomatoes, halved

1 tablespoon fresh lemon juice

¼ teaspoon salt

⅛ teaspoon freshly ground pepper

Kale

Like lettuce, kale comes in shapes and colors from plain to frilly and deep green to red and purple. Dinosaur kale, also known as black kale, *cavolo nero,* or *lacinato,* has large, ruffled leaves. Kale, like other cabbage-family vegetables, is rich in vitamin C and in compounds that help protect against cancer. It is delicious braised, sautéed, or simmered in soups. Look for kale that's bright, crisp, and unbruised.

Artichokes alla Romana

Stuffed artichokes make an appealing and substantial side dish. The simple but flavorful stuffing complements the artichokes' nuttiness without overpowering them. The dish can be made ahead.

2 cups (4 oz/125 g) fresh bread crumbs, preferably whole wheat (wholemeal)

1 tablespoon olive oil

4 large artichokes

2 lemons, halved

⅓ cup (1½ oz/45 g) grated Parmesan cheese

3 cloves garlic, finely chopped

2 tablespoons finely chopped fresh flat-leaf (Italian) parsley

1 tablespoon grated lemon zest

¼ teaspoon freshly ground pepper

1 cup (8 fl oz/250 ml) plus 2–4 tablespoons vegetable stock (page 139), chicken stock (page 138), or broth

1 cup (8 fl oz/250 ml) dry white wine

1 tablespoon minced shallot

1 teaspoon chopped fresh oregano

Preheat the oven to 400°F (200°C). In a bowl, combine the bread crumbs and olive oil. Toss to coat. Spread the crumbs in a shallow baking pan and bake, stirring once halfway through, until the crumbs are lightly golden, about 10 minutes. Set aside to cool.

Working with 1 artichoke at a time, snap off any tough outer leaves and trim the stem flush with the base. Cut off the top third of the leaves with a serrated knife, and trim off any remaining thorns with scissors. Rub the cut edges with a lemon half to prevent discoloration. Separate the inner leaves and pull out the small leaves from the center. Using a melon baller or spoon, scoop out the fuzzy choke, then squeeze some lemon juice into the cavity. Trim the remaining artichokes in the same manner.

In a large bowl, toss the bread crumbs with the Parmesan, garlic, parsley, lemon zest, and pepper. Add the 2–4 tablespoons stock, 1 tablespoon at a time, using just enough for the stuffing to begin to stick together in small clumps

Using two-thirds of the stuffing, mound it slightly in the center of the artichokes. Then, starting at the bottom, spread the leaves open and spoon a rounded ½ teaspoon stuffing near the base of each leaf. (The artichokes can be prepared to this point several hours ahead and kept refrigerated.)

In a Dutch oven with a tight-fitting lid, combine the 1 cup stock, wine, shallot, and oregano. Bring to a boil, then reduce the heat to low. Arrange the artichokes, stem end down, in the liquid in a single layer. Cover and simmer until the outer leaves are tender, about 45 minutes (add water if necessary). Transfer the artichokes to a rack and let cool slightly. Cut each artichoke into quarters and serve warm.

Pyramid Servings

VEGETABLES	◀○○○○●
FRUITS	◀○○○○○
CARBOHYDRATES	○○○○○○○●
PROTEIN & DAIRY	○○○○○○○
FATS	○○○○●

PER SERVING	
calories	117
kilojoules	490
protein	5 g
carbohydrate	14 g
total fat	3 g
saturated fat	1 g
monounsaturated fat	2 g
cholesterol	3 mg
sodium	287 mg
fiber	4 g

Garden Peas with Fresh Mint

The natural sweetness of fresh peas requires little adornment. Here, a handful of chopped mint underscores their straight-from-the-garden appeal. You can also experiment with tarragon or other fresh herbs.

SERVES 6

3 lb (1.5 kg) English peas, shelled (about 3 cups/ 15 oz/470 g), or 1 lb (500 g) frozen shelled peas, thawed

1 tablespoon extra-virgin olive oil

2 tablespoons chopped fresh mint

¼ teaspoon salt

½ teaspoon freshly ground pepper

In a large pot fitted with a steamer basket, bring about 1 inch (2.5 cm) water to a boil. Add the peas, cover, and steam, tossing once, until tender, about 4 minutes. Transfer the peas to a large bowl, and add the olive oil, mint, salt, and pepper. Toss to mix and coat. Serve immediately.

Alternatively, sauté the peas. In a sauté pan, heat the olive oil over medium heat. Add the peas and cook, stirring occasionally, just until tender, about 3 minutes. Stir in the mint. Season with the salt and pepper. Serve immediately.

Pyramid Servings

VEGETABLES	◀ ○ ○ ○ ● ●
FRUITS	◀ ○ ○ ○ ○ ○
CARBOHYDRATES	○ ○ ○ ○ ○ ○ ○
PROTEIN & DAIRY	○ ○ ○ ○ ○ ○ ○
FATS	○ ○ ○ ○ ●

PER SERVING	
calories	86
kilojoules	360
protein	4 g
carbohydrate	12 g
total fat	3 g
saturated fat	0 g
monounsaturated fat	2 g
cholesterol	0 mg
sodium	102 mg
fiber	2 g

Baked Acorn Squash with Pine Nuts and Garlic

SERVES 4

Acorn squash cooks quickly and takes on an elegant appearance when sliced into rings and roasted. For easier cutting, microwave whole unpeeled squash on high for a few minutes to soften them.

Pyramid Servings

VEGETABLES	◀○○○○○
FRUITS	◀○○○○○
CARBOHYDRATES	○○○○○○○●
PROTEIN & DAIRY	○○○○○○○
FATS	○○○○●

PER SERVING

calories	138
kilojoules	577
protein	3 g
carbohydrate	25 g
total fat	5 g
saturated fat	1 g
monounsaturated fat	3 g
cholesterol	0 mg
sodium	154 mg
fiber	7 g

Preheat the oven to 400°F (200°C). Coat a shallow baking dish with cooking spray.

Cut the squash crosswise into rings ½ inch (12 mm) thick, leaving the peel intact. Scrape the seeds out of the center of each ring and discard. Place the rings in the prepared baking dish in a single layer, allowing them to overlap slightly. Brush with 1½ teaspoons of the olive oil, and sprinkle with ⅛ teaspoon of the salt. Bake for 15 minutes.

Meanwhile, in a small bowl, toss the garlic with the remaining 1½ teaspoons olive oil.

Sprinkle the garlic and pine nuts evenly over the squash rings and continue baking until the squash is tender and the pine nuts are lightly browned, 10–15 minutes longer.

Season the squash rings with the remaining ⅛ teaspoon salt and the pepper. Serve immediately.

2 small acorn squash, about 2 lb (1 kg) total weight

1 tablespoon extra-virgin olive oil

¼ teaspoon salt

8 cloves garlic, halved

1 tablespoon pine nuts

¼ teaspoon freshly ground pepper

Sugar Snap Peas with Fresh Marjoram

Sugar snap peas are crisp peas eaten pod and all. Here, they're paired with marjoram and tossed with olive oil and lemon. To save time, look for packaged peas with their strings already removed.

SERVES 4

2 teaspoons extra-virgin olive oil

¾ lb (375 g) sugar snap peas, trimmed of stems and strings

1½ teaspoons chopped fresh marjoram

1 teaspoon fresh lemon juice

¼ teaspoon grated lemon zest

¼ teaspoon salt

⅛ teaspoon freshly ground pepper

In a large frying pan, heat the olive oil over medium heat. Add the peas and sauté until tender-crisp, 4–5 minutes. Stir in the marjoram, lemon juice and zest, salt, and pepper and toss gently to mix. Serve immediately.

Pyramid Servings

VEGETABLES	◀ ○ ○ ○ ● ●
FRUITS	◀ ○ ○ ○ ○ ○
CARBOHYDRATES	○ ○ ○ ○ ○ ○ ○ ○
PROTEIN & DAIRY	○ ○ ○ ○ ○ ○ ○
FATS	○ ○ ○ ○ ○

PER SERVING	
calories	59
kilojoules	247
protein	2 g
carbohydrate	7 g
total fat	2 g
saturated fat	0 g
monounsaturated fat	2 g
cholesterol	0 mg
sodium	155 mg
fiber	2 g

Steamed Summer Squash with Warm Leek Vinaigrette

When you can find them, miniature pattypan and other summer squash are an attractive substitute for full-sized crooknecks and zucchini. The leek vinaigrette is also delicious over grilled fish.

SERVES 6

2 yellow crookneck squash, about ½ lb (250 g) total weight

2 zucchini (courgettes), about ½ lb (250 g) total weight

FOR THE VINAIGRETTE

2 tablespoons extra-virgin olive oil

1 leek, including tender green top, finely chopped (about 1 cup/4 oz/125 g)

1 tablespoon vegetable stock (page 139) or broth

1 tablespoon rice vinegar

1 tablespoon fresh lemon juice

½ teaspoon salt

¼ teaspoon freshly ground pepper

Trim the stems from the crooknecks and zucchini. Halve lengthwise and then cut the halves crosswise on the diagonal into slices ½ inch (12 mm) thick. Set aside.

To make the vinaigrette, in a saucepan, heat the olive oil over medium heat. Add the leek and sauté until soft, 10–12 minutes. Remove from the heat and stir in the vegetable stock, vinegar, lemon juice, salt, and pepper. Cover and keep warm.

Meanwhile, in a large pot fitted with a steamer basket, bring 1 inch (2.5 cm) water to a boil. Add the yellow squash and zucchini, cover, and steam until tender, about 10 minutes.

Transfer the squash to a warmed serving dish. Add the vinaigrette and toss gently to mix. Serve immediately.

Pyramid Servings

VEGETABLES	◀○○○○●
FRUITS	◀○○○○○
CARBOHYDRATES	○○○○○○○○
PROTEIN & DAIRY	○○○○○○○
FATS	○○○○●

PER SERVING	
calories	63
kilojoules	264
protein	1 g
carbohydrate	5 g
total fat	5 g
saturated fat	1 g
monounsaturated fat	3 g
cholesterol	0 mg
sodium	200 mg
fiber	2 g

Two-Potato Gratin

SERVES 6

The buttery flavor of Yukon gold potatoes contrasts nicely with the sweet flavor and firm texture of sweet potatoes in this scalloped potato-style dish. Serve with roasted chicken, pork, or beef.

Pyramid Servings

VEGETABLES	◀○○○○○
FRUITS	◀○○○○○
CARBOHYDRATES	○○○○○●●
PROTEIN & DAIRY	○○○○○○●
FATS	○○○○●

PER SERVING

calories	174
kilojoules	728
protein	5 g
carbohydrate	31 g
total fat	5 g
saturated fat	2 g
monounsaturated fat	3 g
cholesterol	6 mg
sodium	271 mg
fiber	3 g

Preheat the oven to 425°F (220°C). Rub the cut sides of the garlic on the bottom and sides of a large gratin dish or shallow 1½-qt (1.5-l) baking dish. Lightly coat the bottom and sides of the dish with 1 teaspoon of the olive oil.

Arrange half of the white potato slices in a single layer in the bottom of the gratin dish; top with half of the sweet potato slices. Drizzle the melted butter over the potato mixture and sprinkle with ¼ teaspoon of the salt and ⅛ teaspoon of the pepper. Layer the remaining white potato slices over the seasoned potato mixture. Top with the remaining sweet potato slices, ¼ teaspoon salt, and ⅛ teaspoon pepper.

In a small saucepan over medium-low heat, combine the milk and nutmeg. Bring to a boil. Remove from the heat and pour evenly over the potato mixture.

In a food processor, process the bread until small crumbs form. Add the remaining 2½ teaspoons olive oil and pulse to blend. Sprinkle the bread crumb mixture evenly over the potatoes. Bake until the potatoes are tender, 45–50 minutes. Let stand for 5 minutes before serving.

1 clove garlic, halved

3½ teaspoons olive oil

3 Yukon gold or red-skinned potatoes, about 1¼ lb (625 g) total weight, peeled and cut into slices ⅛ inch (3 mm) thick

1 sweet potato, about ½ lb (250 g), peeled and cut into slices ⅛ inch (3 mm) thick

1 tablespoon butter, melted

½ teaspoon salt

¼ teaspoon freshly ground pepper

1¼ cups (10 fl oz/310 ml) nonfat milk

⅛ teaspoon ground nutmeg

1 slice (1 oz/30 g) whole-wheat (wholemeal) bread, torn into pieces

Brussels Sprouts with Shallots and Lemon

SERVES 4

Buy fresh brussels sprouts that are bright green and heavy for their size. In this recipe, quickly caramelized shallots add a sweet note to these diminutive members of the cabbage family.

Pyramid Servings

VEGETABLES	◀○○●●●
FRUITS	◀○○○○○
CARBOHYDRATES	○○○○○○○
PROTEIN & DAIRY	○○○○○○○
FATS	○○○○●

PER SERVING	
calories	108
kilojoules	410
protein	4 g
carbohydrate	14 g
total fat	4 g
saturated fat	1 g
monounsaturated fat	3 g
cholesterol	0 mg
sodium	257 mg
fiber	5 g

In a large, nonstick frying pan, heat 2 teaspoons of the olive oil over medium heat. Add the shallots and sauté until soft and lightly golden, about 6 minutes. Stir in the ⅛ teaspoon salt. Transfer to a bowl and set aside.

In the same frying pan, heat the remaining 1 teaspoon olive oil over medium heat. Add the brussels sprouts and sauté until they begin to brown, 3–4 minutes. Add the vegetable stock and bring to a simmer. Cook, uncovered, until the brussels sprouts are tender, 5–6 minutes. Return the shallots to the pan. Stir in the lemon zest and juice, the ¼ teaspoon salt, and the pepper. Serve immediately.

1 tablespoon extra-virgin olive oil

3 shallots, thinly sliced

¼ teaspoon plus ⅛ teaspoon salt

1 lb (500 g) brussels sprouts, trimmed and cut into quarters

½ cup (4 fl oz/125 ml) vegetable stock (page 139) or broth

¼ teaspoon finely grated lemon zest

1 tablespoon fresh lemon juice

¼ teaspoon freshly ground pepper

Olive Oil

Of the many vegetable oils, olive oil has the widest range of flavors—bland, buttery, sweet, peppery, grassy. Keep at least two types on hand: a mild, low-cost variety for sautéing and roasting, and a quality extra-virgin for salads and other dishes in which the oil is central. An extra-virgin's flavor is not evident in its color or price, so taste a few to find one you like. Olive oils are rich in health-ful monounsaturated fats.

Braised Celery Root

One of the least-known vegetables, though gaining favor, the knobby celery root has a subtle celery flavor that enhances dishes from soup to mashed potatoes. Here, it is finished with a creamy mustard sauce.

SERVES 6

1 cup (8 fl oz/250 ml) vegetable stock (page 139) or broth

1 celery root (celeriac), about 1 lb (500 g), peeled and diced

¼ cup (2 fl oz/60 ml) sour cream

1 teaspoon Dijon mustard

¼ teaspoon salt

¼ teaspoon freshly ground pepper

2 teaspoons fresh thyme leaves

In a large saucepan, bring the stock to a boil over high heat. Stir in the celery root. When the stock returns to a boil, reduce the heat to low. Cover and simmer, stirring occasionally, until the celery root is tender, 10–12 minutes. Using a slotted spoon, transfer to a bowl, cover, and keep warm.

Raise the heat under the saucepan to high and bring the cooking liquid to a boil. Cook, uncovered, until reduced to 1 tablespoon, about 5 minutes. Remove from the heat and whisk in the sour cream, mustard, salt, and pepper. Add the celery root and thyme to the sauce and stir over medium heat until heated through. Transfer to a warmed serving dish and serve immediately.

Pyramid Servings

VEGETABLES	◀ ○ ○ ○ ● ●
FRUITS	◀ ○ ○ ○ ○ ○
CARBOHYDRATES	○ ○ ○ ○ ○ ○ ○
PROTEIN & DAIRY	○ ○ ○ ○ ○ ○ ○
FATS	○ ○ ○ ○ ○

PER SERVING	
calories	58
kilojoules	243
protein	2 g
carbohydrate	8 g
total fat	2 g
saturated fat	1 g
monounsaturated fat	0 g
cholesterol	8 mg
sodium	210 mg
fiber	1 g

Celery Root

Also known as celeriac, celery root is a winter specialty that is equally tasty raw or cooked. Always peel the knobby root before use. Shredded or thinly sliced raw, it adds a pleasing flavor to salads—try it with apple slices and toasted walnuts in a vinaigrette. Cut into cubes, it can be sautéed, steamed, roasted, or puréed. To prevent browning, place the peeled root in water with a squeeze of lemon juice.

Pan-Braised Onions with Rosemary

Slow cooking brings out the sweetness of yellow onions in this rustic dish, while balsamic vinegar adds depth. The recipe can also be doubled. Make ahead or serve hot with roasted chicken.

SERVES 4

1 tablespoon extra-virgin olive oil

2 lb (1 kg) yellow onions, halved lengthwise and cut crosswise into slices ¼ inch (6 mm) thick

2 teaspoons minced fresh rosemary, plus sprigs for garnish

1 bay leaf

¼ cup (2 fl oz/60 ml) vegetable stock (page 139), broth, or dry white wine

½ cup (4 fl oz/125 ml) balsamic vinegar

¼ teaspoon salt

½ teaspoon freshly ground pepper

In a large, nonstick sauté or frying pan, heat the olive oil over medium-high heat. Add the onions, minced rosemary, and bay leaf. Reduce the heat to very low, cover tightly, and cook, stirring occasionally, until the onions are tender and beginning to turn golden, about 30 minutes. If the onions begin to stick at any point during the slow cooking, add a few tablespoons of water.

Add the vegetable stock to the pan and bring to a simmer. Cook until the stock evaporates completely, about 5 minutes. Add the vinegar and simmer until the liquid is completely absorbed, about 5 minutes longer. Season with the salt and pepper.

Transfer to a warmed serving dish and garnish with the rosemary sprigs. Serve immediately.

Pyramid Servings

VEGETABLES	◀ ○ ● ● ● ●
FRUITS	◀ ○ ○ ○ ○ ○
CARBOHYDRATES	○ ○ ○ ○ ○ ○ ○ ○
PROTEIN & DAIRY	○ ○ ○ ○ ○ ○ ○
FATS	○ ○ ○ ○ ●

PER SERVING	
calories	148
kilojoules	582
protein	3 g
carbohydrate	25 g
total fat	4 g
saturated fat	<1 g
monounsaturated fat	3 g
cholesterol	0 mg
sodium	190 mg
fiber	4 g

Broccoli Rabe with Toasted Garlic

SERVES 4

With its little florets, broccoli rabe looks like broccoli. Because the stems can be bitter, some cooks discard them. Here, they're included, and their bold flavor is softened with garlic, olive oil, and a bit of salt.

Pyramid Servings

VEGETABLES	◀○○○○●
FRUITS	◀○○○○○
CARBOHYDRATES	○○○○○○○○
PROTEIN & DAIRY	○○○○○○○
FATS	○○○○●

PER SERVING

calories	72
kilojoules	301
protein	3 g
carbohydrate	6 g
total fat	5 g
saturated fat	1 g
monounsaturated fat	4 g
cholesterol	0 mg
sodium	167 mg
fiber	3 g

Trim off the tough ends of the broccoli rabe stems, then cut the stems into ½-inch (12-mm) pieces. Coarsely chop the leaves; leave the small florets whole.

In a large nonstick sauté or frying pan, heat the olive oil over medium heat. Add the garlic and sauté until lightly golden, 1–2 minutes. Using a slotted spoon, transfer the garlic to a small bowl and set aside.

Add the broccoli rabe stems to the pan and sauté until the stems are slightly softened, about 3 minutes. Stir in ⅛ teaspoon of the salt. Add the leaves and florets and sauté until the leaves wilt and the florets are tender-crisp, 3–4 minutes. Stir in the remaining ⅛ teaspoon salt, the pepper, and the sautéed garlic. Drizzle with the vinegar and toss to mix. Serve immediately.

1 lb (500 g) broccoli rabe, tough stem ends trimmed

1½ tablespoons extra-virgin olive oil

6 cloves garlic, thinly sliced

¼ teaspoon salt

⅛ teaspoon freshly ground pepper

1 tablespoon red wine vinegar

Fruits

Each piece of fruit offers a chance to thrill your taste buds while also helping build your body's defenses.

75   Mixed Fresh Berries with Ginger Sauce

76   Orange Slices with Citrus Syrup

79   Sautéed Bananas with Caramel Sauce

80   Tropical Fruits with Mint and Spices

82   Raspberry Coulis

83   Casaba Melon with Sweet Curry Cream

85   Melon Fool

86   Peach-Nectarine Salsa

89   Grilled Pineapple

90   Ambrosia with Coconut and Toasted Almonds

92   Fresh Figs with Walnuts and Mascarpone

94   Pear and Toasted Pecan Chutney

95   Apple and Sweet Onion Marmalade

96   Baked Apples with Cherries and Almonds

Mixed Fresh Berries
with Ginger Sauce

Make a double batch of this spicy, sweet ginger sauce and refrigerate it for up to 3 days. Spoon it onto angel food cake or fresh melon. If you can't find red currants, use peach slices or strawberries.

SERVES 6

FOR THE SAUCE

4 cups (1 lb/500 g) strawberries, hulled and halved

¼ cup (2 fl oz/60 ml) fresh orange juice

3 tablespoons chopped crystallized ginger

½ teaspoon vanilla extract (essence)

2 cups (8 oz/250 g) blackberries

1 cup (4 oz/125 g) raspberries

1 cup (4 oz/125 g) fresh red currants

Fresh mint leaves for garnish

To make the sauce, in a blender or food processor, combine the strawberries, orange juice, ginger, and vanilla. Process just until blended. Pass the purée through a fine-mesh sieve placed over a small bowl, pressing on the solids with a spatula or the back of a wooden spoon to extract all the juice.

In a large bowl, toss together the blackberries, raspberries, and currants, mixing well. Transfer to a serving bowl or individual bowls. Spoon the ginger sauce over the berries and garnish with the mint. Serve immediately.

Pyramid Servings

VEGETABLES	◖○○○○○
FRUITS	◖○○○○●
CARBOHYDRATES	○○○○○○○○
PROTEIN & DAIRY	○○○○○○○
FATS	○○○○○

PER SERVING	
calories	82
kilojoules	343
protein	1 g
carbohydrate	20 g
total fat	0 g
saturated fat	0 g
monounsaturated fat	0 g
cholesterol	0 mg
sodium	2 mg
fiber	5 g

Orange Slices with Citrus Syrup

SERVES 4

Several orange flavors are combined here to add intensity and depth to fresh orange slices. If you prefer a nonalcoholic version, simply leave out the liqueur; the syrup will still be rich and satisfying.

Pyramid Servings

VEGETABLES	◖○○○○○
FRUITS	◖○○●●●
CARBOHYDRATES	○○○○○○●
PROTEIN & DAIRY	○○○○○○○
FATS	○○○○○

PER SERVING

calories	162
kilojoules	678
protein	2 g
carbohydrate	39 g
total fat	1 g
saturated fat	0 g
monounsaturated fat	0 g
cholesterol	0 mg
sodium	2 mg
fiber	4 g

Working with 1 orange at a time, cut a thin slice off the top and the bottom, exposing the flesh. Stand the orange upright and, using a sharp knife, thickly cut off the peel, following the contour of the fruit and removing all the white pith and membrane. Cut the orange crosswise into slices ½ inch (12 mm) thick. Transfer to a shallow nonaluminum bowl or dish. Repeat with the remaining oranges. Set aside.

In a small saucepan over medium-high heat, combine the julienned zest with water to cover. Bring to a boil and boil for 1 minute. Drain and plunge the zest into a bowl of cold water. Set aside.

To make the syrup, combine the orange juice and honey in a large saucepan over medium-high heat. Bring to a boil, stirring to dissolve the honey. Reduce the heat to medium-low and simmer, uncovered, until the mixture thickens to a light syrup, about 5 minutes. Drain the orange zest and add to the syrup. Cook until the zest is translucent, 3–5 minutes.

Pour the orange syrup mixture over the oranges. Cover and refrigerate until well chilled or for up to 3 hours.

To serve, divide the orange slices among individual plates. Pour the syrup and zest over the orange slices, dividing it evenly. Drizzle each serving with 1½ teaspoons of the orange liqueur, if using. Garnish with the mint and serve immediately.

4 oranges

Zest of 1 orange, cut into julienne 4 inches (10 cm) long and ⅛ inch (3 mm) wide

FOR THE SYRUP

1½ cups (12 fl oz/375 ml) fresh orange juice, strained

2 tablespoons dark honey

2 tablespoons orange liqueur such as Grand Marnier or Cointreau (optional)

4 fresh mint sprigs

Sautéed Bananas with Caramel Sauce

With a glaze of caramel sauce, this banana dish is a sweet ending to any meal. Rich-flavored walnut oil lends an exotic accent. Apple juice is a good substitute for the rum in a nonalcoholic version.

SERVES 6

FOR THE SAUCE

1 tablespoon butter

1 tablespoon walnut oil or canola oil

1 tablespoon honey

2 tablespoons firmly packed brown sugar

3 tablespoons 1-percent low-fat milk

1 tablespoon dark raisins or golden raisins (sultanas)

4 firm bananas, about 1 lb (500 g) total weight

½ teaspoon canola oil

2 tablespoons dark rum or apple juice

To make the sauce, in a small saucepan melt the butter over medium heat. Whisk in the oil, honey, and brown sugar. Cook, stirring continuously, until the sugar is dissolved, about 3 minutes. Stir in the milk, 1 tablespoon at a time, and then cook, stirring continuously, until the sauce thickens slightly, about 3 minutes. Remove from the heat and stir in the raisins. Set aside and keep warm.

Peel the bananas, then cut each crosswise into 3 sections. Cut each section in half lengthwise.

Lightly coat a large nonstick frying pan with the canola oil and place over medium-high heat. Add the bananas and sauté until they begin to brown, 3–4 minutes. Transfer to a plate and keep warm.

Add the rum to the pan, bring to a boil, and deglaze the pan, stirring with a wooden spoon to scrape up any browned bits from the bottom of the pan. Cook until reduced by half, 30–45 seconds. Return the bananas to the pan to rewarm.

To serve, divide the bananas among individual bowls or plates. Drizzle with the warm sauce and serve immediately.

Pyramid Servings

VEGETABLES	◀○○○○○
FRUITS	◀○○○●●
CARBOHYDRATES	○○○○○○○○
PROTEIN & DAIRY	○○○○○○○
FATS	○○○○●

PER SERVING	
calories	146
kilojoules	611
protein	1 g
carbohydrate	27 g
total fat	5 g
saturated fat	1 g
monounsaturated fat	1 g
cholesterol	5 mg
sodium	25 mg
fiber	3 g

Tropical Fruits with Mint and Spices

SERVES 8

This flavorful mix of six different fruits is as colorful as it is nutritious. The richly spiced syrup, aromatic with vanilla, can be prepared up to a day ahead and is delicious on pancakes, too.

Pyramid Servings

VEGETABLES	◀ ○ ○ ○ ○ ○
FRUITS	◀ ○ ○ ○ ● ●
CARBOHYDRATES	○ ○ ○ ○ ○ ○ ○ ○
PROTEIN & DAIRY	○ ○ ○ ○ ○ ○ ○
FATS	○ ○ ○ ○

PER SERVING

calories	159
kilojoules	665
protein	2 g
carbohydrate	39 g
total fat	0 g
saturated fat	0 g
monounsaturated fat	0 g
cholesterol	0 mg
sodium	14 mg
fiber	4 g

To make the syrup, in a saucepan, combine the orange juice, the 3 tablespoons lemon juice, the honey, the spices, and the vanilla bean over high heat. Bring to a boil, stirring to dissolve the honey. Reduce the heat to medium-low, and simmer until the liquid is reduced to 1 cup (8 fl oz/250 ml), about 8 minutes. Remove from the heat. Strain through a medium-mesh sieve into a small bowl. Cover the syrup and refrigerate until well chilled, about 1 hour.

Peel the rind from the cantaloupe, and slice the flesh into ½-inch (12-mm) cubes. In a small bowl, toss the banana slices with the 1 teaspoon lemon juice to prevent discoloration.

In a large bowl, combine the cantaloupe, banana, blueberries, kiwifruits, mango, and papaya. Add the lemon zest and the chilled syrup and toss to coat. Cover and refrigerate for at least 1 hour or up to 8 hours.

Stack the mint leaves and roll up tightly lengthwise. Slice crosswise into thin shreds. To serve, spoon the fruit mixture into individual bowls, garnish with the fresh mint chiffonade, and serve immediately.

FOR THE SYRUP

1½ cups (12 fl oz/375 ml) fresh orange juice

3 tablespoons fresh lemon juice

¼ cup (3 oz/90 g) dark honey

½ teaspoon ground cinnamon

½ teaspoon ground ginger

¼ teaspoon ground coriander

1 vanilla bean, split lengthwise

1 large cantaloupe, 3 lb (1.5 kg), halved and seeded

1 large banana, peeled and sliced crosswise

1 teaspoon fresh lemon juice

1 cup (4 oz/125 g) blueberries or raspberries

2 large kiwifruits, peeled and cut into ½-inch (12-mm) dice

1 mango, peeled, pitted, and cut into ½-inch (12-mm) dice

1 papaya, halved, seeded, peeled, and cut into ½-inch (12-mm) dice

1 tablespoon grated lemon zest

5 or 6 fresh mint leaves

Raspberry Coulis

SERVES 4

This popular and vividly colored sauce of puréed fresh raspberries takes on extra depth with the addition of sweet spices and a splash of balsamic vinegar. Stir it into yogurt or spoon it over fresh fruit.

Pyramid Servings

VEGETABLES	◀○○○○○
FRUITS	◀○○○○●
CARBOHYDRATES	○○○○○○○
PROTEIN & DAIRY	○○○○○○○
FATS	○○○○○

PER SERVING

calories	77
kilojoules	322
protein	1 g
carbohydrate	19 g
total fat	0 g
saturated fat	0 g
monounsaturated fat	0 g
cholesterol	0 mg
sodium	1 mg
fiber	4 g

In a blender or food processor, combine all the ingredients and purée until smooth.

Pass the purée through a fine-mesh sieve placed over a bowl, pressing firmly on the solids with a rubber spatula or the back of a wooden spoon to extract all the juice. Scrape the inside of the sieve periodically to dislodge any seeds that may be plugging the holes. Keep pushing the pulp firmly through the sieve until all that is left is a small number of seeds. Cover the purée and refrigerate until ready to use. Makes about 1 cup (8 fl oz/250 ml).

3 cups (12 oz/375 g) raspberries

2 tablespoons honey

1 tablespoon balsamic vinegar

¼ teaspoon ground cinnamon

Generous pinch of ground nutmeg

Making Peach Coulis

Fresh peaches and apricots can be easily turned into a velvety purée, or coulis. To make 1 cup (8 fl oz/250 ml), peel, pit, and chop 1 pound (500 g) of fruit. Place it and honey or sugar in a blender or food processor with a small amount of water. Process until smooth. Strain into a saucepan over low heat and simmer until reduced by a third. Serve as a sauce for frozen yogurt, fruit, or angel food cake.

Casaba Melon with Sweet Curry Cream

Sweet curry is made with a blend of ground spices without pepper or heat from added chiles. Combined with yogurt, it makes a light creamy sauce that complements ripe, juicy melon.

SERVES **6**

FOR THE SAUCE

1 cup (8 oz/250 g) low-fat vanilla yogurt

1 teaspoon grated lemon zest

1 teaspoon fresh lemon juice

1 teaspoon dark honey

1 teaspoon garam masala or ¼ teaspoon ground cardamom, ¼ teaspoon ground cinnamon, ¼ teaspoon ground ginger, ⅛ teaspoon ground cloves, and a pinch of ground nutmeg

1 large casaba, cantaloupe, or honeydew melon, 3½ lb (1.75 kg)

Fresh mint leaves for garnish

To make the sweet curry cream, in a bowl, whisk together the yogurt, lemon zest and juice, honey, and garam masala or spice mixture. Cover and refrigerate for 30 minutes to allow the flavors to blend.

Halve the melon, and using a spoon remove and discard the seeds. Using a melon baller, scoop out the melon flesh and place it in a large bowl.

Just before serving, place 1 cup (6 oz/185 g) melon balls in each individual bowl. Spoon about 2 tablespoons curry cream over each serving and garnish with the fresh mint. Pass the remaining sauce at the table.

Pyramid Servings

VEGETABLES	◀○○○○○
FRUITS	◀○○○○●
CARBOHYDRATES	○○○○○○○
PROTEIN & DAIRY	○○○○○○○
FATS	○○○○○

PER SERVING	
calories	90
kilojoules	377
protein	4 g
carbohydrate	18 g
total fat	1 g
saturated fat	<1 g
monounsaturated fat	0 g
cholesterol	2 mg
sodium	48 mg
fiber	2 g

Melons

Related to cucumbers and squashes, melons are classified in two groups: the muskmelons—mainly cantaloupe, casaba, Crenshaw, and honeydew—and watermelons. A ripe melon has a sweet aroma and shows a clean break at its stem end (not a short length of stem) indicating that the melon was picked ripe, not cut free while ripening. Unripe melons will soften with time but never sweeten.

Melon Fool

Make the yogurt cheese and the lemon-mint syrup a day ahead, and this puréed fruit dessert will go together in minutes. Don't hurry the draining of the yogurt; fresh ripe melons are extremely juicy.

SERVES 6

1 cup (8 oz/250 g) low-fat lemon yogurt, without gum additives or stabilizers

1 cup (8 oz/250 g) nonfat plain yogurt, without gum additives or stabilizers

¼ cup (2 fl oz/60 ml) water

¼ cup (2 fl oz/60 ml) fresh lemon juice

Zest of 1 lemon, removed in wide strips

2 tablespoons sugar

4 fresh mint leaves, plus extra for garnish

2 tablespoons whipped cream cheese

1 small cantaloupe, 1–1½ lb (500–750 g), halved and seeded

1 small honeydew melon, ½–1 lb (250–500 g), halved and seeded

Set a fine or medium-mesh sieve lined with a paper coffee filter over a bowl. Without stirring the yogurts, gently spoon both of them into the sieve. Place in the refrigerator to drain for 8 hours or up to overnight. Discard the liquid in the bowl, and spoon the yogurt cheese in the sieve into a container with a tight-fitting lid. Refrigerate until ready to use.

In a small saucepan, combine the water, lemon juice and zest, sugar, and the 4 mint leaves. Bring the mixture to a boil over medium-high heat. Remove from the heat and let stand for 30 minutes. Scoop the mint and lemon zest out of the mixture with a slotted spoon. Return the mixture to a boil over high heat. Boil until the liquid is reduced to 1 tablespoon, 3–4 minutes. Transfer the syrup to a small bowl, cover, and refrigerate until cold, about 30 minutes.

Whisk the cream cheese and chilled lemon-mint syrup into the yogurt cheese.

Cut the rind off the cantaloupe and honeydew melons and cut the flesh into chunks. Set aside a 1-inch (2.5-cm) cube of each melon. In a blender or food processor, combine the remaining melon pieces and purée until smooth. Add the yogurt cheese mixture to the food processor and pulse a few times to blend.

Cut each reserved melon cube into 6 pieces. To serve, divide the fruit mixture evenly among small ramekins or Champagne flutes. Garnish with 1 piece of each kind of melon and mint leaves.

Pyramid Servings

VEGETABLES	◀ ○○○○○
FRUITS	◀ ○○○●●
CARBOHYDRATES	○○○○○○○
PROTEIN & DAIRY	○○○○○○○
FATS	○○○○○

PER SERVING	
calories	117
kilojoules	490
protein	5 g
carbohydrate	21 g
total fat	2 g
saturated fat	1 g
monounsaturated fat	0 g
cholesterol	6 mg
sodium	76 mg
fiber	1 g

Peach-Nectarine Salsa

SERVES **8**

A blend of sweet, spicy, and tart flavors makes this savory salsa a perfect accompaniment to salmon or any grilled fresh fish. It's also a delicious topping for dishes such as bean burritos or tacos.

Pyramid Servings

VEGETABLES ◀○○○○○
FRUITS ◀○○○○●
CARBOHYDRATES ○○○○○○○○
PROTEIN & DAIRY ○○○○○○○
FATS ○○○○○

PER SERVING	
calories	42
kilojoules	176
protein	1 g
carbohydrate	10 g
total fat	0 g
saturated fat	0 g
monounsaturated fat	0 g
cholesterol	0 mg
sodium	75 mg
fiber	2 g

In a large bowl, combine all the ingredients except the salt and pepper. Toss gently to mix. Cover and refrigerate for at least 30 minutes to allow the flavors to blend.

Stir in the salt and pepper just before serving. Serve at room temperature. Makes 4 cups (32 fl oz/1 l).

2 peaches, peeled, pitted, and diced

2 nectarines, peeled, pitted, and diced

¼ cup (1½ oz/45 g) minced red onion

2 tablespoons chopped fresh mint

2 tablespoons chopped fresh flat-leaf (Italian) parsley

1½ tablespoons seeded and minced jalapeño chile

2 teaspoons grated orange zest

2 tablespoons fresh orange juice

2 tablespoons fresh lime juice

¼ teaspoon salt

⅛ teaspoon freshly ground pepper

Grilled Pineapple

Brushed with a Caribbean-style marinade and placed over hot coals, pineapple develops a smoky sweetness. You can grill the fruit several hours ahead of time and wrap it in aluminum foil until ready to serve.

SERVES 8

FOR THE MARINADE

2 tablespoons dark honey

1 tablespoon olive oil

1 tablespoon fresh lime juice

1 teaspoon ground cinnamon

¼ teaspoon ground cloves

1 firm yet ripe pineapple

8 wooden skewers, soaked in water for 30 minutes, or metal skewers

1 tablespoon dark rum (optional)

1 tablespoon grated lime zest

Prepare a hot fire in a charcoal grill or preheat a gas grill or broiler (grill). Away from the heat source, lightly coat the grill rack or broiler pan with cooking spray. Position the cooking rack 4–6 inches (10–15 cm) from the heat source.

To make the marinade, in a small bowl, combine the honey, olive oil, lime juice, cinnamon, and cloves and whisk to blend. Set aside.

Cut off the crown of leaves and the base of the pineapple. Stand the pineapple upright and, using a large, sharp knife, pare off the skin, cutting downward just below the surface in long, vertical strips and leaving the small brown "eyes" on the fruit. Lay the pineapple on its side. Aligning the knife blade with the diagonal rows of eyes, cut a shallow furrow, following a spiral pattern around the pineapple, to remove all the eyes. Stand the peeled pineapple upright and cut it in half lengthwise. Place each pineapple half cut side down and cut it lengthwise into 4 long wedges; slice away the core. Cut each wedge crosswise into 3 pieces. Thread the 3 pineapple pieces onto each skewer.

Lightly brush the pineapple with the marinade. Grill or broil, turning once and basting once or twice with the remaining marinade, until tender and golden, about 5 minutes on each side.

Remove the pineapple from the skewers and place on a platter or individual serving plates. Brush with the rum, if using, and sprinkle with the lime zest. Serve hot or warm.

Pyramid Servings

VEGETABLES	◖○○○○
FRUITS	◖○○○●
CARBOHYDRATES	○○○○○○○
PROTEIN & DAIRY	○○○○○○
FATS	○○○○○

PER SERVING	
calories	79
kilojoules	331
protein	<1 g
carbohydrate	15 g
total fat	2 g
saturated fat	<1 g
monounsaturated fat	1 g
cholesterol	0 mg
sodium	1 mg
fiber	1 g

Ambrosia with Coconut and Toasted Almonds

SERVES 8

This Southern classic is pretty and refreshing for dessert or as a snack. The simplicity of its flavors demands the sweetest fruit you can find. Sprinklings of toasted almonds and coconut offer richness with little fat.

Pyramid Servings

VEGETABLES	◀○○○○○
FRUITS	◀○○○●●
CARBOHYDRATES	○○○○○○○○○
PROTEIN & DAIRY	○○○○○○○
FATS	○○○○●

PER SERVING	
calories	146
kilojoules	611
protein	2 g
carbohydrate	26 g
total fat	4 g
saturated fat	1 g
monounsaturated fat	1 g
cholesterol	0 mg
sodium	1 mg
fiber	4 g

Preheat the oven to 325°F (165°C). Spread the almonds on a baking sheet and bake, stirring occasionally, until golden and fragrant, about 10 minutes. Transfer immediately to a plate to cool. Add the coconut to the sheet and bake, stirring often, until lightly browned, about 10 minutes. Transfer immediately to a plate to cool.

Cut off the crown of leaves and the base of the pineapple. Stand the pineapple upright and, using a large, sharp knife, pare off the skin, cutting downward just below the surface in long, vertical strips and leaving the small brown "eyes" on the fruit. Lay the pineapple on its side. Aligning the knife blade with the diagonal rows of eyes, cut a shallow furrow, following a spiral pattern around the pineapple, to remove all the eyes. Cut the pineapple crosswise into slices ¾ inch (2 cm) thick, and remove the core with a small, sharp knife or small cookie cutter. Cut into cubes and set aside.

Working with 1 orange at a time, cut a thin slice off the top and the bottom, exposing the flesh. Stand the orange upright and, using a sharp knife, thickly cut off the peel, following the contour of the fruit and removing all the white pith and membrane. Holding the orange over a bowl, carefully cut along both sides of each section to free it from the membrane. As you work, discard any seeds and let the sections fall into the bowl. Repeat with the remaining oranges.

In a large bowl, combine the pineapple, oranges, apples, banana, and sherry. Toss gently to mix well. Divide the fruit mixture evenly among individual bowls. Sprinkle evenly with the toasted almonds and coconut and garnish with the mint. Serve immediately.

½ cup (2½ oz/75 g) slivered almonds

½ cup (2 oz/60 g) unsweetened flaked coconut

1 small pineapple

5 oranges

2 red apples, cored and diced

1 banana, halved lengthwise, peeled, and sliced crosswise

2 tablespoons cream sherry

Fresh mint leaves for garnish

Fresh Figs
with Walnuts and Mascarpone

SERVES 6

Fresh figs are available just twice a year, from June through July and from September to mid-October, so it's worth going out of your way to find them. Serve these figs for an elegant end to any meal.

Pyramid Servings

VEGETABLES	◀○○○○○
FRUITS	◀○○○●●
CARBOHYDRATES	○○○○○○○○
PROTEIN & DAIRY	○○○○○○○
FATS	○○○○●

PER SERVING

calories	154
kilojoules	644
protein	1 g
carbohydrate	29 g
total fat	5 g
saturated fat	1 g
monounsaturated fat	1 g
cholesterol	4 mg
sodium	3 mg
fiber	3 g

Put the walnuts in a small, dry frying pan over medium-low heat. Cook, stirring often, until lightly toasted, 3–5 minutes. Transfer immediately to a plate to cool.

Slice the stems off the figs. Cut an X in the top of each fig, cutting down into the fruit about 1 inch (2.5 cm). Carefully squeeze each fig from the bottom to open it slightly. Spoon ½ teaspoon of the cheese into the opening of each fig and sprinkle with the nutmeg.

To serve, divide the figs among individual plates. Sprinkle with the toasted walnuts, dividing evenly. Drizzle each serving with 2 teaspoons of the honey.

¼ cup (1 oz/30 g) chopped walnuts

12 ripe figs, about 1 lb (500 g) total weight

2 tablespoons mascarpone cheese or whipped cream cheese

Pinch of ground nutmeg

¼ cup (3 oz/90 g) orange honey or other honey

Pear and Toasted Pecan Chutney

SERVES 8

A relish of fruit simmered with vinegar and spices, chutney is usually sweetened with sugar. In this quick recipe, fruit juice is used instead. Serve with curries or use to dress up grilled chicken or a sandwich.

Pyramid Servings

VEGETABLES	◀︎○○○○○
FRUITS	◀︎○○○○●
CARBOHYDRATES	○○○○○○○○
PROTEIN & DAIRY	○○○○○○○
FATS	○○○○●

PER SERVING

calories	98
kilojoules	410
protein	1 g
carbohydrate	18 g
total fat	3 g
saturated fat	0 g
monounsaturated fat	2 g
cholesterol	0 mg
sodium	5 mg
fiber	3 g

In a saucepan over high heat, bring the grape juice to a boil. Reduce the heat to low and simmer until reduced by half, 5–10 minutes.

Add the pears, vinegar, ginger, cinnamon, mustard seed, and red pepper flakes. Raise the heat to medium and bring the mixture to a boil. Reduce heat to low and simmer, uncovered, stirring occasionally, until the pears are tender and the juices have thickened, about 20 minutes. Remove from the heat and let cool to room temperature.

Stir in the pecans. Cover and refrigerate for up to 1 week. Bring to room temperature before serving. Makes about 2 cups (16 fl oz/500 ml).

1 cup (8 fl oz/250 ml) white grape juice or apple juice

4 firm yet ripe Bosc pears, peeled, cored, and coarsely chopped

¼ cup (2 fl oz/60 ml) cider vinegar

1½ teaspoons peeled and minced fresh ginger or ½ teaspoon ground ginger

½ teaspoon ground cinnamon

½ teaspoon mustard seed

¼ teaspoon red pepper flakes

¼ cup (1 oz/30 g) chopped pecans, lightly toasted

Toasting Nuts

To add flavor and crunch to nuts, place a small amount in a small, dry frying pan over medium-low heat and toast, stirring constantly, until golden brown and fragrant, 3–5 minutes. Or spread larger quantities on a baking sheet and toast in a 350°F (180°C) oven, stirring often, until lightly browned, 8–10 minutes. Transfer to a plate to cool. The same method can be used with sesame seeds.

Apple and Sweet Onion Marmalade

Sweet onions such as Vidalia, Maui, and Walla Walla are worth the search. Vidalia and Maui are in markets in spring, while Walla Walla appear in late summer. Serve this marmalade with roasted chicken or pork.

SERVES 8

1 tablespoon olive oil

1 teaspoon mustard seed

2 large Vidalia onions, diced

½ cup (4 fl oz/125 ml) apple juice

½ cup (4 fl oz/125 ml) chicken stock (page 138), vegetable stock (page 139), or broth

2 Granny Smith apples, peeled, cored, and cut into ½-inch (12-mm) dice

¼ teaspoon salt

¼ teaspoon freshly ground pepper

⅛ teaspoon ground allspice

2 tablespoons chopped fresh flat-leaf (Italian) parsley

In a sauté pan, heat the olive oil over medium heat. Add the mustard seed and onions and cook, stirring occasionally, until the onions are lightly golden, about 12 minutes.

Add the apple juice and stock and bring to a boil over high heat. Add the apples, salt, pepper, and allspice. Reduce the heat to low and simmer, uncovered, until the apples are tender, about 12 minutes.

Remove from the heat and stir in the parsley. Serve warm or at room temperature, or transfer to a container with a tight-fitting lid and refrigerate for up to 1 week. Bring the marmalade to room temperature before serving. Makes about 2 cups (16 fl oz/500 ml).

Pyramid Servings

VEGETABLES	◖○○○○○
FRUITS	◖○○○○●
CARBOHYDRATES	○○○○○○○○
PROTEIN & DAIRY	○○○○○○○
FATS	○○○○○

PER SERVING

calories	68
kilojoules	283
protein	1 g
carbohydrate	13 g
total fat	2 g
saturated fat	<1 g
monounsaturated fat	2 g
cholesterol	0 mg
sodium	36 mg
fiber	2 g

Apples

Apples deserve their great reputation. They contain pectin, a soluble fiber that helps lower heart disease risk by preventing the buildup of artery-clogging placques, while their insoluble fiber helps maintain digestive health. Cortland, Empire, Fuji, Granny Smith, Gravenstein, Jonagold, Jonathan, McIntosh, and Pippin are good both raw and cooked. Store apples in a plastic bag in the fridge.

Baked Apples
with Cherries and Almonds

SERVES 6

Any good baking apple, such as Golden Delicious, Rome, or Granny Smith, will hold its shape beautifully for this dish. Serve it as a light dessert, or alongside roasted pork or pork tenderloin.

Pyramid Servings

VEGETABLES	◀○○○○○
FRUITS	◀○○○●●
CARBOHYDRATES	○○○○○○○
PROTEIN & DAIRY	○○○○○○○
FATS	○○○○●

PER SERVING

calories	179
kilojoules	749
protein	2 g
carbohydrate	37 g
total fat	4 g
saturated fat	0 g
monounsaturated fat	2 g
cholesterol	0 mg
sodium	5 mg
fiber	5 g

Preheat the oven to 350°F (180°C).

In a small bowl, toss together the cherries, almonds, wheat germ, brown sugar, cinnamon, and nutmeg until all the ingredients are evenly distributed. Set aside.

The apples can be left unpeeled, if you like. To peel the apples in a decorative fashion, with a vegetable peeler or a sharp knife, remove the peel from each apple in a circular motion, skipping every other row so that rows of peel alternate with rows of apple flesh. Working from the stem end, core each apple, stopping ¾ inch (2 cm) from the bottom.

Divide the cherry mixture evenly among the apples, pressing the mixture gently into each cavity.

Arrange the apples upright in a heavy ovenproof frying pan or small baking dish just large enough to hold them. Pour the apple juice and water into the pan. Drizzle the honey and oil evenly over the apples, and cover the pan snugly with aluminum foil. Bake until the apples are tender when pierced with a knife, 50–60 minutes.

Transfer the apples to individual plates and drizzle with the pan juices. Serve warm or at room temperature.

⅓ cup (1½ oz/45 g) dried cherries, coarsely chopped

3 tablespoons chopped almonds

1 tablespoon wheat germ

1 tablespoon firmly packed brown sugar

½ teaspoon ground cinnamon

⅛ teaspoon ground nutmeg

6 small Golden Delicious apples, about 1¾ lb (875 g) total weight

½ cup (4 fl oz/125 ml) apple juice

¼ cup (2 fl oz/60 ml) water

2 tablespoons dark honey

2 teaspoons walnut oil or canola oil

Salads

Never before have markets offered such a variety of fresh greens rich with disease-fighting antioxidants.

100   Seared Scallops with New Potatoes and Field Greens

102   Warm Coleslaw with Honey Dressing

105   Grilled Pear and Watercress Salad

106   Mesclun Salad with Radishes, Avocado, and Blood Oranges

108   Chicken Salad with Thai Flavors

109   Ratatouille with Roasted Tomato Vinaigrette

111   Greek Salad

112   Yellow Pear and Cherry Tomato Salad

114   Avocado Salad with Ginger-Miso Dressing

115   Fattoush

117   Grilled Flank Steak Salad with Roasted Corn Vinaigrette

118   Fennel and Leeks with Roasted Onion Vinaigrette

Seared Scallops with New Potatoes and Field Greens

SERVES 4

This warm salad makes for a quick, light supper. Be careful not to overcook the scallops, or they will lose their subtle texture. If you can, make the lemon dressing earlier in the day to allow flavors to blend.

Pyramid Servings

VEGETABLES	◀○○○○●
FRUITS	◀○○○○○
CARBOHYDRATES	○○○○○○○●
PROTEIN & DAIRY	○○○○○●●
FATS	○○○○●

PER SERVING

calories	344
kilojoules	1,439
protein	32 g
carbohydrate	31 g
total fat	12 g
saturated fat	2 g
monounsaturated fat	7 g
cholesterol	47 mg
sodium	619 mg
fiber	5 g

To make the dressing, in a blender or food processor, combine the tofu, lemon zest and juice, mustard, anchovy paste, garlic, salt, and pepper. Process until smooth. With the motor running, slowly add the extra-virgin olive oil in a thin stream until emulsified. Cover and refrigerate until needed.

Put the potatoes in a saucepan, add water to cover, and bring to a boil over high heat. Reduce the heat to medium and cook, uncovered, until the potatoes are tender, 15–20 minutes. Drain and let stand until just cool enough to handle. Cut each potato in half (or quarters, if the potatoes are large). In a bowl, toss the potatoes gently with half of the dressing. Set aside and keep warm.

Season the scallops with the salt and ground pepper. In a large frying pan, heat the olive oil over medium-high heat. Place the scallops in the hot pan and sear on one side until golden, about 1 minute. Turn and cook on the other side until the scallops begin to turn opaque at the center, 1–2 minutes longer. Remove from the heat.

To serve, toss the greens with the remaining dressing and divide among individual plates. Scatter the potatoes and scallops over the greens. Sprinkle with the chives and cracked pepper. Serve immediately.

FOR THE DRESSING

1 cup (8 oz/250 g) silken or soft tofu

1 teaspoon lemon zest

1 tablespoon fresh lemon juice

1½ teaspoons Dijon mustard

½ teaspoon anchovy paste

1 clove garlic, minced

¼ teaspoon salt

¼ teaspoon freshly ground pepper

2 tablespoons extra-virgin olive oil

1 lb (500 g) Yukon gold or red-skinned new potatoes

1¼ lb (625 g) sea scallops

¼ teaspoon salt

¼ teaspoon freshly ground pepper

1 tablespoon olive oil

8 cups (8 oz/250 g) mixed field greens such as baby lettuces, sorrel, and tatsoi

6 tablespoons (½ oz/15 g) chopped fresh chives

2 teaspoons cracked pepper

Warm Coleslaw with Honey Dressing

SERVES 6

Cabbage is one of the healthful cruciferous vegetables. For this slaw, sliced vegetables are quickly stir-fried, then tossed in a hot dressing. Serve with Pork Medallions with Five-Spice Powder (page 265).

Pyramid Servings

VEGETABLES	◀○○○●●
FRUITS	◀○○○○○
CARBOHYDRATES	○○○○○○○○
PROTEIN & DAIRY	○○○○○○○
FATS	○○○○●

PER SERVING	
calories	91
kilojoules	381
protein	2 g
carbohydrate	12 g
total fat	5 g
saturated fat	<1 g
monounsaturated fat	3 g
cholesterol	0 mg
sodium	221 mg
fiber	3 g

In a large nonstick sauté pan, heat 2 teaspoons of the olive oil over medium-high heat until hot but not smoking. Add the onion and mustard and sauté until the onion is soft and lightly golden, about 6 minutes. Transfer to a large bowl.

Reduce the heat to medium and add 2 more teaspoons of the olive oil to the pan. Add the carrot and toss and stir constantly until the carrot is tender-crisp, about 3 minutes. Transfer to the bowl with the onion.

Add the remaining 2 teaspoons oil to the pan over medium heat. Add the cabbage and toss and stir constantly until the cabbage just begins to wilt, about 3 minutes. Quickly transfer the cabbage to the bowl with the other vegetables.

Quickly add the vinegar and honey to the pan over medium heat, stirring until combined and bubbly and the honey is dissolved. Pour over the slaw. Add the salt and pepper and toss well. Garnish with the caraway seed and parsley and serve warm.

6 teaspoons olive oil

1 yellow onion, finely chopped

1 teaspoon dry mustard

1 large carrot, peeled and cut into julienne

½ head napa cabbage, cored and thinly sliced crosswise (about 5 cups/14 oz/440 g)

3 tablespoons cider vinegar

1 tablespoon dark honey

½ teaspoon salt

¼ teaspoon freshly ground pepper

½ teaspoon caraway seed

1 tablespoon chopped fresh flat-leaf (Italian) parsley

Grilled Pear and Watercress Salad

Its interesting, assertive flavor makes watercress a perfect partner for the richness of blue cheese and sweetness of spiced walnuts. This first-course salad can also be served as a main course for lunch.

SERVES 6

2 tablespoons firmly packed brown sugar

1 tablespoon water

¼ teaspoon freshly ground pepper

2 tablespoons chopped walnuts

2 firm yet ripe pears, cored and cut into 6 lengthwise wedges, peel intact

Lemon juice for brushing

FOR THE VINAIGRETTE

2 tablespoons fresh lemon juice, plus extra for brushing

1 tablespoon rice vinegar

1 teaspoon Dijon mustard

1 tablespoon minced shallot

¼ teaspoon salt

¼ teaspoon freshly ground pepper

1 tablespoon extra-virgin olive oil

6 cups (7 oz/220 g) watercress sprigs, tough stems removed

3 tablespoons crumbled blue cheese

Prepare a hot fire in a charcoal grill or preheat a gas grill or broiler (grill). Away from the heat source, lightly coat the grill rack or broiler pan with cooking spray. Position the cooking rack 4–6 inches (10–15 cm) from the heat source.

In a small frying pan over medium heat, combine the brown sugar, water, and pepper. Cook, stirring constantly, until the sugar dissolves. Stir in the walnuts, reduce the heat to low, and cook for 30 seconds. Remove from the heat and quickly spread the nuts on a sheet of parchment (baking) paper or a plate. Set aside and let cool.

Brush the pear wedges with lemon juice and arrange on the grill or broiler pan. Grill or broil, turning once, until the pears begin to brown, 3–4 minutes total. Set aside.

To make the vinaigrette, in a small bowl, whisk together the 2 tablespoons lemon juice, the rice vinegar, the mustard, and the shallot. Add the salt and pepper and whisk to blend. While whisking, slowly add the olive oil in a thin stream until emulsified.

In a large bowl, combine the watercress and blue cheese. Pour the vinaigrette over the salad and toss gently to mix well and coat evenly.

To serve, divide the salad among individual plates. Place 2 pear wedges on each, then sprinkle with the walnuts.

Pyramid Servings

VEGETABLES	◀○○○○○
FRUITS	◀○○○○●
CARBOHYDRATES	○○○○○○○○
PROTEIN & DAIRY	○○○○○○○
FATS	○○○○●

PER SERVING	
calories	101
kilojoules	423
protein	2 g
carbohydrate	13 g
total fat	5 g
saturated fat	1 g
monounsaturated fat	2 g
cholesterol	3 mg
sodium	184 mg
fiber	2 g

Mesclun Salad with Radishes, Avocado, and Blood Oranges

SERVES 6

The mix of gourmet salad greens called mesclun may include oakleaf lettuce, arugula (rocket), frisée, mizuna, mâche, radicchio, and sorrel. Here, it is brightened with the red flesh of blood oranges.

Pyramid Servings

VEGETABLES	◀○○○○●
FRUITS	◀○○○○●
CARBOHYDRATES	○○○○○○○○
PROTEIN & DAIRY	○○○○○○○
FATS	○○○○●

PER SERVING

calories	105
kilojoules	439
protein	3 g
carbohydrate	14 g
total fat	5 g
saturated fat	1 g
monounsaturated fat	3 g
cholesterol	2 mg
sodium	170 mg
fiber	4 g

Working with 1 orange at a time, cut a thin slice off the top and the bottom, exposing the flesh. Stand the orange upright and, using a sharp knive, thickly cut off the peel, following the contour of the fruit and removing all the white pith and membrane. Holding the orange over a small bowl, carefully cut along both sides of each section to free it from the membrane. As you work, discard any seeds and let the sections and any juice fall into the bowl. Repeat with the second orange. When both oranges are sectioned, squeeze the membranes into the bowl to extract all of the juice.

To make the vinaigrette, in a small bowl, whisk together 2 tablespoons of the captured blood orange juice, the vinegar, and the mustard. While whisking, slowly add the olive oil in a thin stream until emulsified. Whisk in the salt and pepper. Reserve any remaining orange juice for another use.

In a large bowl, combine the mesclun, radishes, and orange sections. Pour the vinaigrette over the salad and toss gently to mix well and coat evenly.

To serve, divide the salad among individual plates. Top each portion with slices of avocado and sprinkle with the cheese.

2 small blood oranges or other oranges

1 tablespoon rice vinegar

½ teaspoon Dijon mustard

1 tablespoon extra-virgin olive oil

¼ teaspoon salt

¼ teaspoon freshly ground pepper

6 cups (6 oz/185 g) mesclun or mixed young salad greens

4 red radishes, trimmed and very thinly sliced

½ small avocado, peeled and thinly sliced

2 tablespoons crumbled blue cheese

Chicken Salad with Thai Flavors

SERVES 4

This salad is a worthy centerpiece for a luncheon, but you can also serve it wrapped in whole-wheat (wholemeal) tortillas or tucked inside warm pita bread. Try using all cabbage instead of the spinach mix.

Pyramid Servings

VEGETABLES ◀ ○ ○ ● ● ●
FRUITS ◀ ○ ○ ○ ○ ○
CARBOHYDRATES ○ ○ ○ ○ ○ ○ ○
PROTEIN & DAIRY ○ ○ ○ ○ ○ ● ●
FATS ○ ○ ○ ○ ●

PER SERVING	
calories	340
kilojoules	1,423
protein	40 g
carbohydrate	11 g
total fat	15 g
saturated fat	2 g
monounsaturated fat	2 g
cholesterol	82 mg
sodium	790 mg
fiber	2 g

In a large saucepan, combine the stock, lemongrass, ginger, halved green onion, and cilantro sprigs. Bring to a boil over high heat, reduce the heat to low, and simmer for 5 minutes. Add the chicken breasts, raise the heat to high, and return to a boil. Again reduce the heat to low and simmer the chicken for 3 minutes. Remove from the heat and cover. Uncover after 5 minutes and allow the chicken to cool in the stock. Remove the chicken from the stock when cool enough to handle. Reserve the stock. Using your fingers, shred the chicken with the grain into strips about ½ inch (12 mm) thick and 2 inches (5 cm) long. Cover and refrigerate.

Strain the cooled stock and discard the solids. Return 1½ cups (12 fl oz/375 ml) of the stock to the saucepan; discard the remaining liquid. Bring to a boil over medium-high heat and cook, uncovered, until reduced to ½ cup (4 fl oz/125 ml), 5–6 minutes. Cool slightly.

In a blender, combine the lime juice, vinegar, fish sauce, soy sauce, shallot, peanut butter, garlic, and reduced stock. Blend until smooth. With the motor running, slowly add the olive oil. The dressing will be somewhat thin. Set aside.

Remove the stems from the spinach and cut out the core from the cabbage. Stack the spinach and cabbage leaves separately, roll up lengthwise, and cut crosswise into ¼-inch (6-mm) chiffonade.

In a large bowl, toss together the spinach, cabbage, shredded chicken, carrot, chopped cilantro, and sliced green onions. Pour half of the dressing over the salad. Divide the salad evenly among individual plates. Garnish with the peanuts. Pass the remaining dressing at the table.

2 cups (16 fl oz/500 ml) chicken stock (page 138), vegetable stock (page 139), or broth

2 stalks lemongrass, bottom 6 inches (15 cm) only, thinly sliced

½-inch (12-mm) piece fresh ginger, thinly sliced

1 green (spring) onion, halved lengthwise, plus 2 green onions, thinly sliced

3 fresh cilantro (fresh coriander) sprigs, plus 3 tablespoons chopped

1¼ lb (625 g) skinless, boneless chicken breasts

2 tablespoons fresh lime juice

2 tablespoons rice vinegar

1 tablespoon fish sauce

1 tablespoon reduced-sodium soy sauce

1 tablespoon minced shallot

1 tablespoon peanut butter

1 clove garlic

3 tablespoons extra-virgin olive oil

½ bunch spinach

½ small head green cabbage

1 large carrot, peeled, halved lengthwise, and thinly sliced on the diagonal

1 tablespoon unsalted dry-roasted peanuts, crushed

Ratatouille with Roasted Tomato Vinaigrette

Traditionally, ratatouille is a mélange of eggplant, onions, zucchini, bell peppers, and tomatoes simmered into a stew with garlic and herbs. This version adds roasted peppers and grated lemon zest.

SERVES 8

- 1 eggplant (aubergine), about 1 lb (500 g), cut into ½-inch (12-mm) dice
- 7 teaspoons extra-virgin olive oil
- 2 zucchini (courgettes), about ½ lb (250 g) total weight, cut into ½-inch (12-mm) dice
- 2 plum (Roma) tomatoes, halved lengthwise
- 1 yellow bell pepper (capsicum), roasted and seeded (page 165)
- 1 red bell pepper (capsicum), roasted and seeded (page 165)
- 1 shallot, coarsely chopped
- ¼ cup (2 fl oz/60 ml) balsamic vinegar
- ½ teaspoon salt
- ½ teaspoon freshly ground pepper
- 1 tablespoon grated lemon zest
- 1 tablespoon chopped fresh basil
- 1 tablespoon chopped fresh flat-leaf (Italian) parsley

Position racks in the lower third and middle of the oven and preheat to 450°F (230°C). Lightly coat 2 baking sheets with olive oil cooking spray.

In a bowl, toss the eggplant with 1 teaspoon of the olive oil. Spread the eggplant in a single layer on 1 of the prepared baking sheets. On the other prepared baking sheet, spread the zucchini in a single layer and arrange the tomato halves cut side up. Drizzle the zucchini and tomatoes with 1 teaspoon of the olive oil. Place the eggplant on the lower rack and the zucchini and tomatoes on the middle rack of the oven. Roast for 8 minutes. Turn the eggplant, zucchini, and tomatoes and roast until softened, about 8 minutes longer. Set aside to cool.

Peel the roasted bell peppers and cut into ½-inch (12-mm) dice. Set aside.

In a blender or food processor, combine the roasted tomatoes, shallot, vinegar, salt, and pepper. Process until smooth. With the motor running, slowly add the remaining 5 teaspoons olive oil in a thin stream until emulsified.

In a large bowl, stir together the roasted eggplant, zucchini, and bell peppers and the lemon zest. Add the vinaigrette and toss just to combine. Sprinkle with the basil and parsley. Cover and refrigerate or serve at room temperature.

Pyramid Servings

VEGETABLES	◐○○○○●
FRUITS	◐○○○○
CARBOHYDRATES	○○○○○○○○
PROTEIN & DAIRY	○○○○○○○
FATS	○○○○●

PER SERVING	
calories	71
kilojoules	255
protein	1 g
carbohydrate	8 g
total fat	4 g
saturated fat	1 g
monounsaturated fat	2 g
cholesterol	0 mg
sodium	153 mg
fiber	3 g

Greek Salad

The simple flavors of this Mediterranean salad provide the perfect opportunity to showcase a fruity extra-virgin olive oil in a lemony dressing. For variety, try romaine (cos) lettuce instead of spinach.

SERVES 8

FOR THE VINAIGRETTE

1 tablespoon red wine vinegar

1 tablespoon fresh lemon juice

2 teaspoons chopped fresh oregano or ¾ teaspoon dried oregano

½ teaspoon salt

¼ teaspoon freshly ground pepper

2½ tablespoons extra-virgin olive oil

1 large eggplant (aubergine), about 1½ lb (750 g), trimmed and cut into ½-inch (12-mm) cubes

1 lb (500 g) spinach, stemmed and torn into bite-sized pieces

1 English (hothouse) cucumber, peeled, seeded, and diced

1 tomato, seeded and diced

½ red onion, diced

2 tablespoons pitted, chopped black Greek olives

2 tablespoons crumbled feta cheese

Position a rack in the lower third of the oven and preheat to 450°F (230°C). Lightly coat a baking sheet with olive oil cooking spray.

To make the vinaigrette, in a small bowl, whisk together the vinegar, lemon juice, oregano, salt, and pepper. While whisking, slowly add the olive oil in a thin stream until emulsified. Set aside.

Spread the eggplant cubes in a single layer on the prepared baking sheet. Spray the eggplant with olive oil cooking spray. Roast for 10 minutes. Turn the cubes and roast until softened and lightly golden, 8–10 minutes longer. Set aside and let cool completely.

In a large bowl, combine the spinach, cucumber, tomato, onion, and cooled eggplant. Pour the vinaigrette over the salad and toss gently to mix well and coat evenly. Divide the salad among individual plates. Sprinkle with the olives and feta. Serve immediately.

Pyramid Servings

VEGETABLES ◀ ○ ○ ● ●
FRUITS ◀ ○ ○ ○ ○
CARBOHYDRATES ○ ○ ○ ○ ○ ○ ○
PROTEIN & DAIRY ○ ○ ○ ○ ○ ○
FATS ○ ○ ○ ○ ●

PER SERVING	
calories	88
kilojoules	368
protein	3 g
carbohydrate	9 g
total fat	5 g
saturated fat	1 g
monounsaturated fat	3 g
cholesterol	2 mg
sodium	245 mg
fiber	3 g

Yellow Pear and Cherry Tomato Salad

SERVES 6

Ripe tomatoes, fresh basil, and olive oil always make a superb salad. But the combination looks especially spectacular when composed with brightly colored yellow pear, orange, and red cherry tomatoes.

Pyramid Servings

VEGETABLES	◀ ○○○○●
FRUITS	◀ ○○○○○
CARBOHYDRATES	○○○○○○○○
PROTEIN & DAIRY	○○○○○○○
FATS	○○○○●

PER SERVING

calories	47
kilojoules	197
protein	1 g
carbohydrate	6 g
total fat	3 g
saturated fat	0 g
monounsaturated fat	2 g
cholesterol	0 mg
sodium	108 mg
fiber	1 g

To make the vinaigrette, in a small bowl, combine the vinegar and shallot and let stand for 15 minutes. Add the olive oil, salt, and pepper and whisk until well blended.

In a large serving or salad bowl, toss together all the tomatoes. Pour the vinaigrette over the tomatoes, add the basil shreds, and toss gently to mix well and coat evenly. Serve immediately.

FOR THE VINAIGRETTE

2 tablespoons sherry vinegar or red wine vinegar

1 tablespoon minced shallot

1 tablespoon extra-virgin olive oil

¼ teaspoon salt

⅛ teaspoon freshly ground pepper

1½ cups (9 oz/280 g) yellow pear tomatoes, halved

1½ cups (9 oz/280 g) orange cherry tomatoes, halved

1½ cups (9 oz/280 g) red cherry tomatoes, halved

4 large fresh basil leaves, cut into chiffonade

Avocado Salad with Ginger-Miso Dressing

SERVES 6

Four classic soy foods—tofu, soy milk, miso, and soy sauce—flavor this creamy dressing. A perfect complement to the avocado in this salad, the dressing is equally delicious on sliced tomatoes or grilled salmon.

Pyramid Servings

VEGETABLES	◀○○○○●
FRUITS	◀○○○○○
CARBOHYDRATES	○○○○○○○○
PROTEIN & DAIRY	○○○○○○○
FATS	○○○○●

PER SERVING

calories	82
kilojoules	343
protein	2 g
carbohydrate	8 g
total fat	5 g
saturated fat	1 g
monounsaturated fat	2 g
cholesterol	0 mg
sodium	104 mg
fiber	4 g

To make the dressing, in a blender or food processor, combine the tofu, soy milk, ginger, soy sauce, miso, and mustard. Process just until smooth and creamy. Transfer to a bowl and stir in the cilantro and green onion. Cover and refrigerate for at least 1 hour.

In a small bowl, toss the avocado slices in the lemon juice to prevent browning. Set aside. In a large bowl, combine the lettuces, red and green onions, and cilantro and toss to mix. Add two-thirds of the dressing and toss lightly to coat.

Divide the salad among individual plates. Arrange 2 avocado slices on top of each portion in a crisscross pattern. Top each avocado cross with a dollop of the remaining dressing. Serve immediately.

FOR THE DRESSING

⅓ cup (3 oz/90 g) plain silken tofu

⅓ cup (3 fl oz/80 ml) low-fat plain soy milk (soya milk)

1 tablespoon peeled and minced fresh ginger

1½ teaspoons reduced-sodium soy sauce

1 teaspoon light miso

1 teaspoon Dijon mustard

1 tablespoon chopped fresh cilantro (fresh coriander)

1 tablespoon chopped green (spring) onion, including tender green top

1 small avocado, pitted, peeled, and cut into 12 thin slices

1 tablespoon fresh lemon juice

¾ lb (375 g) mixed baby lettuces

¼ cup (1 oz/30 g) julienned red onion

1 green (spring) onion, including tender green top, thinly sliced on the diagonal

1 tablespoon chopped fresh cilantro (fresh coriander)

Fattoush

Fattoush is a traditional Lebanese salad seasoned with sumac, a tart, deep red spice made from the dried berries of the sumac bush. It can be found in Middle Eastern groceries and well-stocked supermarkets.

SERVES 8

FOR THE DRESSING

¼ cup (2 fl oz/60 ml) fresh lemon juice

3 cloves garlic, minced

1 teaspoon ground cumin

1 teaspoon ground sumac (optional)

½ teaspoon salt

½ teaspoon red pepper flakes

¼ teaspoon freshly ground black pepper

7 tablespoons (3½ fl oz/ 105 ml) extra-virgin olive oil

2 whole-wheat (wholemeal) pita breads, 6 inches (15 cm) in diameter, torn into ½-inch (12-mm) pieces

1 head romaine (cos) lettuce, diced (about 4 cups/ 6 oz/185 g)

2 tomatoes, seeded and diced

2 small cucumbers, peeled, seeded, and diced

1 red bell pepper (capsicum), seeded and diced

3 green (spring) onions, including tender green tops, minced

1 tablespoon chopped fresh mint

¼ cup (⅓ oz/10 g) chopped fresh flat-leaf (Italian) parsley

To make the dressing, in a blender or a food processor, combine the lemon juice, garlic, cumin, sumac (if using), salt, red pepper flakes, and black pepper. Process until smooth. With the motor running, slowly add the olive oil in a thin stream until emulsified. Set the dressing aside.

Preheat the oven to 400°F (200°C). Spread the pita bread pieces in a single layer on a baking sheet and bake until crisp and lightly golden, about 8 minutes. Set aside to cool.

In a large bowl, combine the lettuce, tomatoes, cucumbers, bell pepper, green onions, mint, and parsley and toss. Add one-third of the dressing and toss lightly to coat evenly. Transfer the remaining dressing to a container with a tight-fitting lid and refrigerate for another use. It will keep for up to 1 week. Divide the salad among individual plates. Top with the pita croutons, dividing evenly. Serve immediately.

Pyramid Servings

VEGETABLES	◀○○○○●
FRUITS	◀○○○○○
CARBOHYDRATES	○○○○○○●
PROTEIN & DAIRY	○○○○○○○
FATS	○○○○●

PER SERVING	
calories	102
kilojoules	427
protein	3 g
carbohydrate	14 g
total fat	5 g
saturated fat	<1 g
monounsaturated fat	3 g
cholesterol	0 mg
sodium	141 mg
fiber	3 g

Grilled Flank Steak Salad with Roasted Corn Vinaigrette

Many seasonings meld in this harmonious main dish. Cook the black beans for the salad as you would the cannellini beans in the Tuscan White Bean Stew (page 125), or use good-quality canned beans.

SERVES 6

3 cups (18 oz/560 g) fresh corn kernels (cut from 4 or 5 ears corn) or frozen corn kernels, thawed

½ cup (4 fl oz/125 ml) vegetable stock (page 139) or broth

2 tablespoons fresh lime juice

2 tablespoons chopped red bell pepper (capsicum)

2 tablespoons extra-virgin olive oil

1 teaspoon salt

½ teaspoon freshly ground black pepper

¼ cup (⅓ oz/10 g) chopped fresh cilantro (fresh coriander)

1 tablespoon ground cumin

2 teaspoons dried oregano

¼ teaspoon red pepper flakes

¾ lb (375 g) flank steak

1 large head romaine (cos) lettuce, trimmed and torn into bite-sized pieces

4 cups (1½ lb/750 g) cherry tomatoes, halved

¾ cup (3 oz/90 g) thinly sliced red onion

1½ cups (10½ oz/330 g) cooked black beans

Place a dry, large cast-iron or heavy nonstick frying pan over medium-high heat. Add the corn and cook, stirring often, until the corn begins to brown, 4–5 minutes. Remove from the heat and set aside.

In a food processor, combine the stock, lime juice, bell pepper, and 1 cup (6 oz/185 g) of the roasted corn. Pulse to purée. Add the olive oil, ½ teaspoon of the salt, ¼ teaspoon of the black pepper, and the cilantro. Pulse once to blend. Set the vinaigrette aside.

Prepare a hot fire in a charcoal grill or preheat a gas grill or broiler (grill). Away from the heat source, lightly coat the grill rack or broiler pan with cooking spray. Position the cooking rack 4–6 inches (10–15 cm) from the heat source.

In a small bowl, mix together the cumin, oregano, red pepper flakes, and the remaining ½ teaspoon salt and ¼ teaspoon black pepper. Rub on both sides of the steak.

Place the steak on the grill rack or broiler pan and grill or broil, turning once, until browned, 4–5 minutes on each side. Cut into the center to check for doneness. Let stand for 5 minutes. Cut across the grain into thin slices. Cut the slices into pieces 2 inches (5 cm) long.

In a large bowl, combine the lettuce, tomatoes, onion, black beans, and remaining roasted corn. Add the vinaigrette and toss gently to mix well and coat evenly.

To serve, divide the salad among individual plates. Top each serving with slices of grilled steak.

Pyramid Servings

VEGETABLES	◖○○○●●
FRUITS	◖○○○○○
CARBOHYDRATES	○○○○○○●●
PROTEIN & DAIRY	○○○○○○●
FATS	○○○○●

PER SERVING

calories	335
kilojoules	1,402
protein	22 g
carbohydrate	43 g
total fat	11 g
saturated fat	3 g
monounsaturated fat	6 g
cholesterol	29 mg
sodium	481 mg
fiber	9 g

Fennel and Leeks with Roasted Onion Vinaigrette

SERVES 8

Here is a great make-ahead salad, as the vegetables can be cooked and the dressing prepared up to a day in advance. This flavorful salad may be served at room temperature or chilled. Assemble just before serving.

Pyramid Servings

VEGETABLES	◀○○○●●
FRUITS	◀○○○○○
CARBOHYDRATES	○○○○○○
PROTEIN & DAIRY	○○○○○○
FATS	○○○○●

PER SERVING	
calories	75
kilojoules	314
protein	2 g
carbohydrate	12 g
total fat	3 g
saturated fat	0 g
monounsaturated fat	2 g
cholesterol	0 mg
sodium	96 mg
fiber	3 g

Split the leeks in half lengthwise to within 1½ inches (4 cm) of the root end, leaving the root intact. Discard the outer leaves and rinse the leeks well.

In a large pot with a tight-fitting lid, combine the stock, vinegar, water, oregano, and peppercorns. Bring to a boil over medium-high heat. Add the fennel and leeks; the liquid may not cover. Return to a boil, reduce the heat to low, cover, and simmer until the vegetables are just tender, about 15 minutes. Remove from the heat and let cool in the pot, uncovered, for 1 hour. Remove the vegetables with a slotted spoon and set aside. Reserve the poaching liquid.

While the vegetables are cooling, preheat the oven to 400°F (200°C). Arrange the onion wedges on a baking sheet and drizzle with 1 teaspoon of the olive oil. Roast for 15 minutes. Turn the onion wedges over and bake until browned and caramelized, about 15 minutes longer. Set aside to cool.

Strain the reserved poaching liquid and pour 1 cup (8 fl oz/250 ml) into a small saucepan. The remaining liquid may be reserved for soup or another use. Bring to a boil over high heat and cook, uncovered, until reduced by half, 5–10 minutes. Remove from the heat and let cool.

In a blender or food processor, combine the roasted onion with the reduced poaching liquid and mustard. Process until smooth. (Add 1 tablespoon water if the mixture is too thick to process.) With the motor running, add the remaining 5 teaspoons olive oil in a thin stream until emulsified.

Cut each leek and fennel half crosswise into 8 slices (or cut thinner if desired). Divide the vegetables evenly among individual plates. Drizzle about 1 tablespoon of the vinaigrette on each salad. Garnish with the olives and fennel leaves.

3 leeks, green tops trimmed to about 7 inches (18 cm), bottom trimmed but intact

2 cups (16 fl oz/500 ml) chicken stock (page 138), vegetable stock (page 139), or broth

1 cup (8 fl oz/250 ml) white wine vinegar

1 cup (8 fl oz/250 ml) water

1 tablespoon chopped fresh oregano

5 peppercorns

2 fennel bulbs, trimmed and cut in half vertically; green tops reserved for garnish

½ yellow onion, cut into 4 wedges

2 tablespoons extra-virgin olive oil

1 teaspoon Dijon mustard

2 tablespoons pitted, chopped Kalamata olives

1 tablespoon chopped fennel tops or fresh flat-leaf (Italian) parsley

Soups

Soup can span a daily menu's whole spectrum, from quick lunch to light side dish to hearty dinner.

122   Corn Chowder with Roasted Poblanos

125   Tuscan White Bean Stew

126   Miso Soup with Watercress and Shiitakes

127   Fresh Tomato Soup with Crispy Herb Toasts

129   Split Pea Soup

130   Gingery Chicken Noodle Soup

132   Chicken Adobo Soup with Bok Choy

133   Curried Carrot Soup

135   Posole with Fresh Corn Gorditas

136   Summer Vegetable Soup

138   Easy Chicken Stock

139   Easy Vegetable Stock

Curried Carrot Soup, page 133

Corn Chowder with Roasted Poblanos

SERVES 4

Dark green poblanos, traditionally used for *chiles rellenos,* take on a smoky flavor when roasted. That smokiness makes them a perfect contrast for the sweet corn flavor of this filling main course.

Pyramid Servings

VEGETABLES	◖○○●●●
FRUITS	◖○○○○○
CARBOHYDRATES	○○○○○○●●
PROTEIN & DAIRY	○○○○○○○
FATS	○○○●●

PER SERVING

calories	304
kilojoules	1,272
protein	9 g
carbohydrate	50 g
total fat	10 g
saturated fat	2 g
monounsaturated fat	6 g
cholesterol	2 mg
sodium	380 mg
fiber	6 g

Preheat a gas grill or broiler (grill). Position the cooking rack 4–6 inches (10–15 cm) from the heat source.

Arrange the chiles, skin side down on the grill rack, or skin side up on a broiler pan lined with aluminum foil or parchment (baking) paper. Grill or broil until the skins begin to blacken, 5–7 minutes. Transfer to a bowl, cover with plastic wrap, and let steam until the skins loosen, about 10 minutes. Peel the chiles and chop coarsely. Set aside.

Put the potatoes in a saucepan, add water to cover, and bring to a boil over high heat. Reduce the heat to medium and cook, uncovered, until the potatoes are tender, 15–20 minutes. Drain and transfer to a small bowl. With a potato masher, partially mash the potatoes and set aside.

In a large saucepan, heat the olive oil over medium heat. Add the onion, celery, and bell pepper and sauté until the vegetables are softened, about 5 minutes. Stir in ¼ teaspoon of the salt and cook for 3–4 minutes longer. Stir in the roasted chiles and the mashed potatoes. Add the corn, stock, milk, pepper, and the remaining ¼ teaspoon salt and simmer, uncovered, until the soup thickens, 25–30 minutes.

Ladle into warmed individual bowls and sprinkle with the cilantro and oregano. Serve immediately.

2 poblano or Anaheim chiles, halved lengthwise and seeded

2 or 3 Yukon gold or red-skinned potatoes, about 1 lb (500 g) total weight, peeled and cut into 1½ -inch (4-cm) chunks

2 tablespoons olive oil

1 small yellow onion, chopped

¼ cup (1 oz/30 g) diced celery

½ red bell pepper (capsicum), seeded and diced

½ teaspoon salt

2½ cups (15 oz/470 g) fresh corn kernels (cut from about 4 ears corn) or frozen corn kernels, thawed

2 cups (16 fl oz/500 ml) vegetable stock (page 139) or broth

1 cup (8 fl oz/250 ml) 1-percent low-fat milk

¼ teaspoon freshly ground pepper

2 tablespoons chopped fresh cilantro (fresh coriander)

2 teaspoons chopped fresh oregano or ½ teaspoon dried oregano

Tuscan White Bean Stew

The white beans called cannellini, along with garlic and rosemary or sage, are traditional ingredients in many soups and stews in Tuscany. Serve as a main course with a simple salad of mixed greens.

SERVES 6

FOR THE CROUTONS

1 tablespoon extra-virgin olive oil

2 cloves garlic, quartered

1 slice (1 oz/30 g) whole-grain peasant bread, cut into ½-inch (12-mm) cubes

2 cups (14 oz/440 g) dried cannellini or other white beans, picked over and rinsed, soaked overnight, and drained

6 cups (48 fl oz/1.5 l) water

1 teaspoon salt

1 bay leaf

2 tablespoons olive oil

1 yellow onion, coarsely chopped

3 carrots, peeled and coarsely chopped

6 cloves garlic, chopped

¼ teaspoon freshly ground pepper

1 tablespoon chopped fresh rosemary, plus 6 sprigs

1½ cups (12 fl oz/375 ml) vegetable stock (page 139) or broth

To make the croutons, in a large frying pan, heat the olive oil over medium heat. Add the garlic and sauté for 1 minute. Remove from the heat and let stand for 10 minutes to infuse the garlic flavor into the oil. Remove the garlic and discard. Return the pan to medium heat. Add the bread cubes and sauté, stirring frequently, until lightly browned, 3–5 minutes. Transfer to a small bowl and set aside.

In a soup pot over high heat, combine the white beans, water, ½ teaspoon of the salt, and the bay leaf. Bring to a boil over high heat. Reduce the heat to low, cover partially, and simmer until the beans are tender, 60–75 minutes. Drain the beans, reserving ½ cup (4 fl oz/125 ml) of the cooking liquid. Discard the bay leaf.

In a small bowl, combine the reserved cooking liquid and ½ cup (3½ oz/105 g) of the cooked beans. Mash with a fork to form a paste. Stir the bean paste into the cooked beans.

Return the pot to the stove top and add the olive oil. Heat over medium-high heat. Stir in the onion and carrots and sauté until the carrots are tender-crisp, 6–7 minutes. Stir in the garlic and cook until softened, about 1 minute. Stir in the remaining ½ teaspoon salt, the pepper, the chopped rosemary, the bean mixture, and the stock. Bring to a boil, then reduce the heat to low and simmer until the stew is heated through, about 5 minutes.

Ladle into warmed individual bowls and sprinkle with the croutons. Garnish each bowl with a rosemary sprig and serve immediately.

Pyramid Servings

VEGETABLES	◀○○○○●
FRUITS	◀○○○○
CARBOHYDRATES	○○○○○○●
PROTEIN & DAIRY	○○○○●●
FATS	○○○○○

PER SERVING	
calories	328
kilojoules	1,372
protein	15 g
carbohydrate	51 g
total fat	8 g
saturated fat	1 g
monounsaturated fat	5 g
cholesterol	0 mg
sodium	423 mg
fiber	19 g

Miso Soup
with Watercress and Shiitakes

SERVES 6

Miso, a Japanese flavoring, is made by fermenting cooked soybeans. White and yellow misos are mild; dark varieties have more complex flavors. Look for miso in the cold case of well-stocked supermarkets.

Pyramid Servings

VEGETABLES	◀○●●●●
FRUITS	◀○○○○○
CARBOHYDRATES	○○○○○○○○
PROTEIN & DAIRY	○○○○○○○
FATS	○○○○○

PER SERVING	
calories	98
kilojoules	410
protein	8 g
carbohydrate	7 g
total fat	4 g
saturated fat	<1 g
monounsaturated fat	2 g
cholesterol	0 mg
sodium	495 mg
fiber	1 g

In a large saucepan, heat the olive oil over medium heat. Add the yellow onion and sauté until soft and translucent, about 4 minutes. Add the tomatoes, ginger, and garlic and sauté until the tomatoes are softened, about 5 minutes. Add the stock and bring to boil. Reduce the heat to a simmer.

Whisk in the miso until dissolved. Add the tofu, mushrooms, and watercress and simmer until the tofu is heated through and the mushrooms and watercress are softened, about 1 minute.

Ladle into warmed individual bowls and garnish with the green onion. Serve immediately.

1 tablespoon olive oil

1 yellow onion, finely chopped

3 plum (Roma) tomatoes, peeled and seeded (page 127), then diced

1 tablespoon peeled and finely chopped fresh ginger

3 cloves garlic, minced

4 cups (32 fl oz/1 l) chicken stock (page 138), vegetable stock (page 139), or broth

2 tablespoons white miso

¼ lb (125 g) firm tofu, drained and cut into ¼-inch (6-mm) dice

3 oz (90 g) fresh shiitake mushrooms, stemmed, brushed clean, and caps thinly sliced

1 cup (1 oz/30 g) watercress leaves

1 green (spring) onion, including tender green top, thinly sliced

Fresh Tomato Soup with Crispy Herb Toasts

When fresh tomatoes are at their peak, their intense flavor makes this soup a treat. Serve it with grilled vegetables for a light summer lunch or supper. In winter, substitute vine-ripened hothouse tomatoes.

SERVES 4

8 slices whole-grain baguette, ½ inch (12 mm) thick

1 tablespoon chopped fresh basil

2 teaspoons chopped fresh oregano

4 teaspoons grated Parmesan cheese

4 tomatoes

2 teaspoons olive oil

½ small yellow onion, diced

1 tablespoon tomato paste

1½ cups (12 fl oz/375 ml) 1-percent low-fat milk

½ teaspoon salt

⅛ teaspoon freshly ground pepper

Preheat the broiler (grill). Arrange the baguette slices on a broiler pan and top each slice with a sprinkling of basil, oregano, and cheese. Place about 4 inches (10 cm) from the heat source and broil (grill) until the cheese is melted, 45–60 seconds. Watch carefully to prevent burning. Set aside.

Peel, seed, and dice the tomatoes. In a large, heavy saucepan, heat the olive oil over medium heat. Add the onion and sauté until soft and translucent, about 4 minutes. Add the tomatoes and tomato paste and bring to a boil. Reduce the heat to medium-low and simmer, uncovered, until the soup thickens, 20–25 minutes.

In a blender or food processor, purée the soup in batches until smooth and return to the pan. Stir in the milk, salt, and pepper and reheat gently. Ladle into individual bowls, garnish each with 2 herb toasts, and serve.

Pyramid Servings

VEGETABLES	◀ ○ ○ ○ ○ ●
FRUITS	◀ ○ ○ ○ ○ ○
CARBOHYDRATES	○ ○ ○ ○ ○ ○ ●
PROTEIN & DAIRY	○ ○ ○ ○ ○ ○ ●
FATS	○ ○ ○ ○ ○

PER SERVING	
calories	188
kilojoules	787
protein	8 g
carbohydrate	28 g
total fat	6 g
saturated fat	2 g
monounsaturated fat	3 g
cholesterol	5 mg
sodium	487 mg
fiber	4 g

Peeling Tomatoes

Fill a pan with enough water to cover the tomatoes and bring to a boil. Using a small, sharp knife, cut out the core from each tomato's stem end. Cut a shallow X in the other end. Submerge in the boiling water until the skin wrinkles, about 20 seconds. Using a slotted spoon, transfer to a bowl of cold water. Peel when cool. Cut in half crosswise, then squeeze gently and shake to dislodge the seeds.

Split Pea Soup

When you want a quick, hearty meal, this soup, made with yellow split peas, pairs well with crusty whole-grain bread or a fresh-vegetable medley. Or accompany it with Spinach Frittata (page 261).

SERVES 4

FOR THE CHIVE CREAM

3 tablespoons coarsely chopped fresh chives, plus long cuts for garnish

3 tablespoons nonfat plain yogurt

1 tablespoon low-fat buttermilk

¼ teaspoon sugar

Pinch of salt

2 tablespoons olive oil

1 yellow onion, chopped

½ teaspoon salt

1 large carrot, peeled and chopped

2 cloves garlic, minced

1½ cups (10½ oz/330 g) dried yellow or green split peas, picked over, rinsed, and drained

3 cups (24 fl oz/750 ml) water

3 cups (24 fl oz/750 ml) vegetable stock (page 139) or broth

¼ teaspoon freshly ground pepper

½ cup (30 oz/90 g) chopped lean ham

To make the chive cream, in a small blender or food processor, combine the chopped chives, yogurt, buttermilk, sugar, and the pinch of salt. Process until well blended. Cover and refrigerate until needed.

In a large saucepan, heat the olive oil over medium heat. Add the onion and sauté until soft and lightly golden, about 6 minutes. Stir in ¼ teaspoon of the salt. Add the carrot and sauté until the carrot is softened, about 5 minutes. Add the garlic and sauté for 1 minute. Stir in the split peas, water, stock, the remaining ¼ teaspoon salt, and the pepper and bring to a boil. Reduce the heat to low, cover partially, and simmer until the peas are tender, 60–65 minutes.

In a blender or food processor, purée the soup in batches until smooth and return to the saucepan over medium heat. Reheat gently.

Ladle into warmed individual bowls. Top each serving with a drizzle or swirl of chive cream and garnish with a sprinkle of chopped ham and a few long cuts of fresh chives. Serve immediately.

Pyramid Servings

VEGETABLES	◁○○○●●
FRUITS	◁○○○○○
CARBOHYDRATES	○○○○○○○○
PROTEIN & DAIRY	○○○○●●●
FATS	○○○○○

PER SERVING	
calories	393
kilojoules	1,644
protein	23 g
carbohydrate	56 g
total fat	11 g
saturated fat	1 g
monounsaturated fat	6 g
cholesterol	7 mg
sodium	695 mg
fiber	12 g

Gingery Chicken Noodle Soup

SERVES 8

This souped-up version of the ultimate comfort food features edamame, or fresh soybeans. For a vegetarian version, substitute cubes of extra-firm tofu for the chicken and use vegetable stock (page 139).

Pyramid Servings

VEGETABLES	◀○○○○●
FRUITS	◀○○○○○
CARBOHYDRATES	○○○○○○○●
PROTEIN & DAIRY	○○○○○○●
FATS	○○○○○

PER SERVING

calories	184
kilojoules	773
protein	22 g
carbohydrate	11 g
total fat	5 g
saturated fat	1 g
monounsaturated fat	2 g
cholesterol	33 mg
sodium	267 mg
fiber	2 g

Bring a saucepan three-fourths full of water to a boil, add the noodles, and cook until just tender, about 5 minutes. Drain and set aside until needed.

In a large saucepan, heat the olive oil over medium heat. Add the onion and sauté until soft and translucent, about 4 minutes. Add the ginger and carrot and sauté for 1 minute. Add the garlic and sauté for 30 seconds; do not let the garlic brown. Add the stock and soy sauce and bring to a boil. Add the chicken and edamame and return to a boil. Reduce the heat to medium-low and simmer until the chicken is cooked and the edamame are tender, about 4 minutes. Add the soba noodles and soy milk and cook until heated through; do not let boil.

Remove from the heat and stir in the cilantro. Ladle into warmed individual bowls and serve immediately.

3 oz (90 g) dried soba noodles

1 tablespoon olive oil

1 large yellow onion, chopped

1 tablespoon peeled and minced fresh ginger

1 carrot, peeled and finely chopped

1 clove garlic, minced

4 cups (32 fl oz/1 l) chicken stock (page 138) or broth

2 tablespoons reduced-sodium soy sauce

1 lb (500 g) skinless, boneless chicken breasts, chopped

1 cup (5 oz/155 g) shelled edamame

1 cup (8 fl oz/250 ml) plain soy milk (soya milk)

¼ cup (⅓ oz/10 g) chopped fresh cilantro (fresh coriander)

Chicken Adobo Soup with Bok Choy

SERVES 4

Adobo, the national dish of the Philippines, is a tangy stew made with pork or chicken. This version, a soup that's a complete meal, has the original blend of soy sauce, vinegar, and garlic, plus Chinese greens.

Pyramid Servings

VEGETABLES	◀○○○●●
FRUITS	◀○○○○○
CARBOHYDRATES	○○○○○○○●
PROTEIN & DAIRY	○○○○○○●
FATS	○○○○●

PER SERVING	
calories	295
kilojoules	1,234
protein	29 g
carbohydrate	30 g
total fat	6 g
saturated fat	1 g
monounsaturated fat	3 g
cholesterol	48 mg
sodium	769 mg
fiber	5 g

In a small saucepan, combine the soy sauce, vinegar, garlic, and bay leaf over medium-high heat. Heat the mixture until it just comes to a boil. Remove from the heat and set aside.

In a large saucepan, heat the olive oil over medium heat. Add the yellow onion and sauté until soft and lightly golden, about 6 minutes. Add the chicken stock and bring to a boil. Add the soy sauce mixture, chicken, and couscous. Return to a boil, reduce the heat to medium, and simmer for 2 minutes. Add the bok choy and simmer until the bok choy is tender, about 2 minutes. Discard the bay leaf.

Ladle into warmed individual bowls and garnish with the green onions. Serve immediately.

⅓ cup (3 fl oz/80 ml) reduced-sodium soy sauce

⅓ cup (3 fl oz/80 ml) rice vinegar

2 cloves garlic, sliced

1 bay leaf

1 teaspoon olive oil

½ yellow onion, chopped

4 cups (32 fl oz/1 l) chicken stock (page 138) or broth

1½ cups (9 oz/280 g) skinned and shredded roasted or boiled chicken breast meat

½ cup (3 oz/90 g) uncooked whole-wheat (wholemeal) couscous or 1 cup (5 oz/155 g) cooked brown rice

½ lb (250 g) baby bok choy, halved lengthwise and sliced crosswise ½ inch (12 mm) wide

2 green (spring) onions, including tender green tops, thinly sliced

Curried Carrot Soup

A splash of lime juice and a blend of spices transform an everyday carrot soup into a sophisticated indulgence. Accompany the soup with a green salad and crusty whole-grain bread for a complete meal.

SERVES 6

1 tablespoon olive oil

1 teaspoon mustard seed

½ yellow onion, chopped

1 lb (500 g) carrots, peeled and cut into ½-inch (12-mm) pieces

1 tablespoon plus 1 teaspoon peeled and chopped fresh ginger

½ jalapeño chile, seeded

2 teaspoons curry powder

5 cups (40 fl oz/1.25 l) chicken stock (page 138), vegetable stock (page 139), or broth

¼ cup (⅓ oz/10 g) chopped fresh cilantro (fresh coriander), plus leaves for garnish

2 tablespoons fresh lime juice

½ teaspoon salt (optional)

3 tablespoons low-fat sour cream or nonfat plain yogurt

Grated zest of 1 lime

In a large saucepan, heat the olive oil over medium heat. Add the mustard seed. When the seeds just start to pop, after about 1 minute, add the onion and sauté until soft and translucent, about 4 minutes. Add the carrots, ginger, jalapeño, and curry powder and sauté until the seasonings are fragrant, about 3 minutes.

Add 3 cups (24 fl oz/750 ml) of the stock, raise the heat to high, and bring to a boil. Reduce the heat to medium-low and simmer, uncovered, until the carrots are tender, about 6 minutes.

In a blender or food processor, purée the soup in batches until smooth and return to the saucepan. Stir in the remaining 2 cups (16 fl oz/500 ml) stock. Return the soup to medium heat and reheat gently. Just before serving, stir in the chopped cilantro and lime juice. Season with the salt, if desired.

Ladle into warmed individual bowls. Garnish with a drizzle of yogurt, a sprinkle of lime zest, and cilantro leaves.

Pyramid Servings

VEGETABLES	◀ ○ ○ ○ ● ●
FRUITS	◀ ○ ○ ○ ○ ○
CARBOHYDRATES	○ ○ ○ ○ ○ ○ ○ ○
PROTEIN & DAIRY	○ ○ ○ ○ ○ ○ ○
FATS	○ ○ ○ ○ ●

PER SERVING	
calories	80
kilojoules	335
protein	6 g
carbohydrate	5 g
total fat	4 g
saturated fat	1 g
monounsaturated fat	2 g
cholesterol	3 mg
sodium	147 mg
fiber	1 g

Posole with Fresh Corn Gorditas

Posole, a southwestern main-course soup, is typically made with pork shoulder that is simmered with hominy—large, dried corn kernels that have had their skin removed. Here, lean pork tenderloin is used.

SERVES 6

½ cup (3 oz/90 g) fresh corn kernels (cut from 1 ear) or frozen kernels, thawed

⅔ cup (3 oz/90 g) *masa harina* or cornmeal

2 tablespoons whole-wheat (wholemeal) flour

1 teaspoon baking powder

¼ teaspoon red pepper flakes

¼ teaspoon salt

1 tablespoon plus 1½ teaspoons canola oil

3–4 tablespoons water

1 small onion, chopped

4 cloves garlic, minced

3 cups (24 fl oz/750 ml) vegetable stock (page 139) or broth

2 cups (16 fl oz/500 ml) water

1 cup (6 oz/185 g) dried hominy, soaked overnight and drained, or 3 cups canned hominy

3 Anaheim chiles, seeded, roasted, and peeled (page 165), then chopped

½ lb (250 g) pork tenderloin, trimmed of fat and cut into ¾-inch (2-cm) cubes

¼ cup (⅓ oz/10 g) chopped fresh cilantro (fresh coriander)

Sliced radishes and red onions and shredded lettuce for serving

Preheat the oven to 400°F (200°C). Place the corn kernels in a blender or food processor and pulse to purée partially. Set aside. In a small bowl, combine the *masa harina,* flour, baking powder, red pepper flakes, and salt and stir until well blended. Add the puréed corn and the 1 tablespoon canola oil and stir to combine. Add the water, 1 tablespoon at a time, until the dough comes together.

Turn the dough out onto a lightly floured surface and roll out ¼ inch (6 mm) thick. Using a 1½-inch (4-cm) round cookie cutter, cut out 24 rounds. Arrange the rounds on a nonstick baking sheet and bake until light brown, 10–12 minutes. Transfer the gorditas to a wire rack to cool.

In a soup pot, heat the 1½ teaspoons oil over medium heat. Add the onion and sauté until soft and lightly golden, about 6 minutes. Stir in the garlic and sauté for 1 minute. Add the stock, water, and hominy. Bring to a boil. Reduce the heat to low, cover, and simmer until all the hominy kernels have burst, 75–85 minutes. (If using canned hominy, skip the long cooking and proceed directly to adding the chiles and pork.) Add the chiles and pork, return to a simmer, cover, and cook until the pork is just faintly pink at the center, about 4 minutes. Add the gorditas to the soup pot, cover, and let stand off the heat for 4 minutes. Stir in the cilantro.

Ladle into warmed individual bowls. Pass the radishes, onion, and lettuce at the table.

Pyramid Servings

VEGETABLES	◖○○○○○
FRUITS	◖○○○○○
CARBOHYDRATES	○○○○○○●●
PROTEIN & DAIRY	○○○○○○●
FATS	○○○○●

PER SERVING	
calories	285
kilojoules	1,192
protein	13 g
carbohydrate	43 g
total fat	8 g
saturated fat	1 g
monounsaturated fat	4 g
cholesterol	25 mg
sodium	427 mg
fiber	4 g

Summer Vegetable Soup

SERVES 8

The midsummer wealth of vegetables and herbs makes it a pleasure to prepare this satisfying soup. Despite the bountiful ingredients, the soup is quick to make. For a heartier version, add shredded chicken.

Pyramid Servings

VEGETABLES	◀○○○●●
FRUITS	◀○○○○○
CARBOHYDRATES	○○○○○○○○
PROTEIN & DAIRY	○○○○○○○
FATS	○○○○○

PER SERVING

calories	60
kilojoules	251
protein	2 g
carbohydrate	9 g
total fat	2 g
saturated fat	<1 g
monounsaturated fat	1 g
cholesterol	0 mg
sodium	311 mg
fiber	2 g

In a large saucepan, heat the olive oil over medium heat. Add the onion and sauté until soft and translucent, about 4 minutes. Add the garlic and sauté for 30 seconds; do not let the garlic brown. Add the tomatoes, oregano, and cumin and sauté until the tomatoes are softened, about 4 minutes.

Add the stock and the bay leaf and bring to a boil, then reduce the heat to medium-low and bring to a simmer. Add the carrot and bell pepper and cook for 2 minutes. Add the zucchini and simmer until the vegetables are tender, about 3 minutes longer. Stir in the lemon zest and cilantro. Season with the salt and pepper. Discard the bay leaf.

Ladle into individual bowls or mugs and serve immediately.

1 tablespoon olive oil

1 yellow onion, chopped

3 cloves garlic, chopped

4 plum (Roma) tomatoes, peeled and seeded (page 127), then diced

1 tablespoon chopped fresh oregano or 1 teaspoon dried oregano

1 teaspoon ground cumin

4 cups (32 fl oz/1 l) vegetable stock (page 139) or broth

1 bay leaf

1 carrot, peeled, halved lengthwise, and thinly sliced crosswise

1 yellow bell pepper (capsicum), seeded and diced

1 zucchini (courgette), halved lengthwise and thinly sliced crosswise

1 tablespoon grated lemon zest

2 tablespoons chopped fresh cilantro (fresh coriander)

¼ teaspoon salt

¼ teaspoon freshly ground pepper

Easy Chicken Stock

SERVES 12

Making stock at home is the surefire way to avoid the high sodium content of most prepared broths. Browning the ingredients before simmering imparts color and flavor to the finished stock.

Pyramid Servings

VEGETABLES	◀○○○○●
FRUITS	◀○○○○○
CARBOHYDRATES	○○○○○○○○
PROTEIN & DAIRY	○○○○○○○
FATS	○○○○○

PER SERVING	
calories	20
kilojoules	84
protein	1 g
carbohydrate	2 g
total fat	<1 g
saturated fat	<1 g
monounsaturated fat	0 g
cholesterol	11 mg
sodium	118 mg
fiber	0 g

Preheat the oven to 450°F (230°C). Rinse the bones in cold water and place in a large roasting pan. Roast the bones until browned on one side, about 20 minutes. Turn the bones, add the carrots, celery, and onion to the pan, and roast until evenly browned, about 20 minutes longer.

Transfer the vegetables and bones to a stockpot. Deglaze the hot roasting pan with a little water, stirring with a wooden spoon to scrape up any browned bits, and add the liquid to the stockpot. Add the peppercorns, parsley, and cold water and slowly bring to a boil over medium-high heat. Reduce the heat to low, cover partially, and simmer for 1½ hours, using a spoon to regularly skim off the foam that rises to the surface. Remove from the heat and let cool slightly.

Carefully strain the stock into a bowl through a colander or sieve lined with paper towels or cheesecloth (muslin). Discard the bones and solids. Let cool at room temperature for about 1 hour.

Cover and refrigerate the stock overnight. With a large spoon, lift off any solidified fat from the surface and discard. Use the stock immediately, cover and refrigerate for up to 2 days, or freeze in airtight containers for up to 3 months. Makes about 12 cups (96 fl oz/3l).

3 lb (1.5 kg) chicken bones, trimmed of fat

3 carrots, cut into 2-inch (5-cm) pieces

2 celery stalks, cut into 2-inch (5-cm) pieces

1 large yellow onion, cut into chunks

¼ teaspoon peppercorns

5 fresh flat-leaf (Italian) parsley sprigs

4 qt (4 l) water

Easy Vegetable Stock

Since vegetables yield their flavors quickly, in little more than half an hour you can have a pot full of flavorful stock to use in everything from Split Pea Soup (page 129) to Braised Celery Root (page 67).

SERVES 6

3 teaspoons olive oil

12–14 fresh white mushrooms, brushed clean and coarsely chopped

1 large yellow onion, cut into 1-inch (2.5-cm) pieces

3 large carrots, cut into 1-inch (2.5-cm) pieces

2 celery stalks with leaves, cut into 1-inch (2.5-cm) pieces

6 cloves garlic, halved

8 cups (64 fl oz/2 l) water

6 fresh flat-leaf (Italian) parsley sprigs

4 fresh thyme sprigs

1 bay leaf

⅛ teaspoon salt

In a stockpot, heat 2 teaspoons of the olive oil over medium-high heat. Add the mushrooms and sauté until they begin to brown, 4–5 minutes. Push the mushrooms to the side of the pot and add the remaining 1 teaspoon oil, the onion, the carrots, the celery, and the garlic. Raise the heat to high and sauté, stirring often, until the vegetables are deeply browned, about 10 minutes. (The browner the vegetables, the richer the flavor of the stock.) Add the water, parsley, thyme, bay leaf, and salt. Bring to a boil, then reduce the heat to medium-low and simmer, uncovered, for 25–30 minutes. Remove from the heat and let cool slightly.

Carefully strain the stock into a bowl through a colander or sieve lined with paper towels or cheesecloth (muslin). Use immediately, cover and refrigerate for up to 3 days, or freeze in airtight containers for up to 3 months. Makes about 6 cups (48 fl oz/1.5 l).

Pyramid Servings

VEGETABLES	◀○○○○●
FRUITS	◀○○○○
CARBOHYDRATES	○○○○○○○
PROTEIN & DAIRY	○○○○○○
FATS	○○○○○

PER SERVING	
calories	24
kilojoules	100
protein	0 g
carbohydrate	1 g
total fat	2 g
saturated fat	0 g
monounsaturated fat	2 g
cholesterol	0 mg
sodium	52 mg
fiber	0 g

Homemade Stock

Homemade stock, rich with the flavors of onion, carrot, and other seasonings, is always tastier than canned broth. It's healthier, too, with little or no added salt. Of course, no one makes stock for every recipe that calls for it, so when time is short, canned broth is an acceptable substitute. Always purchase fat-free, reduced-sodium varieties. When in doubt check the label's "Nutrition Facts."

Pasta & Grains

Grains are the soul of many meals, from cereal to sandwiches to pasta, but it's whole grains that we need.

143   Tabbouleh

144   Farfalle with Fresh Tomato Sauce

147   Spaghetti with Summer Squash and Peppers

148   Quinoa Risotto with Arugula and Parmesan

150   Linguine with Mushrooms

151   Brown Rice Pilaf

153   Spinach Lasagne with Sun-Dried Tomato Sauce

154   Corn Tamales with Avocado-Tomatillo Salsa

156   Bulgur and Chickpeas with Preserved-Lemon Vinaigrette

158   Savory Buckwheat Pilaf with Toasted Spices

159   Barley and Roasted Tomato Risotto

161   Orzo with Cherry Tomatoes, Capers, and Lemon

162   Double-Corn Spoon Bread

164   Curried Vegetable Couscous

165   Creamy Polenta with Roasted Red Pepper Coulis

167   Banana-Oatmeal Hotcakes with Spiced Maple Syrup

168   Muesli Breakfast Bars

170   Whole-Grain Buttermilk Biscuits

171   Cranberry-Walnut Oatmeal

173   Three-Grain Raspberry Muffins

174   Sweet-Potato Waffles with Blueberry Syrup

176   Irish Brown Bread

177   Nutty Berry Granola

179   Pumpkin-Hazelnut Tea Cake

Tabbouleh

Wrap this traditional Middle Eastern salad in lettuce, tuck it in a pita pocket, or serve it as a side dish. This version has more vegetables than grain. Add extra parsley, if you like, or use the curly-leaf variety.

SERVES 8

1 cup (8 fl oz/250 ml) vegetable stock (page 139) or broth or water

1 cup (6 oz/185 g) fine-grind bulgur

2 cups (12 oz/375 g) cherry tomatoes, halved, or 2 tomatoes, seeded and diced

½ cucumber, peeled, seeded, and diced

¼ cup (2 fl oz/60 ml) fresh lemon juice

¼ cup (⅓ oz/10 g) chopped fresh flat-leaf (Italian) parsley

3 tablespoons chopped fresh mint

2 tablespoons extra-virgin olive oil

2 green (spring) onions, including tender green tops, finely chopped

1 tablespoon grated lemon zest

1 clove garlic, minced

¾ teaspoon salt

¼ teaspoon freshly ground pepper

¼ teaspoon ground allspice

In a small saucepan, bring the vegetable stock to a boil. Place the bulgur in a large, heatproof bowl and pour in the boiling stock. Let stand until the bulgur is tender and the liquid is completely absorbed, about 15 minutes.

Add all the remaining ingredients and toss gently just until the ingredients are evenly distributed. Cover and refrigerate for 2 hours to allow the flavors blend. Serve chilled.

Pyramid Servings

VEGETABLES	◀ ○ ○ ○ ○ ●
FRUITS	◀ ○ ○ ○ ○
CARBOHYDRATES	○ ○ ○ ○ ○ ○ ○ ●
PROTEIN & DAIRY	○ ○ ○ ○ ○ ○ ○
FATS	○ ○ ○ ○ ●

PER SERVING	
calories	109
kilojoules	456
protein	3 g
carbohydrate	18 g
total fat	4 g
saturated fat	1 g
monounsaturated fat	3 g
cholesterol	0 mg
sodium	286 mg
fiber	4 g

Farfalle with Fresh Tomato Sauce

SERVES 4

For this perfect dish for summer nights, the sauce that coats the pasta is uncooked, or what Italians call *salsa cruda*. Be sure to use your best-quality extra-virgin olive oil; its fruity flavor will be evident.

Pyramid Servings

VEGETABLES	◁○○●●●
FRUITS	◁○○○○○
CARBOHYDRATES	○○○○○●●●
PROTEIN & DAIRY	○○○○○○○
FATS	○○○●●

PER SERVING

calories	372
kilojoules	1,556
protein	10 g
carbohydrate	58 g
total fat	12 g
saturated fat	2 g
monounsaturated fat	8 g
cholesterol	0 mg
sodium	463 mg
fiber	5 g

To make the sauce, in a large bowl, combine the tomatoes, julienned basil, onion, olive oil, vinegar, garlic, salt, and pepper. Toss gently to mix.

Fill a large pot three-fourths full with water and bring to a boil. Add the farfalle and cook until al dente, 10–12 minutes, or according to package directions. Drain the pasta thoroughly.

Divide the pasta among warmed individual bowls. Top each serving with sauce and garnish with a fresh basil leaf.

4 tomatoes, about 2 lbs (1 kg) total weight, peeled and seeded (page 127), then cut into ½-inch (12-mm) dice

½ cup (¾ oz/20 g) fresh basil cut into chiffonade, plus whole leaves for garnish

3 tablespoons chopped red onion

3 tablespoons extra-virgin olive oil

1 tablespoon red wine vinegar

1 clove garlic, finely minced

¾ teaspoon salt

¼ teaspoon freshly ground pepper

½ lb (250 g) farfalle

Spaghetti with Summer Squash and Peppers

This garlicky primavera–style dish gets its rich, nutty flavor from the whole-grain pasta and chopped walnuts. If you can't find whole-wheat noodles to suit your taste, try a half-wheat, half-regular blend.

SERVES 4

1 slice (1½ oz/45 g) day-old whole-grain peasant bread

2½ tablespoons extra-virgin olive oil

4 cloves garlic, thinly sliced

1½ tablespoons finely chopped walnuts

¼ cup (⅓ oz/10 g) chopped fresh flat-leaf (Italian) parsley

1 teaspoon salt

1 small yellow squash, cut into 2-inch (5-cm) julienne

1 small zucchini (courgette), cut into 2-inch (5-cm) julienne

1 cup (5 oz/155 g) shredded carrot

1 small red bell pepper (capsicum), cut into julienne

¼ cup (1 oz/30 g) diced yellow bell pepper (capsicum)

½ teaspoon freshly ground pepper

½ lb (250 g) whole-wheat (wholemeal) spaghetti

In a blender or food processor, process the bread to make fine crumbs. In a large nonstick frying pan, heat 1½ teaspoons of the olive oil over medium heat. Add the sliced garlic and sauté until lightly golden, about 1 minute. Stir in the bread crumbs and cook until lightly browned and crunchy, 3–4 minutes. Transfer to a bowl and stir in the walnuts, parsley, and ½ teaspoon of the salt; set aside.

Add the remaining 2 tablespoons oil to the pan and heat over medium heat. Add the yellow squash, zucchini, and carrot and sauté until the vegetables are tender-crisp, about 5 minutes. Transfer to a plate and keep warm.

Add the bell peppers to the pan and sauté until they begin to soften, about 2 minutes. Stir in the remaining ½ teaspoon salt and the pepper. Return the squash mixture to the pan and toss to mix. Set aside and keep warm.

Fill a large pot three-fourths full with water and bring to a boil. Add the spaghetti and cook until al dente, 10–12 minutes, or according to package directions. Drain the pasta thoroughly.

In a warmed shallow serving bowl, combine the spaghetti, vegetables, and bread crumb mixture. Toss gently to mix. Serve immediately.

Pyramid Servings

VEGETABLES	◀○○○●●
FRUITS	◀○○○○○
CARBOHYDRATES	○○○○○●●●
PROTEIN & DAIRY	○○○○○○○
FATS	○○○●●

PER SERVING	
calories	353
kilojoules	1,477
protein	11 g
carbohydrate	56 g
total fat	12 g
saturated fat	2 g
monounsaturated fat	7 g
cholesterol	0 mg
sodium	661 mg
fiber	11 g

Quinoa Risotto with Arugula and Parmesan

SERVES 6

Quinoa (pronounced KEEN-wah), native to Peru, is much like wheat. Its subtle nutty flavor pairs well with a wide range of seasonings. To serve this dish as a main course, double the portions.

Pyramid Servings

VEGETABLES	◁○○○●●
FRUITS	◁○○○○
CARBOHYDRATES	○○○○○○○●
PROTEIN & DAIRY	○○○○○○○
FATS	○○○○●

PER SERVING

calories	147
kilojoules	612
protein	8 g
carbohydrate	23 g
total fat	3 g
saturated fat	1 g
monounsaturated fat	1 g
cholesterol	3 mg
sodium	292 mg
fiber	2 g

In a large saucepan, heat the olive oil over medium heat. Add the onion and sauté until soft and translucent, about 4 minutes. Add the garlic and quinoa and cook for about 1 minute, stirring occasionally. Do not let the garlic brown.

Add the stock and bring to a boil. Reduce the heat to low and simmer until the quinoa is almost tender to the bite but slightly hard in the center, about 12 minutes. The mixture will be brothy. Stir in the arugula, carrot, and mushrooms and simmer until the quinoa grains have turned from white to translucent, about 2 minutes longer.

Stir in the cheese and season with the salt and pepper. Serve immediately.

1 tablespoon olive oil

½ yellow onion, chopped

1 clove garlic, minced

1 cup (6 oz/185 g) quinoa, well rinsed

2¼ cups (18 fl oz/560 ml) chicken stock (page 138), vegetable stock (page 139), or broth

2 cups (3 oz/90 g) chopped, stemmed arugula (rocket)

1 small carrot, peeled and finely shredded

½ cup (1½ oz/45 g) thinly sliced fresh shiitake mushrooms

¼ cup (1 oz/30 g) grated Parmesan cheese

½ teaspoon salt

¼ teaspoon freshly ground pepper

Linguine with Mushrooms

SERVES 4

With its mix of mushrooms, this vegetarian pasta takes on an almost meaty flavor. If you can't find cremini mushrooms, use portobellos. Dried porcini (found in the produce aisle) lend depth to the sauce.

Pyramid Servings

VEGETABLES	◀○●●●●
FRUITS	◀○○○○○
CARBOHYDRATES	○○○○○○●●
PROTEIN & DAIRY	○○○○○○○
FATS	○○○●●

PER SERVING

calories	340
kilojoules	1,423
protein	14 g
carbohydrate	47 g
total fat	11 g
saturated fat	3 g
monounsaturated fat	6 g
cholesterol	54 mg
sodium	683 mg
fiber	6 g

In a small, heatproof glass measuring pitcher or bowl, combine the dried porcini and 1 cup boiling water. Let stand for 20 minutes. Remove the mushrooms with a slotted spoon and coarsely chop. Set aside.

Line a fine-mesh sieve with a paper coffee filter or cheesecloth (muslin) and strain the mushroom soaking liquid to remove the grit; reserve the liquid.

In a large sauté or frying pan, heat the olive oil over medium heat. Add the shallots and sauté until soft and translucent, 2–3 minutes. Add the garlic and sauté for 1 minute. Add the shiitake mushrooms and sauté until they brown around the edges, 3–4 minutes. Stir in the cremini mushrooms, porcini, reserved porcini soaking liquid, stock, and ½ teaspoon of the salt. Cover and cook until the mushrooms are tender, about 5 minutes. Uncover and stir in the butter, chopped thyme, the remaining ½ teaspoon salt, and the pepper. Set aside and keep warm.

Fill a large pot three-fourths full with water and bring to a boil. Add the linguine and cook until al dente, 8–10 minutes, or according to package directions. Drain the pasta thoroughly.

Divide the pasta among warmed individual shallow bowls and top with the mushroom sauce. Garnish with the fresh thyme sprigs.

2 tablespoons dried porcini mushrooms (ceps)

1 cup (8 fl oz/250 ml) boiling water

5 teaspoons extra-virgin olive oil

3 shallots, chopped

2 cloves garlic, minced

½ lb (250 g) fresh shiitake mushrooms, stemmed, brushed clean, and thinly sliced

¾ lb (375 g) fresh cremini mushrooms, brushed clean and thinly sliced

1 cup (8 fl oz/250 ml) vegetable stock (page 139) or broth

1 teaspoon salt

1 tablespoon butter

2 tablespoons chopped fresh thyme, plus sprigs for garnish

¼ teaspoon freshly ground pepper

9 oz (280 g) fresh linguine or ½ lb (250 g) dried linguine

Brown Rice Pilaf

Any brown rice will work in this recipe, but darker-toned Wehani looks particularly good. Invest in the pistachio oil if you can. Its flavor is so intense that just a bit makes this light side dish taste incredibly rich.

SERVES 8

1⅛ cups (8 oz/250 g) dark brown rice, rinsed and drained

2 cups (16 fl oz/500 ml) water

¾ teaspoon salt

¼ teaspoon saffron threads or ground turmeric

½ teaspoon grated orange zest

3 tablespoons fresh orange juice

1½ tablespoons pistachio oil or canola oil

¼ cup (1 oz/30g) chopped pistachio nuts

¼ cup (1½ oz/45 g) dried apricots, chopped

In a saucepan over high heat, combine the rice, water, ¼ teaspoon of the salt, and the saffron. Bring to a boil. Reduce the heat to low, cover, and simmer until the water is absorbed and the rice is tender, about 45 minutes. Transfer to a large bowl and keep warm.

In a small bowl, combine the orange zest and juice, pistachio oil, and the remaining ½ teaspoon salt. Whisk to blend. Pour the orange mixture over the warm rice. Add the nuts and apricots and toss gently to mix and coat. Serve immediately.

Pyramid Servings

VEGETABLES	◀ ○ ○ ○ ○ ○
FRUITS	◀ ○ ○ ○ ●
CARBOHYDRATES	○ ○ ○ ○ ○ ○ ●
PROTEIN & DAIRY	○ ○ ○ ○ ○ ○ ○
FATS	○ ○ ○ ○ ●

PER SERVING

calories	156
kilojoules	653
protein	3 g
carbohydrate	25 g
total fat	5 g
saturated fat	1 g
monounsaturated fat	2 g
cholesterol	0 mg
sodium	221 mg
fiber	2 g

Brown Rice

Because it retains its bran, brown rice is flavorful and a little chewy. Unlike white rice, it contains the grain's fiber, B vitamins, minerals, and oils. Brown arborio is a creamy short-grain variety good in risotto. Brown basmati is long-grain with a floral aroma. Wehani is also aromatic, with a nutty flavor. The bran's oils cause brown rice to spoil more easily, so store airtight and use within a few months.

Spinach Lasagne with Sun-Dried Tomato Sauce

This hearty main dish can be prepared ahead, refrigerated, and baked later. Add the time-saving "no-boil" noodles directly to the dish. Alternatively, cook ¾ pound (375 g) regular spinach lasagne sheets.

SERVES 8

2 tablespoons plus 2 teaspoons olive oil

1½ tablespoons all-purpose (plain) flour

2 cloves garlic, minced

1 cup (8 fl oz/250 ml) plain soy milk (soya milk)

1 cup (8 fl oz/250 ml) vegetable stock (page 139) or chicken stock (page 138)

2 green (spring) onions, including tender green tops, sliced

½ cup (4 oz/125 g) dry-packed sun-dried tomatoes, soaked in water to rehydrate, drained, and chopped

10 oz (315 g) fresh cremini or shiitake mushrooms, sliced

1 shallot, minced

1 tablespoon chopped fresh flat-leaf (Italian) parsley

¼ teaspoon salt

6 cups (12 oz/375 g) baby spinach leaves, chopped

2 cups (16 oz/500 g) nonfat ricotta cheese

¾ cup (3 oz/90 g) grated Parmesan cheese

1 egg white

12 no-boil spinach lasagne sheets, about 7 by 3½ inches (18 by 9 cm)

1 tablespoon chopped fresh basil

In a saucepan, heat the 2 tablespoons olive oil over medium-high heat. Whisk in the flour and cook for 1–2 minutes, stirring constantly. Add the garlic and continue to whisk until the garlic is fragrant, about 30 seconds. Whisk in the soy milk and stock all at once. Cook and stir until slightly thickened. Remove from the heat and stir in the green onions and sun-dried tomatoes. Set the sauce aside.

In a large nonstick frying pan, heat 1 teaspoon of the olive oil over medium-high heat. Add the mushrooms and shallot and sauté until lightly browned, about 10 minutes. Stir in the parsley and salt. Transfer to a bowl and set aside to cool.

In the same pan, heat the remaining 1 teaspoon olive oil over medium-high heat. Add the spinach and stir quickly until the spinach is wilted but still bright green. Remove from the heat. Let cool slightly.

In a large bowl, beat together the ricotta, ½ cup (2 oz/60 g) of the Parmesan, and the egg white. Stir in the spinach and set aside.

Preheat the oven to 375°F (190°C). Lightly coat a 9-by-13-inch (23-by-33-cm) baking dish with cooking spray. Spread ½ cup (4 fl oz/125 ml) of the sauce in the dish and cover with 3 sheets of the pasta. Spoon half of the spinach mixture onto the pasta and spread gently. Cover with 3 more pasta sheets. Top with another ½ cup of sauce. Spread the mushroom mixture on top and cover with another ½ cup of sauce, then another layer of pasta. Spoon in the remaining spinach filling and top with the last 3 pasta sheets. Add the remaining sauce and the remaining ¼ cup (1 oz/30 g) Parmesan. Cover loosely with foil and bake for 25 minutes. Remove the foil and bake until golden, about 10 minutes longer. Let stand for 10 minutes before serving. Garnish with the basil.

Pyramid Servings

VEGETABLES	◖○○●●●
FRUITS	◖○○○○○
CARBOHYDRATES	○○○○○○○●
PROTEIN & DAIRY	○○○○○○○●
FATS	○○○○●

PER SERVING	
calories	288
kilojoules	803
protein	17 g
carbohydrate	39 g
total fat	8 g
saturated fat	2 g
monounsaturated fat	4 g
cholesterol	6 mg
sodium	526 mg
fiber	4 g

Corn Tamales
with Avocado-Tomatillo Salsa

SERVES 6

Most well-stocked supermarkets have a selection of Mexican items, including dried corn husks, tomatillos, and *masa harina* (a specialized corn flour). Or shop for them at a Latin grocery.

Pyramid Servings

VEGETABLES	◄ ○ ○ ○ ○ ●
FRUITS	◄ ○ ○ ○ ○ ○
CARBOHYDRATES	○ ○ ○ ○ ○ ● ● ●
PROTEIN & DAIRY	○ ○ ○ ○ ○ ○ ○
FATS	○ ○ ○ ○ ●

PER SERVING

calories	297
kilojoules	1,243
protein	7 g
carbohydrate	49 g
total fat	11 g
saturated fat	1 g
monounsaturated fat	5 g
cholesterol	0 mg
sodium	375 mg
fiber	7 g

Place the corn husks in a bowl of water to soften for 10 minutes. Drain and rinse well. Pat dry and set aside.

In a food processor, process 2½ cups (15 oz/470 g) of the corn kernels until coarsely puréed.

In a large bowl, combine the puréed corn, *masa harina,* lukewarm water, baking powder, the ½ teaspoon salt, and the oil. Mix until well blended, using your hands if necessary.

Place a dry nonstick frying pan over medium heat. Add the bell peppers, onion, and remaining ½ cup (3 oz/90 g) corn kernels and sauté until tender-crisp, 6–8 minutes. Stir in the red pepper flakes and remove from the heat.

To assemble a tamale, place 3 tablespoons of *masa* mixture in the center of a soaked corn husk. Flatten with your hand and form a small well in the center. Add 1 tablespoon of the sautéed vegetables to the well. Fold the long side over the filling to cover, then fold over the ends, overlapping them. Tie with a thin strip torn from an extra soaked husk. Repeat to make 18 tamales in all.

In a large pot fitted with a steamer basket, bring 2 inches (5 cm) water to a boil. Layer the wrapped tamales in the steamer basket. Cover with a damp kitchen towel and steam until the filling becomes firm and the tamales are heated through, 50–60 minutes. (Add more water as needed.)

While the tamales are steaming, make the salsa. In a small bowl, combine the avocado, tomatillos, lime juice, cilantro, jalapeño, and the ¼ teaspoon salt. Toss gently.

To serve, place 3 tamales on each plate. Accompany each serving with a generous spoonful of salsa on the side.

18 dried corn husks, plus extra husks to make ties

3 cups (18 oz/560 g) fresh corn kernels or frozen kernels, thawed

2 cups (10 oz/315 g) *masa harina*

½ cup (4 fl oz/125 ml) lukewarm water

1 teaspoon baking powder

½ teaspoon salt

3 tablespoons canola oil

¼ cup (1 oz/30 g) diced red bell pepper (capsicum)

¼ cup (1 oz/30 g) diced green bell pepper (capsicum)

2 tablespoons diced yellow onion

⅛ teaspoon red pepper flakes

FOR THE SALSA

¼ cup (1 oz/30 g) chopped avocado

5 oz (155 g) tomatillos, husked under warm running water and chopped

1 tablespoon fresh lime juice

2 tablespoons chopped fresh cilantro (fresh coriander)

½ teaspoon seeded, minced jalapeño chile

¼ teaspoon salt

Bulgur and Chickpeas with Preserved-Lemon Vinaigrette

SERVES **8**

This dish is loaded with texture and flavor. Wrap it in a whole-grain pita for lunch, take it on a picnic, or serve it as a side dish at dinner. If using canned chickpeas, be sure to rinse and drain thoroughly.

Pyramid Servings

VEGETABLES	◀○○○○○
FRUITS	◀○○○○○
CARBOHYDRATES	○○○○○○○●
PROTEIN & DAIRY	○○○○○○●
FATS	○○○○○

PER SERVING

calories	163
kilojoules	682
protein	6 g
carbohydrate	24 g
total fat	5 g
saturated fat	<1 g
monounsaturated fat	3 g
cholesterol	0 mg
sodium	273 mg
fiber	6 g

In a small saucepan, bring the vegetable stock to a boil. Place the bulgur in a large, heatproof bowl and pour in the boiling stock. Cover and let stand until the bulgur is tender and the liquid is completely absorbed, about 15 minutes.

Add the chickpeas, onion, tomatoes, olives, parsley, cilantro, salt, and pepper and stir to combine.

In a small bowl, combine the lemon juice, garlic, preserved lemon, cumin, paprika, and ground coriander. Whisk in the olive oil until emulsified.

Pour the vinaigrette over the salad and toss gently to mix and coat evenly. Transfer the mixture to a serving bowl and serve immediately.

1 cup (8 fl oz/250 ml) vegetable stock (page 139)

1 cup (6 oz/185 g) coarse-grind bulgur wheat

1½ cups (10½ oz/330 g) cooked chickpeas (garbanzo beans; page 198)

½ red onion, chopped

2 tablespoons dry-packed sun-dried tomatoes, soaked in water to rehydrate, drained, and chopped

2 tablespoons chopped pitted Niçoise olives

1 tablespoon chopped fresh flat-leaf (Italian) parsley

1 tablespoon chopped fresh cilantro (fresh coriander)

½ teaspoon salt

¼ teaspoon freshly ground pepper

¼ cup (2 fl oz/60 ml) fresh lemon juice

3 cloves garlic, minced

1½ teaspoons minced preserved lemon or 1 tablespoon grated lemon zest

1 teaspoon ground cumin

½ teaspoon paprika

½ teaspoon ground coriander

2 tablespoons extra-virgin olive oil

Savory Buckwheat Pilaf with Toasted Spices

SERVES 6 | Similar to rice pilaf, this richly flavored side dish features buckwheat groats plumped up in simmering vegetable stock and seasoned with fresh herbs and pungent spices.

Pyramid Servings

VEGETABLES	◀○○○○●
FRUITS	◀○○○○○
CARBOHYDRATES	○○○○○○○●
PROTEIN & DAIRY	○○○○○○
FATS	○○○○●

PER SERVING

calories	139
kilojoules	582
protein	4 g
carbohydrate	25 g
total fat	3 g
saturated fat	<1 g
monounsaturated fat	2 g
cholesterol	0 mg
sodium	198 mg
fiber	3 g

In a saucepan, heat the olive oil over medium heat. Add the onion and sauté until soft and translucent, about 4 minutes. Add the buckwheat groats, garlic, cumin seed, mustard seed, and cardamom. Sauté, stirring constantly, until the spices and garlic are fragrant and the buckwheat is lightly toasted, about 3 minutes.

Carefully pour in the stock. Bring to a boil, then reduce the heat to medium-low, cover, and simmer until the liquid is absorbed, about 10 minutes. Remove from the heat and let stand, covered, for 2 minutes.

Stir in the tomato and salt. Transfer to a serving bowl and sprinkle with the cilantro. Serve immediately.

1 tablespoon olive oil

1 yellow onion, chopped

1 cup (8 oz/250 g) buckwheat groats

3 cloves garlic, minced

½ teaspoon cumin seed

½ teaspoon mustard seed

¼ teaspoon ground cardamom

2 cups (16 fl oz/500 ml) vegetable stock (page 139) or broth

1 tomato, peeled and seeded (page 127), then diced

½ teaspoon salt

2 tablespoons chopped fresh cilantro (fresh coriander)

Buckwheat Groats

Not a true grain, buckwheat, native to China, is the nutty-flavored seed of an annual herb related to sorrel and rhubarb. Whole seeds stripped of their inedible coating are called groats and are sold raw or toasted. Crushed groats, known as kasha, are served in side dishes and cereals. Buckwheat is also milled into flour, used in pancakes. Look for kasha and flour in natural-foods stores.

Barley and Roasted Tomato Risotto

When cooked slowly, barley takes on a creamy texture like that of the short-grain Arborio rice used in Italian risottos—but with a lot more fiber. Serve as a hearty side dish or light vegetarian main course.

SERVES 8

10 large plum (Roma) tomatoes, about 2 lbs (1 kg) total weight, peeled (page 127) and each cut into 4 wedges

2 tablespoons extra-virgin olive oil

1 teaspoon salt

½ teaspoon freshly ground pepper

4 cups (32 fl oz/1 l) vegetable stock (page 139) or broth

3 cups (24 fl oz/750 ml) water

2 shallots, chopped

¼ cup (2 fl oz/60 ml) dry white wine (optional)

2 cups (14 oz/440 g) pearl barley

3 tablespoons chopped fresh basil, plus whole leaves for garnish

3 tablespoons chopped fresh flat-leaf (Italian) parsley

1½ tablespoons chopped fresh thyme

½ cup (2 oz/60 g) grated Parmesan cheese, plus extra ungrated Parmesan for making curls for garnish

Preheat the oven to 450°F (230°C).

Arrange the tomatoes on a nonstick baking sheet. Drizzle with 1 tablespoon of the olive oil and sprinkle with ¼ teaspoon of the salt and ¼ teaspoon of the pepper. Toss gently to mix. Roast until the tomatoes are softened and beginning to brown, 25–30 minutes. Set aside 16 tomato wedges to use for a garnish.

In a saucepan, combine the vegetable stock and water and bring to a boil over high heat. Reduce the heat to low and keep at a simmer.

In a large, heavy saucepan, heat the remaining 1 tablespoon olive oil over medium heat. Add the chopped shallots and sauté until soft and translucent, 2–3 minutes. Stir in the white wine, if using, and cook until most of the liquid evaporates, 2–3 minutes. Stir in the barley and cook, stirring, for 1 minute. Stir in ½ cup (4 fl oz/125 ml) of the stock mixture and cook until the liquid is completely absorbed, stirring occasionally. Continue stirring in the stock mixture in ½ cup increments, cooking each time until the liquid is absorbed before adding more, until the barley is tender, 45–50 minutes total. Remove from the heat and fold in the tomatoes, chopped basil, parsley, thyme, and grated cheese. Add the remaining ¾ teaspoon salt and ¼ teaspoon pepper and stir to combine.

Divide the risotto among warmed individual shallow bowls. Garnish with the reserved roasted tomato wedges and the whole basil leaves. Using a vegetable peeler, cut a curl or two of Parmesan cheese for topping each serving.

Pyramid Servings

VEGETABLES	◖○○○●●
FRUITS	◖○○○○
CARBOHYDRATES	○○○○○○●
PROTEIN & DAIRY	○○○○○○●
FATS	○○○○●

PER SERVING	
calories	285
kilojoules	1,192
protein	9 g
carbohydrate	46 g
total fat	8 g
saturated fat	2 g
monounsaturated fat	4 g
cholesterol	6 mg
sodium	480 mg
fiber	9 g

Orzo with Cherry Tomatoes, Capers, and Lemon

This simple pasta dish lends itself to variation. Try it with different herbs, add slivers of spinach, or replace the tomatoes with sautéed mushrooms. Orzo is a rice-shaped pasta that readily absorbs flavors.

SERVES 4

2 teaspoons extra-virgin olive oil

2 cups (12 oz/375 g) cherry tomatoes, halved

1 clove garlic, minced

1 cup (7 oz/220 g) orzo

2 cups (16 fl oz/500 ml) chicken stock (page 138), vegetable stock (page 139), or broth

2 teaspoons chopped fresh thyme

2 teaspoons capers, drained and finely chopped

1 tablespoon pine nuts, finely chopped

1 tablespoon grated Parmesan cheese

1 tablespoon grated lemon zest

¼ teaspoon salt

¼ teaspoon freshly ground pepper

In a frying pan, heat the olive oil over medium heat. Add the tomatoes and garlic and cook until the tomatoes are tender, about 3 minutes. Set aside.

In a large saucepan, combine the orzo and chicken stock over medium-high heat. Bring to a boil, then reduce the heat to low, cover, and simmer until the pasta is al dente, about 7 minutes. Remove from the heat and let stand, covered, until almost all of the liquid is absorbed, about 3 minutes.

Add the thyme, capers, pine nuts, cheese, lemon zest, salt, and pepper and toss gently to mix. Add the tomato mixture and toss until all the ingredients are evenly distributed. Spoon the pasta into warmed individual bowls and serve immediately.

Pyramid Servings

VEGETABLES	◀ ○ ○ ● ● ●
FRUITS	◀ ○ ○ ○ ○ ○
CARBOHYDRATES	○ ○ ○ ○ ○ ● ●
PROTEIN & DAIRY	○ ○ ○ ○ ○ ○ ○
FATS	○ ○ ○ ○ ●

PER SERVING	
calories	215
kilojoules	900
protein	9 g
carbohydrate	38 g
total fat	5 g
saturated fat	<1 g
monounsaturated fat	1 g
cholesterol	1 mg
sodium	295 mg
fiber	2 g

Double-Corn Spoon Bread

SERVES **8**

Spoon bread is made from cornmeal that is cooked on the stove top before folding in whipped eggs. It is then cooked again, in the oven, like a soufflé. In this light version, only the egg whites are used.

Pyramid Servings

VEGETABLES	◖○○○○○
FRUITS	◖○○○○○
CARBOHYDRATES	○○○○○○○●
PROTEIN & DAIRY	○○○○○○●
FATS	○○○○○

PER SERVING

calories	159
kilojoules	665
protein	7 g
carbohydrate	22 g
total fat	5 g
saturated fat	<1 g
monounsaturated fat	3 g
cholesterol	1 mg
sodium	300 mg
fiber	3 g

Preheat the oven to 375°F (190°C). Lightly coat a 3-qt (3-l) soufflé dish with olive oil cooking spray.

In a saucepan over medium heat, combine the soy milk, stock, olive oil, and honey. Heat until very hot but not boiling. Reduce the heat to low so the mixture simmers. Add the cornmeal in a stream while whisking constantly. Cook, stirring constantly, until the mixture thickens, about 5 minutes. Transfer to a large bowl. Add the corn kernels, shallot, thyme, baking powder, and salt and stir to combine.

In a large, spotlessly clean bowl, using an electric mixer on high speed, beat the egg whites until stiff peaks form. Gently whisk one-third of the whites into the cornmeal mixture to lighten it. Using a rubber spatula, gently fold the remaining egg whites into the batter, mixing just until incorporated.

Pour the batter into the prepared soufflé dish and sprinkle with the cheese. Bake until puffed and lightly golden, about 35 minutes. Let stand in the dish for 5 minutes before serving. Serve hot.

2 cups (16 fl oz/500 ml) plain soy milk (soya milk)

2 cups (16 fl oz/500 ml) chicken stock (page 138), vegetable stock (page 139), or broth

3 tablespoons olive oil

1 tablespoon dark honey

1 cup (5 oz/155 g) cornmeal, preferably stone-ground

1¼ cups (7½ oz/235 g) fresh corn kernels (cut from 2 or 3 ears corn)

1 tablespoon minced shallot

1 tablespoon chopped fresh thyme

1 teaspoon baking powder

½ teaspoon salt

4 egg whites

1 tablespoon grated Parmesan cheese

Curried Vegetable Couscous

With its colorful vegetables and fresh herbs, this quick and healthful couscous is as attractive as it is delicious. Serve it as a side dish to dress up grilled fish or roasted chicken.

Pyramid Servings

VEGETABLES	◖○○●●●
FRUITS	◖○○○○○
CARBOHYDRATES	○○○○○○●
PROTEIN & DAIRY	○○○○○○○
FATS	○○○○●

PER SERVING

calories	189
kilojoules	791
protein	6 g
carbohydrate	35 g
total fat	3 g
saturated fat	<1 g
monounsaturated fat	2 g
cholesterol	0 mg
sodium	203 mg
fiber	6 g

In a food processor, combine the celery, carrot, onion, bell pepper, ginger, and garlic. Pulse until the vegetables are very finely minced. Do not purée. Set aside.

In a large nonstick sauté or frying pan, heat the olive oil over medium heat. Add the minced vegetables and sauté until they begin to soften, about 3 minutes. Add the curry powder and sauté until fragrant, about 1 minute longer.

Add the couscous and stock and stir well. Bring the mixture to a boil over high heat. Reduce the heat to very low and cover the pan. After 5 minutes, remove from the heat.

Uncover and fluff the couscous with a fork. Add the salt and cilantro and toss to mix. Transfer to a serving bowl and serve immediately.

4-inch (10-cm) piece celery stalk, cut into 1-inch (2.5-cm) pieces

4-inch (10-cm) piece carrot, peeled and cut into 1-inch (2.5-cm) pieces

½ yellow onion, coarsely chopped

½ red bell pepper (capsicum), seeded and coarsely chopped

¼-inch (6-mm) piece fresh ginger, about 1 inch (2.5 cm) in diameter, peeled and thinly sliced

1 clove garlic

1 tablespoon extra-virgin olive oil

1 teaspoon curry powder

1 cup (6 oz/185 g) whole-wheat (wholemeal) couscous

2 cups (16 fl oz/500 ml) chicken stock (page 138), vegetable stock (page 139), or broth

½ teaspoon salt

2 tablespoons chopped fresh cilantro (fresh coriander)

Creamy Polenta
with Roasted Red Pepper Coulis

Polenta, coarse-grind Italian cornmeal, can be served hot and creamy, cut into shapes and grilled, or baked until set. Here, it is mixed with a red pepper coulis for added flavor and color.

SERVES 6

1 red bell pepper (capsicum), roasted and seeded (see box below)

1 clove garlic

1¾ cups (14 fl oz/430 ml) water

1¾ cups (14 fl oz/430 ml) plain soy milk (soya milk) or 1-percent low-fat milk

1 tablespoon extra-virgin olive oil

½ teaspoon salt

1 cup (7 oz/220 g) polenta, preferably stone-ground

2 tablespoons grated Parmesan cheese

1 tablespoon chopped thyme

In a blender or food processor, combine the roasted pepper, garlic, and 1 tablespoon of the water. Process until smooth; set the coulis aside.

Preheat the oven to 450°F (230°C). Lightly coat a 9-inch (23-cm) round cake pan with olive oil cooking spray.

In a large saucepan, combine the soy milk, the remaining water, olive oil, and salt. Whisk in the polenta and place over medium heat. Whisk constantly until the polenta begins to thicken. Reduce the heat to low and resume stirring with a wooden spoon. Cook, stirring frequently, until the polenta pulls away from the sides of the pan, about 15 minutes. Add the coulis and stir to combine. Pour the mixture into the prepared cake pan and sprinkle with the cheese. Bake until firm, about 15 minutes. Let stand in the pan for 10 minutes before serving. Cut into 6 wedges and sprinkle with the thyme.

Pyramid Servings

VEGETABLES	◖○○○○
FRUITS	◖○○○○
CARBOHYDRATES	○○○○○●
PROTEIN & DAIRY	○○○○○●
FATS	○○○○○

PER SERVING	
calories	164
kilojoules	687
protein	5 g
carbohydrate	29 g
total fat	4 g
saturated fat	1 g
monounsaturated fat	3 g
cholesterol	1 mg
sodium	252 mg
fiber	4 g

Roasting Red Peppers

Preheat the broiler (grill). Position the rack 4 inches (10 cm) from the heat source. Place the bell pepper on a baking sheet lined with aluminum foil. Broil (grill), turning frequently with tongs, until the skin blackens all over, about 10 minutes. Transfer the pepper to a bowl, cover, and let steam until the skin loosens, about 10 minutes. Peel, cover, and refrigerate until needed.

Banana-Oatmeal Hotcakes with Spiced Maple Syrup

Mashed bananas and cooked oats help keep these pancakes moist and flavorful. If you don't love syrup, warm some sliced bananas in a frying pan with a small amount of butter or oil and spoon them on top.

SERVES 6

½ cup (5½ oz/170 g) maple syrup

½ cinnamon stick

3 whole cloves

½ cup (1½ oz/45 g) old-fashioned rolled oats

1 cup (8 fl oz/250 ml) water

2 tablespoons firmly packed light brown sugar

2 tablespoons canola oil

½ cup (2½ oz/75 g) whole-wheat (wholemeal) flour

½ cup (2½ oz/75 g) all-purpose (plain) flour

1½ teaspoons baking powder

¼ teaspoon baking soda (bicarbonate of soda)

¼ teaspoon salt

¼ teaspoon ground cinnamon

½ cup (4 fl oz/125 ml) 1-percent low-fat milk

¼ cup (2 oz/60 g) nonfat plain yogurt

1 banana, peeled and mashed

1 egg, lightly beaten

In a small saucepan, combine the maple syrup, cinnamon stick, and cloves. Place over medium heat and bring to a boil. Remove from the heat and let steep for 15 minutes. Remove the cinnamon stick and cloves with a slotted spoon. Set the syrup aside and keep warm.

In a large microwave-safe bowl, combine the oats and water. Microwave on high until the oats are creamy and tender, about 3 minutes. Stir in the brown sugar and canola oil. Set aside to cool slightly.

In a bowl, combine the flours, baking powder, baking soda, salt, and ground cinnamon. Whisk to blend.

Add the milk, yogurt, and mashed banana to the oats and stir until well blended. Beat in the egg. Add the flour mixture to the oat mixture and stir just until moistened.

Place a nonstick frying pan or griddle over medium heat. When a drop of water sizzles as it hits the pan, spoon ¼ cup (2 fl oz/60 ml) pancake batter into the pan. Cook until the top surface of the pancake is covered with bubbles and the edges are lightly browned, about 2 minutes. Turn and cook until the bottom is well browned and the pancake is cooked through, 1–2 minutes longer. Repeat with the remaining pancake batter.

Place the pancakes on warmed individual plates. Drizzle with the warm syrup and serve immediately.

Pyramid Servings

VEGETABLES	◁○○○○○
FRUITS	◁○○○○●
CARBOHYDRATES	○○○○○○●●
PROTEIN & DAIRY	○○○○○○○
FATS	○○○○●

PER SERVING	
calories	268
kilojoules	1,121
protein	6 g
carbohydrate	48 g
total fat	6 g
saturated fat	1 g
monounsaturated fat	3 g
cholesterol	36 mg
sodium	230 mg
fiber	3 g

Muesli Breakfast Bars

The original breakfast cereal called muesli (a German word meaning "mixture") combined rolled oats with nuts and fruit. The bars here are perfect for breakfast-on-the-go or for a healthful snack anytime.

Pyramid Servings

VEGETABLES	◀○○○○○
FRUITS	◀○○○○●
CARBOHYDRATES	○○○○○○○●
PROTEIN & DAIRY	○○○○○○○
FATS	○○○○●

PER BAR	
calories	162
kilojoules	678
protein	5 g
carbohydrate	25 g
total fat	5 g
saturated fat	1 g
monounsaturated fat	3 g
cholesterol	1 mg
sodium	60 mg
fiber	3 g

Preheat the oven to 325°F (165°C). Lightly coat a 9-by-13-inch (23-by-33-cm) baking pan with olive oil cooking spray.

In a large bowl, combine the oats, flour, dry milk, wheat germ, almonds, apples, raisins, and salt. Stir well to blend, and set aside.

In a small saucepan, stir together the honey, peanut butter, and olive oil over medium-low heat until well blended. Do not let the mixture boil. Stir in the vanilla. Add the warm honey mixture to the dry ingredients and stir quickly until well combined. The mixture should be sticky but not wet.

Pat the mixture evenly into the prepared baking pan. Press firmly to remove any air pockets. Bake just until the edges begin to brown, about 25 minutes. Let cool in the pan on a wire rack for 10 minutes, then cut into 24 bars. When just cool enough to handle, remove the bars from the pan and place on the rack to cool completely. Store in airtight containers in the refrigerator.

2½ cups (7½ oz/235 g) old-fashioned rolled oats

½ cup (2 oz/60 g) soy flour

½ cup (1½ oz/45 g) nonfat dry milk

½ cup (1½ oz/45 g) toasted wheat germ

½ cup (2 oz/60 g) sliced (flaked) almonds or chopped pecans, toasted (page 94)

½ cup (1½ oz/45 g) dried apples, chopped

½ cup (3 oz/90 g) raisins

½ teaspoon salt

1 cup (12 oz/375 g) dark honey

½ cup (5 oz/155 g) natural unsalted peanut butter

1 tablespoon olive oil

2 teaspoons vanilla extract (essence)

Whole-Grain Buttermilk Biscuits

MAKES 16 BISCUITS

Serve these fluffy and light biscuits with Spinach Frittata (page 261) for an easy breakfast. Or cook up a batch for supper with Beef Stew with Fennel and Shallots (page 264).

Pyramid Servings

VEGETABLES	◀○○○○○
FRUITS	◀○○○○○
CARBOHYDRATES	○○○○○○●
PROTEIN & DAIRY	○○○○○○○
FATS	○○○○

PER BISCUIT

calories	77
kilojoules	322
protein	3 g
carbohydrate	11 g
total fat	3 g
saturated fat	1 g
monounsaturated fat	1 g
cholesterol	6 mg
sodium	142 mg
fiber	1 g

Preheat the oven to 400°F (200°C). Have ready an ungreased nonstick baking sheet.

In a large bowl, combine the flours, wheat germ, baking powder, baking soda, and salt. Whisk to blend. Add the butter to the flour mixture. With a pastry blender or 2 knives, cut the butter into the dry ingredients until the mixture resembles coarse crumbs. Add the buttermilk and stir just until a moist dough forms. Do not overmix. Cover the bowl with plastic wrap and refrigerate for 30 minutes.

Turn the dough out onto a generously floured work surface and, with floured hands, knead gently for 6–8 times until smooth and manageable.

Using a rolling pin, roll the dough into a rectangle ½ inch (12 mm) thick. Using a 2½-inch (6-cm) round biscuit cutter dipped in flour, cut out biscuits. Cut close together for a minumum of scraps. Gather the scraps and roll out to make additional biscuits.

Place the biscuits about 1 inch (2.5 cm) apart on the baking sheet. Bake until the biscuits rise to twice their unbaked height and are lightly golden, 8–10 minutes. Serve hot.

1 cup (5 oz/155 g) whole-wheat (wholemeal) flour

¾ cup (4 oz/125 g) all-purpose (plain) flour, plus extra for kneading

3 tablespoons wheat germ

2 teaspoons baking powder

½ teaspoon baking soda (bicarbonate of soda)

¼ teaspoon salt

3 tablespoons chilled butter, cut into small pieces

1 cup (8 fl oz/250 ml) low-fat buttermilk

Cranberry-Walnut Oatmeal

Steel-cut oats make a creamy, delicious oatmeal. If you have time, toast the walnuts (page 94) to bring out their flavor. Try substituting other dried fruits—raisins, apricots, or apples—for the cranberries.

SERVES 4

1 cup (6 oz/185 g) steel-cut oats

⅓ cup (2 oz/60 g) sweetened dried cranberries

¼ teaspoon salt

¼ teaspoon ground cinnamon

2 cups (16 fl oz/500 ml) water

4 teaspoons chopped walnuts

4 teaspoons firmly packed brown sugar

In a saucepan, combine the oats, cranberries, salt, cinnamon, and water. Bring to a boil over high heat, then reduce the heat to low and simmer, uncovered, until the oats are tender, about 20 minutes.

Spoon the oatmeal into warmed individual bowls and sprinkle each serving with 1 teaspoon of the walnuts and 1 teaspoon of the brown sugar. Serve immediately.

Pyramid Servings

VEGETABLES ◀○○○○○
FRUITS ◀○○○●●
CARBOHYDRATES ○○○○○○○●
PROTEIN & DAIRY ○○○○○○○
FATS ○○○○●

PER SERVING	
calories	215
kilojoules	900
protein	6 g
carbohydrate	40 g
total fat	4 g
saturated fat	1 g
monounsaturated fat	1 g
cholesterol	0 mg
sodium	150 mg
fiber	4 g

Steel-Cut Oats

Markets nowadays carry several kinds of oats. Steel-cut versions, sold as Irish oatmeal or Scotch oats, are hulled whole oats cut into pieces. They cook in 20 to 40 minutes, depending on their size, and have a nutty taste and firm texture. Old-fashioned oats, popular in cookies and hot cereal, are sliced, steamed, and rolled flat. They cook in about 5 minutes. Quick-cooking oats are rolled extra thin.

Three-Grain Raspberry Muffins

Cornmeal gives these muffins a crunchy texture that pairs well with any sweet berry, from raspberries to blueberries. If one dozen muffins sounds like too many, freeze any extras in a lock-top plastic bag.

MAKES **12** MUFFINS

½ cup (1½ oz/45 g) rolled oats

1 cup (8 fl oz/250 ml) 1-percent low-fat milk or plain soy milk (soya milk)

¾ cup (4 oz/125 g) all-purpose (plain) flour

½ cup (2½ oz/75 g) cornmeal, preferably stone-ground

¼ cup (½ oz/15 g) wheat bran

1 tablespoon baking powder

¼ teaspoon salt

½ cup (6 oz/185 g) dark honey

3½ tablespoons canola oil

2 teaspoons grated lime zest

1 egg, lightly beaten

⅔ cup (2½ oz/75 g) raspberries

Preheat the oven to 400°F (200°C). Line a 12-cup muffin pan with paper or foil liners.

In a large microwave-safe bowl, combine the oats and milk. Microwave on high until the oats are creamy and tender, about 3 minutes. Set aside.

In a large bowl, combine the flour, cornmeal, bran, baking powder, and salt. Whisk to blend. Add the honey, canola oil, lime zest, oats mixture, and egg. Beat just until moistened but still slightly lumpy. Gently fold in the raspberries.

Spoon the batter into the muffin cups, filling each cup about two-thirds full. Bake until the tops are golden brown and a toothpick inserted into the center of a muffin comes out clean, 16–18 minutes. Transfer the muffins to a wire rack and let cool completely.

Pyramid Servings

VEGETABLES	◀○○○○○
FRUITS	◀○○○○●
CARBOHYDRATES	○○○○○○○●
PROTEIN & DAIRY	○○○○○○○
FATS	○○○○●

PER MUFFIN	
calories	162
kilojoules	678
protein	3 g
carbohydrate	27 g
total fat	5 g
saturated fat	1 g
monounsaturated fat	3 g
cholesterol	19 mg
sodium	156 mg
fiber	2 g

Sweet-Potato Waffles with Blueberry Syrup

SERVES 6

A hint of spices and a blanket of juicy berries make these waffles a breakfast treat. Leftovers can be frozen and popped into the toaster. The syrup will keep, covered and refrigerated, for up to a week.

Pyramid Servings

VEGETABLES	◀ ○ ○ ○ ○ ○
FRUITS	◀ ○ ○ ○ ○ ●
CARBOHYDRATES	○ ○ ○ ○ ○ ○ ○ ●
PROTEIN & DAIRY	○ ○ ○ ○ ○ ○ ●
FATS	○ ○ ○ ○ ●

PER SERVING

calories	263
kilojoules	1,063
protein	6 g
carbohydrate	48 g
total fat	6 g
saturated fat	1 g
monounsaturated fat	4 g
cholesterol	0 mg
sodium	298 mg
fiber	3 g

To make the syrup, in a saucepan, combine the blueberries, water (if using), lemon juice and zest, honey, 1 tablespoon of the molasses, and the cloves. Bring to a boil over medium-high heat, then reduce the heat to low, cover, and simmer until the berries burst and the juices are slightly thickened, about 5 minutes. (Frozen berries may take slightly longer to thicken.) Set aside and keep warm.

If using sweet potato, bring a small saucepan half full of water to a boil. Add the sweet potato, return to a boil, then reduce the heat to medium-low and simmer until very tender, about 10 minutes. Drain and purée in a food processor or mash with a potato masher until smooth. Set aside. If using pumpkin purée, reserve.

In a small bowl, sift together the flours, cornmeal, baking powder, salt, cinnamon, and ginger. In a large bowl, whisk together the soy milk, sweet potato purée, olive oil, and the remaining 2 tablespoons molasses. Add the flour mixture and stir just until combined.

In a spotlessly clean bowl, using an electric mixer on high speed, beat the egg white until stiff peaks form. Gently whisk one-third of the egg white into the batter to lighten it. Using a rubber spatula, gently fold the remaining egg white into the batter, mixing just until incorporated.

Place a baking sheet in the oven and preheat to 225°F (110°C). Preheat a waffle iron. Spoon or ladle about ½ cup (4 fl oz/125 ml) batter into the waffle iron, depending on the size of the iron. Spread evenly and cook according to the manufacturer's instructions. (If the batter thickens, thin with a little soy milk.) Transfer the waffle to the baking sheet in the oven to keep warm. Repeat with the remaining batter to make 6 waffles. Serve topped with the syrup.

FOR THE SYRUP

1½ cups (6 oz/185 g) fresh or frozen blueberries

2 tablespoons water, if using fresh berries

1 tablespoon fresh lemon juice

1 teaspoon grated lemon zest

1 tablespoon dark honey

3 tablespoons light molasses

Pinch of ground cloves

⅓ cup (1½ oz/45 g) peeled and diced sweet potato, or ¼ cup (2 oz/60 g) canned pumpkin purée

¾ cup (4 oz/125 g) all-purpose (plain) flour

¼ cup (1½ oz/45 g) whole-wheat (wholemeal) flour

¼ cup (1½ oz/45 g) cornmeal, preferably stone-ground

1 tablespoon baking powder

½ teaspoon salt

⅛ teaspoon ground cinnamon

⅛ teaspoon ground ginger

1 cup (8 fl oz/250 ml) plain soy milk (soya milk)

2 tablespoons olive oil

1 egg white

Irish Brown Bread

MAKES **24** SLICES

A staple in homes all over Ireland, this hearty round wheat bread is a snap to make. It's typically cut into wedges and served with jam for the morning meal. Don't forget to cut an X into the top of the dough.

Pyramid Servings

VEGETABLES	◖○○○○○
FRUITS	◖○○○○○
CARBOHYDRATES	○○○○○○●
PROTEIN & DAIRY	○○○○○○○
FATS	○○○○○

PER SLICE

calories	83
kilojoules	347
protein	4 g
carbohydrate	15 g
total fat	1 g
saturated fat	0 g
monounsaturated fat	0 g
cholesterol	10 mg
sodium	154 mg
fiber	2 g

Preheat the oven to 400°F (200°C). Have ready a nonstick baking sheet.

In a bowl, combine the flours, wheat germ, baking soda, and salt. Whisk to blend. Beat in the buttermilk and egg and stir just until moistened.

Turn the dough out onto a generously floured work surface and, with floured hands, gently knead it 8–10 times; the dough will be sticky. Gather into a loose ball.

On the baking sheet, form the dough into a 7-inch (18-cm) round. Dust the top of dough with a small amount of flour. Cut a 4-inch (10-cm) X into the top of the dough, cutting about ½ inch (12 mm) deep. Bake until the bread splits open at the X and makes a hollow sound when the underside is tapped, 25–30 minutes. Transfer to a wire rack and let cool for 2 hours before slicing.

2 cups (10 oz/315 g) whole-wheat (wholemeal) flour

1½ cups (7½ oz/235 g) all-purpose (plain) flour, plus extra for kneading and dusting

½ cup (1½ oz/45 g) wheat germ

2 teaspoons baking soda (bicarbonate of soda)

¼ teaspoon salt

2 cups (16 fl oz/500 ml) low-fat buttermilk

1 egg, lightly beaten

Whole-Wheat Flour

Milled from wheat kernels that contain their original germ, or embryo, whole-wheat (wholemeal) flour is nutritionally superior to white flour, with more fiber, more vitamins and minerals, and a bit of heart-healthy oil. It's also more flavorful. But since its trace of oil can spoil, it should be bought in small quantities and stored in a sealed container in the refrigerator. It will keep for up to 6 months.

Nutty Berry Granola

Slowly toasting this granola at a low oven temperature allows for even browning. The wheat germ should be raw (untoasted), or it may burn. Serve with soy milk (soya milk) or yogurt topped with fruit, if desired.

MAKES **20** SERVINGS

4 cups (12 oz/375 g) old-fashioned rolled oats

2 cups (1¼ oz/37 g) puffed brown rice

¾ cup (2 oz/60 g) wheat bran

½ cup (1½ oz/45 g) raw wheat germ

3 tablespoons raw sunflower seeds

3 tablespoons chopped walnuts

¼ cup (¾ oz/20 g) nonfat dry milk

¾ cup (9 oz/280 g) dark honey

⅓ cup (3 fl oz/80 ml) olive oil or canola oil

1 teaspoon vanilla extract (essence)

½ teaspoon pure almond extract (essence)

½ cup (2 oz/60 g) dried cranberries, chopped

½ cup (2 oz/60 g) dried blueberries, chopped

Preheat the oven to 250°F (120°C). Have ready a large, heavy, nonstick baking sheet.

In a large bowl, combine the oats, puffed rice, wheat bran, wheat germ, sunflower seeds, walnuts, and dry milk. Stir until well blended.

In a small saucepan, stir together the honey and oil over medium-low heat until well blended. Do not let the mixture boil. Stir in the vanilla and almond extracts. Add the warm honey mixture to the dry ingredients and stir quickly until well combined.

Spread the mixture evenly on the baking sheet. Bake for 1 hour, stirring every 20 minutes to ensure even browning. Add the berries during the last 10 minutes of baking time and toss gently to mix. Transfer the baking sheet to a wire rack and let the granola cool completely. Store in airtight containers in the refrigerator. Makes about 10 cups (2 lb/1 kg).

Pyramid Servings

VEGETABLES	◐○○○○○
FRUITS	◐○○○○●
CARBOHYDRATES	○○○○○○●
PROTEIN & DAIRY	○○○○○○○
FATS	○○○○●

PER SERVING

calories	161
kilojoules	674
protein	4 g
carbohydrate	27 g
total fat	5 g
saturated fat	<1 g
monounsaturated fat	3 g
cholesterol	0 mg
sodium	5 mg
fiber	3 g

Pumpkin-Hazelnut Tea Cake

If pumpkins are in season, roast a small pie pumpkin and purée the flesh in a blender or food processor for this loaf cake. Otherwise, use canned pumpkin. This cake makes a nice holiday gift.

MAKES **12** SLICES

3 tablespoons canola oil

¾ cup (6 oz/185 g) homemade or canned pumpkin purée

½ cup (6 oz/185 g) honey

3 tablespoons firmly packed brown sugar

2 eggs, lightly beaten

1 cup (5 oz/155 g) whole-wheat (wholemeal) flour

½ cup (2½ oz/75 g) all-purpose (plain) flour

2 tablespoons flaxseed

½ teaspoon baking powder

½ teaspoon ground allspice

½ teaspoon ground cinnamon

½ teaspoon ground nutmeg

¼ teaspoon ground cloves

¼ teaspoon salt

2 tablespoons chopped hazelnuts (filberts)

Preheat the oven to 350°F (180°C). Lightly coat an 8-by-4-inch (20-by-10-cm) loaf pan with cooking spray.

In a large bowl, using an electric mixer on low speed, beat together the canola oil, pumpkin purée, honey, brown sugar, and eggs until well blended.

In a small bowl, whisk together the flours, flaxseed, baking powder, allspice, cinnamon, nutmeg, cloves, and salt. Add the flour mixture to the pumpkin mixture and using the electric mixer on medium speed beat until well blended.

Pour the batter into the prepared pan. Sprinkle the hazelnuts evenly over the top and press down gently to lodge the nuts into the batter. Bake until a toothpick inserted into the center of the loaf comes out clean, 50–55 minutes. Let cool in the pan on a wire rack for 10 minutes. Turn the loaf out of the pan onto the rack and let cool completely. Cut into 12 slices to serve.

Pyramid Servings

VEGETABLES	◀○○○○○
FRUITS	◀○○○○○
CARBOHYDRATES	○○○○○○●●
PROTEIN & DAIRY	○○○○○○○
FATS	○○○○●

PER SLICE	
calories	174
kilojoules	728
protein	4 g
carbohydrate	28 g
total fat	6 g
saturated fat	1 g
monounsaturated fat	3 g
cholesterol	35 mg
sodium	79 mg
fiber	2 g

Beans & Legumes

The nutritional value of beans, peas, and lentils is matched only by their versatility in the kitchen.

183   Black-Eyed Pea and Sweet Corn Salsa

185   Red Bean Chilaquiles

186   Fava Beans with Garlic

188   Chickpea Polenta with Olives

190   Lima Bean Ragout with Tomatoes and Thyme

191   French Green Lentil Salad

193   Cannellini Beans with Wilted Greens

194   Black Bean Burgers with Chipotle Ketchup

196   Stewed Flageolets in Lemon Broth

198   Chickpea Hummus

199   Tofu Hoisin with Baby Bok Choy

201   Sesame-Crusted Tofu

203   Yellow Lentils with Spinach and Ginger

204   Three-Bean Chili

205   Caribbean Red Beans and Brown Rice

207   Lentils with Wild Rice and Crispy Onions

208   Soybeans with Fennel, Thyme, and Oregano

210   Spicy Red Lentils

211   Edamame and Summer Bean Salad

213   Classic Boston Baked Beans

Black-Eyed Pea and Sweet Corn Salsa

A staple in Southern cooking, the black-eyed pea is a cream-colored legume distinguished by a black dot with a white center. This salsa is a perfect partner for grilled fish or chicken. It's also an ideal salad.

SERVES 8

1 cup (7 oz/220 g) dried black-eyed peas, picked over and rinsed, soaked overnight, and drained

3 cups (24 fl oz/750 ml) water

½ teaspoon salt

1 tablespoon olive oil

½ yellow onion, chopped

½ green bell pepper (capsicum), seeded and chopped

1 cup (6 oz/185 g) fresh corn kernels (cut from about 2 ears corn)

1 tomato, seeded and diced

1 clove garlic, minced

Grated zest and juice of 1 lime

1 tablespoon white wine vinegar or sherry vinegar

3 tablespoons chopped fresh cilantro (fresh coriander)

¼ teaspoon freshly ground pepper

In a large saucepan over high heat, combine the peas, water, and ¼ teaspoon of the salt. Bring to a boil. Reduce the heat to low, cover partially, and simmer until the peas are tender, about 45 minutes. Drain the peas, rinse with cool water, drain again, and transfer to a large bowl to cool.

In a large nonstick sauté or frying pan, heat the olive oil over medium-high heat. Add the onion and bell pepper and sauté until softened, about 4 minutes. Add the corn, tomato, and garlic and sauté until the tomato is softened and the corn is tender-crisp, about 4 minutes.

Add the corn mixture to the peas along with the lime zest and juice, vinegar, cilantro, the remaining ¼ teaspoon salt, and the pepper. Toss to mix. Serve immediately, or cover and refrigerate for up to 2 days.

Pyramid Servings

VEGETABLES	◀○○○○○
FRUITS	◀○○○○○
CARBOHYDRATES	○○○○○○○
PROTEIN & DAIRY	○○○○○●
FATS	○○○○○

PER SERVING	
calories	112
kilojoules	469
protein	6 g
carbohydrate	18 g
total fat	2 g
saturated fat	<1 g
monounsaturated fat	1 g
cholesterol	0 mg
sodium	298 mg
fiber	5 g

Red Bean Chilaquiles

In Mexico, a popular way to use up leftover tortillas is in a dish called *chilaquiles*. In this version, the tortillas are layered and baked, lasagne style, with red beans, oven-roasted tomatoes, and some mild cheese.

SERVES 6

1 cup (7 oz/220 g) dried kidney beans, picked over and rinsed, soaked overnight, and drained

3 cups (24 fl oz/750 ml) water

8 corn tortillas, 6 inches (15 cm) in diameter

10 plum (Roma) tomatoes, about 2 lb (1 kg) total weight, cored

1 yellow onion, cut into 8 wedges

2 jalapeño chiles

¼ cup (⅓ oz/10 g) chopped fresh cilantro (fresh coriander)

1 teaspoon salt

3 tablespoons olive oil or canola oil

3 cloves garlic, minced

½ cup (2 oz/60 g) shredded *queso asadero* or Monterey jack cheese

1 green (spring) onion, including tender green top, thinly sliced

In a large saucepan over high heat, combine the beans and water. Bring to a boil. Reduce the heat to low, cover the pan partially, and simmer until tender, 65–75 minutes. Drain.

While the beans are cooking, preheat the oven to 400°F (200°C). Stack the tortillas and cut them to form 48 wedges in all. Place on a baking sheet and bake until crisp, 4–5 minutes. Remove from the oven and set aside.

Preheat the broiler (grill). Position the rack 4 inches (10 cm) from the heat source. On a baking sheet lined with aluminum foil, arrange the tomatoes, yellow onion wedges, and chiles. Broil (grill) until the skins blacken, 4–5 minutes. Turn the vegetables over and broil until blackened, 3–4 minutes longer. Transfer to a bowl, cover, and let stand for about 10 minutes. Reduce the oven temperature to 350°F (180°C). Peel the tomatoes. Wearing gloves, peel and seed the chiles. Place the vegetables in a blender or food processor and pulse until coarsely puréed. Add the cilantro and ½ teaspoon of the salt; pulse to make a chunky sauce. Set aside.

In a large frying pan, heat 2½ tablespoons of the oil over medium-high heat. Add the garlic and sauté until golden, 1–2 minutes. Stir in the cooked beans and the remaining ½ teaspoon salt and cook until heated through, about 3 minutes. Remove from the heat.

Grease a large, oblong baking dish with the remaining 1½ teaspoons oil. Spread ½ cup (4 fl oz/125 ml) of the tomato sauce in the dish. Layer one-third of the tortilla wedges on top and cover with one-third of the bean mixture. Repeat layering, then top with the remaining sauce. Sprinkle with the cheese and bake until browned, 25–30 minutes. Cut into squares, top with the green onion, and serve.

Pyramid Servings

VEGETABLES	◀○○○○●
FRUITS	◀○○○○○
CARBOHYDRATES	○○○○○○●
PROTEIN & DAIRY	○○○○●●
FATS	○○○○●

PER SERVING

calories	343
kilojoules	1,435
protein	15 g
carbohydrate	49 g
total fat	12 g
saturated fat	3 g
monounsaturated fat	5 g
cholesterol	12 mg
sodium	590 mg
fiber	13 g

Fava Beans with Garlic

SERVES 4

The delectable fresh fava bean has a short season in late spring. Once removed from the pods, fava beans are blanched to remove their thin but tough outer skins. This simple recipe lets their flavor shine.

Pyramid Servings

VEGETABLES	◀○○○○○
FRUITS	◀○○○○
CARBOHYDRATES	○○○○○○○○
PROTEIN & DAIRY	○○○○○●
FATS	○○○○●

PER SERVING	
calories	130
kilojoules	544
protein	7 g
carbohydrate	18 g
total fat	4 g
saturated fat	<1 g
monounsaturated fat	3 g
cholesterol	0 mg
sodium	293 mg
fiber	5 g

Bring a large saucepan three-fourths full of water to a boil. Add the fava beans and ¼ teaspoon of the salt and cook for 2 minutes. Drain and rinse immediately with cold water to stop the cooking. To remove the skins, pinch each bean on the side opposite where it was attached to the pod; the bean should slip easily from the skin. Remove and discard the outer skins. Set the beans aside.

In a large saucepan with a tight-fitting lid, heat the olive oil over medium heat. Add the onion and sauté until soft and lightly golden, about 6 minutes. Add the garlic and sauté for 30 seconds; do not let the garlic brown. Add the fava beans and stock and bring to a boil. Reduce the heat to low, cover, and simmer, shaking the pan gently from time to time, until the beans are tender, about 15 minutes.

Season with the remaining ¼ teaspoon salt and the pepper. Sprinkle with the parsley and serve immediately.

2 lb (1 kg) fava (broad) beans, shelled (about 2 cups/ 10 oz/315 g)

½ teaspoon salt

1 tablespoon olive oil

¼ cup (1½ oz/45 g) minced yellow onion

1 clove garlic, minced

½ cup (4 fl oz/125 ml) vegetable stock (page 139), chicken stock (page 138), or broth

¼ teaspoon freshly ground pepper

1 teaspoon chopped fresh flat-leaf (Italian) parsley

Chickpea Polenta with Olives

Panisse, a polenta-like side dish from southern France, is usually cut like French fries and fried. This adaptation is baked, then broiled until crispy. Chickpea flour can be found in Italian or East Indian markets.

Pyramid Servings

VEGETABLES	◀○○○○○
FRUITS	◀○○○○○
CARBOHYDRATES	○○○○○○○○
PROTEIN & DAIRY	○○○○○○●
FATS	○○○○●

PER SERVING

calories	152
kilojoules	636
protein	9 g
carbohydrate	18 g
total fat	5 g
saturated fat	1 g
monounsaturated fat	3 g
cholesterol	1 mg
sodium	275 mg
fiber	3 g

In a blender or food processor, combine the flour, soy milk, stock, olive oil, garlic, thyme, mustard, salt, and pepper. Process until smooth. Pour the batter into a large bowl. Let stand for 1 hour.

Preheat the oven to 425°F (220°C). Lightly coat a 9-by-13-inch (23-by-33-cm) baking pan with cooking spray.

In a large, spotlessly clean bowl, using an electric mixer on high speed, beat the egg whites until stiff peaks form. Gently fold the egg whites into the batter.

Pour the batter into the prepared pan. Bake until puffed and lightly browned around the edges, about 15 minutes. Let cool for 15 minutes.

Preheat the broiler (grill). Position the rack 4 inches (10 cm) from the heat source.

While the polenta is cooling, make the topping. In a small sauté or frying pan, heat the olive oil over medium-high heat. Add the onion and cook until soft and lightly golden, about 6 minutes. Add the olives and tomatoes and cook for 1 minute. Remove from the heat.

Carefully spoon the onion mixture evenly over the baked polenta and sprinkle with the cheese. Broil (grill) until the top is lightly browned. Watch carefully; this takes only about 1 minute. Sprinkle with the parsley. Transfer to a wire rack and let cool for 10 minutes. Cut into 8 squares, then cut the squares on the diagonal into 16 wedges. Serve immediately.

1¾ cups (9 oz/280 g) chickpea (garbanzo bean) flour

2 cups (16 fl oz/500 ml) plain soy milk (soya milk)

1 cup (8 fl oz/250 ml) chicken stock (page 138), vegetable stock (page 139), or broth

1 tablespoon extra-virgin olive oil

3 cloves garlic, chopped

1 tablespoon chopped fresh thyme, oregano, or basil, or 1 teaspoon dried

1 teaspoon dry mustard

½ teaspoon salt

¼ teaspoon freshly ground pepper

3 egg whites

FOR THE TOPPING

1 tablespoon extra-virgin olive oil

½ yellow onion, minced

¼ cup (1 oz/30 g) coarsely chopped pitted Niçoise olives

¼ cup (2 oz/60 g) dry-packed sun-dried tomatoes, soaked in water to rehydrate, drained and chopped

2 tablespoons grated Parmesan cheese

2 tablespoons finely chopped fresh flat-leaf (Italian) parsley

Lima Bean Ragout with Tomatoes and Thyme

SERVES 6

Also known as butter beans, fresh limas are creamy with a mild flavor. Keep an eye out for them at your farmers' market. Fresh fava (broad) beans are a good substitute in this flavorful side dish.

Pyramid Servings

VEGETABLES	◀○○○○●
FRUITS	◀○○○○○
CARBOHYDRATES	○○○○○○○○
PROTEIN & DAIRY	○○○○○○●
FATS	○○○○●

PER SERVING

calories	160
kilojoules	669
protein	6 g
carbohydrate	23 g
total fat	5 g
saturated fat	<1 g
monounsaturated fat	3 g
cholesterol	0 mg
sodium	261 mg
fiber	6 g

Bring a large saucepan three-fourths full of water to a boil. Add the lima beans and cook until just tender-crisp, about 6 minutes. Transfer with a slotted spoon to a bowl of ice water to stop the cooking. Drain and set aside.

In a saucepan, heat 1 tablespoon of the olive oil over medium heat. Add the tomato, onion, garlic, bay leaf, thyme, and salt and sauté until the vegetables soften, about 5 minutes.

Add the stock and bring to a boil over medium-high heat. Reduce the heat to low, add the cooked lima beans, and simmer, uncovered, until heated through, 2–3 minutes. Discard the bay leaf and transfer to a serving bowl. Drizzle with the remaining 1 tablespoon olive oil and sprinkle with the chopped parsley.

4 lb (2 kg) fresh lima beans, shelled, or 2 packages (10 oz/315 g each) frozen lima beans, thawed

2 tablespoons olive oil

1 tomato, peeled and seeded (page 127), then diced

½ yellow onion, chopped

3 cloves garlic, minced

1 bay leaf

1½ teaspoons chopped fresh thyme

¼ teaspoon salt

1 cup (8 fl oz/250 ml) vegetable stock (page 139) or broth

2 tablespoons chopped fresh flat-leaf (Italian) parsley

Fresh Herbs

Thyme and other fresh herbs, now widely sold by the bunch, may seem aromatic yet can be subtle. When cooking with them, always use the full quantity indicated in the recipe, and crush or chop the leaves to release their aromatic oils. Dried herbs, in contrast, often seem mild but may add aggressive flavors. When substituting dried for fresh herbs, use one-third of the amount.

French Green Lentil Salad

French lentils can be hard to find, but their intense, earthy flavors are worth a search. Brown lentils may be substituted; they cook in less time and are more likely to break apart, so watch them closely.

SERVES 6

1 tablespoon olive oil

½ yellow onion, finely chopped

4-inch (10-cm) piece celery stalk, finely chopped

4-inch (10-cm) piece carrot, peeled and finely chopped

3 cloves garlic, minced

1 teaspoon mustard seed

1 teaspoon fennel seed

2 cups (16 fl oz/500 ml) vegetable stock (page 139), chicken stock (page 138), or broth

½ cup (4 fl oz/125 ml) water

1 cup (7 oz/220 g) French green lentils, picked over, rinsed, and drained

1 tablespoon chopped fresh thyme or 1 teaspoon dried thyme

1 bay leaf

1 tablespoon sherry vinegar or red wine vinegar

1 tablespoon Dijon mustard

1 tablespoon extra-virgin olive oil

2 tablespoons fresh flat-leaf (Italian) parsley chiffonade

½ teaspoon salt

¼ teaspoon freshly ground pepper

In a large saucepan, heat the olive oil over medium heat. Add the onion, celery, and carrot and sauté until the vegetables are softened, about 5 minutes. Add the garlic, mustard seed, and fennel seed and sauté until the spices are fragrant, about 1 minute.

Add the stock, water, lentils, thyme, and bay leaf. Raise the heat to medium-high and bring to a boil. Reduce the heat to low, cover partially, and simmer until the lentils are tender but still firm, 25–30 minutes. Drain the lentils, reserving the cooking liquid. Transfer the lentils to a large bowl and discard the bay leaf.

In a small bowl, combine the vinegar, mustard, and ¼ cup (2 fl oz/60 ml) of the reserved cooking liquid. (Discard any remaining liquid or reserve for another use.) Whisk in the extra-virgin olive oil.

Add the vinaigrette, parsley, salt, and pepper to the lentils and toss gently to mix and coat evenly. Serve warm.

Pyramid Servings

VEGETABLES	◀○○○○
FRUITS	◀○○○○
CARBOHYDRATES	○○○○○○○
PROTEIN & DAIRY	○○○○○●
FATS	○○○○●

PER SERVING	
calories	167
kilojoules	699
protein	8 g
carbohydrate	23 g
total fat	5 g
saturated fat	<1 g
monounsaturated fat	4 g
cholesterol	0 mg
sodium	214 mg
fiber	6 g

Cannellini Beans with Wilted Greens

Cannellini are a staple in many Italian recipes, such as minestrone. If you can't find them, substitute small white (navy) beans. You can also replace the escarole with spinach, kale, or chard. Serve as a side dish.

SERVES 8

1¼ cups (9 oz/280 g) dried cannellini beans, picked over and rinsed, soaked overnight, and drained

3 cups (24 fl oz/750 ml) water

1 bay leaf

1 tablespoon chopped fresh oregano

4 cloves garlic, 1 left whole and 3 minced

1 tablespoon extra-virgin olive oil

½ yellow onion, chopped

2 tomatoes, seeded and diced

2 anchovy fillets, rinsed and finely chopped (optional)

1 head escarole, about ½ lb (250 g), stemmed and leaves coarsely chopped

½ teaspoon salt

¼ teaspoon freshly ground pepper

2 tablespoons grated Parmesan cheese

In a large saucepan over high heat, combine the beans, water, bay leaf, oregano, and the whole garlic clove. Bring to a boil. Reduce the heat to low, cover partially, and simmer until the beans are tender, 60–75 minutes. Drain and discard the bay leaf and garlic.

In a large saucepan, heat the olive oil over medium-high heat. Add the onion and sauté until soft and lightly golden, about 6 minutes. Add the tomatoes, minced garlic, and the anchovies, if using. Sauté until the tomatoes are softened, about 4 minutes. Stir in the escarole and cooked beans and cook until the greens are wilted and the beans are heated through, about 3 minutes. Season with the salt and pepper and sprinkle with the Parmesan. Serve immediately.

Pyramid Servings

VEGETABLES
FRUITS
CARBOHYDRATES
PROTEIN & DAIRY
FATS

PER SERVING	
calories	143
kilojoules	598
protein	8 g
carbohydrate	23 g
total fat	3 g
saturated fat	1 g
monounsaturated fat	1 g
cholesterol	1 mg
sodium	179 mg
fiber	6 g

Black Bean Burgers with Chipotle Ketchup

SERVES 6

Spend the time to make the tasty chipotle ketchup, and serve these burgers on whole-grain buns piled with lettuce, tomato, sliced onion, or other extras. Or serve them with a side order of oven-baked fries.

Pyramid Servings

VEGETABLES	◀ ○ ○ ○ ○ ○
FRUITS	◀ ○ ○ ○ ○
CARBOHYDRATES	○ ○ ○ ○ ○ ● ●
PROTEIN & DAIRY	○ ○ ○ ○ ● ●
FATS	○ ○ ○ ○ ●

PER SERVING

calories	389
kilojoules	1,628
protein	16 g
carbohydrate	59 g
total fat	11 g
saturated fat	1 g
monounsaturated fat	5 g
cholesterol	35 mg
sodium	791 mg
fiber	15 g

In a large saucepan over high heat, combine the beans, water, and bay leaf. Bring to a boil. Reduce the heat to low, cover partially, and simmer until the beans are tender, 60–70 minutes. Drain and discard the bay leaf.

While the beans are cooking, combine the tomatoes, half of the yellow onion, half of the garlic, the tomato paste, vinegar, chipotle chile, ¾ teaspoon of the cumin, and ¼ teaspoon of the salt in a small saucepan over medium-high heat. Bring the mixture to a boil. Reduce the heat to medium and simmer uncovered, stirring occasionally, until the liquid is reduced and the mixture is a thick sauce, about 5 minutes. Set the chipotle ketchup aside to cool.

In a frying pan, heat ½ tablespoon of the canola oil over medium heat. Add the remaining yellow onion and sauté until soft and translucent, about 4 minutes. Add the bell pepper and the remaining garlic and sauté until they begin to soften, about 3 minutes. Stir in ¼ teaspoon of the salt, transfer the mixture to a bowl, and let cool. Set the pan aside.

In a food processor, combine the drained beans, the onion mixture, the brown rice, pecans, green onion, the remaining 1 teaspoon cumin, and the remaining ½ teaspoon salt. Pulse several times until the mixture is coarsely puréed. Fold in the beaten egg and bread crumbs. Form the mixture into patties each ¾ inch (2 cm) thick.

In the same pan used for the onion mixture, heat the remaining 1 tablespoon canola oil over medium-high heat. Add the patties and cook, turning once, until nicely browned on both sides and heated through, 7–9 minutes total.

Serve each burger on a bun topped with 1 tomato slice, 1 onion slice, ½ lettuce leaf, and a dollop of the ketchup.

1¼ cups (9 oz/280 g) dried black beans, picked over and rinsed, soaked overnight, and drained

3 cups (24 fl oz/750 ml) water

1 bay leaf

2 plum (Roma) tomatoes, peeled and seeded (page 127), then diced

1 yellow onion, chopped

4 cloves garlic, minced

1 tablespoon tomato paste

1 tablespoon wine vinegar

1 chipotle chile in adobo sauce, minced

1¾ teaspoons ground cumin

1 teaspoon salt

1½ tablespoons canola oil

½ red bell pepper (capsicum), seeded and chopped

½ cup (2½ oz/75 g) cooked brown rice

¼ cup (1 oz/30 g) chopped pecans

1 green (spring) onion, thinly sliced

1 egg, lightly beaten

¾ cup (1½ oz/45 g) fresh whole-grain bread crumbs

6 whole-grain hamburger buns

6 slices tomato

6 slices red onion

3 Bibb lettuce leaves, halved

Stewed Flageolets in Lemon Broth

Although one rarely finds them fresh, the tender French beans for this easy side dish are available dried, canned, and sometimes frozen. Great Northern or small white (navy) beans can be substituted.

Pyramid Servings

VEGETABLES	◀○○○○●
FRUITS	◀○○○○
CARBOHYDRATES	○○○○○○○○
PROTEIN & DAIRY	○○○○○○●
FATS	○○○○○

PER SERVING

calories	130
kilojoules	544
protein	8 g
carbohydrate	24 g
total fat	1 g
saturated fat	<1 g
monounsaturated fat	<1 g
cholesterol	0 mg
sodium	198 mg
fiber	6 g

In a large saucepan over high heat, combine the beans, stock, onion, garlic, and oregano. Bring to a boil. Reduce the heat to low, cover partially, and simmer until the beans are tender but still firm, about 2 hours. Check the beans every 30 minutes, adding water as needed to keep them fully covered.

When the beans are tender, stir in the preserved lemon, salt, and pepper. Transfer to a serving dish and garnish with the chopped parsley.

1 cup (7 oz/220 g) dried flageolet beans, picked over and rinsed, soaked overnight, and drained

4 cups (32 fl oz/1 l) vegetable stock (page 139), chicken stock (page 138), or broth

1 small yellow onion, finely diced

1 clove garlic, minced

1 teaspoon chopped fresh oregano

1½ teaspoons minced preserved lemon or 1 tablespoon grated lemon zest

½ teaspoon salt

¼ teaspoon freshly ground pepper

1 tablespoon chopped fresh flat-leaf (Italian) parsley

Chickpea Hummus

SERVES 6

Serve this easy Mediterranean spread with warmed whole-wheat (wholemeal) pita bread. For a more traditional version, replace the vinegar with lemon juice and the olive oil with tahini (sesame paste).

Pyramid Servings

VEGETABLES	◀○○○○○
FRUITS	◀○○○○○
CARBOHYDRATES	○○○○○○○
PROTEIN & DAIRY	○○○○○○●
FATS	○○○○○

PER SERVING	
calories	103
kilojoules	431
protein	4 g
carbohydrate	14 g
total fat	4 g
saturated fat	0 g
monounsaturated fat	2 g
cholesterol	0 mg
sodium	300 mg
fiber	4 g

In a large saucepan over high heat, combine the chickpeas, water, garlic cloves, bay leaf, and ½ teaspoon of the salt. Bring to a boil. Reduce the heat to low, cover partially, and simmer until the beans are very tender, 50–60 minutes. Drain and discard the bay leaf, reserving the garlic and ½ cup (4 fl oz/125 ml) of the cooking liquid.

In a blender or food processor, combine the chickpeas, cooked garlic, olive oil, the ¾ cup green onion, vinegar, cilantro, cumin, and the remaining ¼ teaspoon salt. Process to purée. Add the reserved cooking liquid, 1 tablespoon at a time, until the mixture has the consistency of a thick spread.

In a small serving bowl, stir together the chickpea mixture and the remaining 2 tablespoons green onion. Serve immediately, or cover and refrigerate until ready to serve. Makes about 1½ cups (12 oz/375 g).

⅔ cup (4½ oz/140 g) dried chickpeas (garbanzo beans), picked over and rinsed, soaked overnight, and drained

3 cups (24 fl oz/750 ml) water

2 cloves garlic

1 bay leaf

¾ teaspoon salt

1 tablespoon olive oil

¾ cup (2 oz/60 g) plus 2 tablespoons sliced green (spring) onion

2 tablespoons sherry vinegar

3 tablespoons chopped fresh cilantro (fresh coriander)

1 teaspoon ground cumin

Chickpea Choices

If you're short on time, skip the instructions for dried chickpeas (above) and substitute one 15-ounce (470-g) can chickpeas, rinsed and drained. In dishes with dried black, kidney, or white (navy) beans, or black-eyed peas, replace each 1 cup (7 oz/220 g) dried beans with two 15-ounce (470-g) cans of beans or 3 cups of home-cooked beans. Canned beans can be salty; shop for low-sodium versions.

Tofu Hoisin with Baby Bok Choy

This easy oven-baked tofu has a subtle barbecue-like flavor. Steam the bok choy while the tofu bakes, and dinner can be on the table in less than 30 minutes. For a heartier meal, steam some brown rice for a side dish.

1 lb (500 g) firm tofu, drained

3 tablespoons hoisin sauce

2 tablespoons rice vinegar

1 tablespoon firmly packed brown sugar

1 tablespoon soy sauce

1 teaspoon Dijon mustard

½ teaspoon chile garlic sauce

1 clove garlic, minced

4 heads baby bok choy, halved

1 teaspoon sesame oil

⅛ teaspoon salt

Preheat the oven to 450°F (230°C). Cut the tofu lengthwise into 4 slices. Cut each slice into 2 triangles. Place the tofu triangles on a plate and cover with plastic wrap. Top with a second plate and a heavy weight and let stand for 10 minutes.

In a small bowl, whisk together the hoisin sauce, vinegar, brown sugar, soy sauce, mustard, chile garlic sauce, and garlic. Spread one-third of the mixture in an oblong baking dish. Drain the tofu, arrange the triangles in the dish, and top with the remaining hoisin mixture. Bake until heated through, 10–15 minutes.

While the tofu is baking, bring 1 inch (2.5 cm) water to a boil in a large pot fitted with a steamer basket. Add the bok choy, cover, and steam until tender, 6–8 minutes. Transfer to a plate. Sprinkle with the sesame oil and salt. Serve 2 bok choy halves and 2 tofu triangles on each individual plate.

Pyramid Servings

VEGETABLES	◖○○○○●
FRUITS	◖○○○○
CARBOHYDRATES	○○○○○○○
PROTEIN & DAIRY	○○○○○●
FATS	○○○○●

PER SERVING

calories	157
kilojoules	659
protein	12 g
carbohydrate	15 g
total fat	7 g
saturated fat	1 g
monounsaturated fat	2 g
cholesterol	2 mg
sodium	628 mg
fiber	2 g

Firm Tofu

Made of cooked soybeans, tofu comes in a range of textures, making the bean curd an adaptable ingredient. Firm and extra-firm tofu, like chicken, picks up flavors in stir-fries and on the grill. Soft tofu is ideal for blending with other ingredients in soups and smoothies. Creamy silken tofu is perfect for custardy desserts. All tofu is rich in protein and a source of B vitamins and iron.

Sesame-Crusted Tofu

Serve these "steaks" with soy sauce and a green-onion garnish. Be sure to use firm tofu. Brown it gently so it loses some moisture before coating it with bread crumbs and sesame seeds, then browning again.

SERVES 4

1 lb (500 g) firm tofu, drained

¼ cup (2 fl oz/60 ml) nonfat milk

2 egg whites, lightly beaten

½ teaspoon salt

¼ teaspoon freshly ground pepper

3 tablespoons plain dried bread crumbs

2 tablespoons white sesame seeds

1 tablespoon black sesame seeds

½ teaspoon sesame oil or canola oil

12 green (spring) onions, ends trimmed, cut in half crosswise, then halved again lengthwise

Cut the tofu crosswise into 12 slices. Place the tofu slices in a large nonstick frying pan over medium heat and cook for 5 minutes on each side. The tofu will brown slightly and lose some of its liquid. Transfer to a plate and let cool.

In a bowl, whisk together the milk, egg whites, ¼ teaspoon of the salt, and the pepper until well blended. On a large plate, combine the bread crumbs, white and black sesame seeds, and the remaining ¼ teaspoon salt. Mix until well blended. Dip a tofu slice into the milk mixture, then dredge in the sesame seed mixture. Repeat dipping and dredging with the remaining tofu slices.

In a large nonstick frying pan, heat the oil over medium heat. Arrange the tofu slices in the pan and cook, turning once, until lightly browned, about 3 minutes on each side. Transfer to a plate and keep warm. Add the green onions to the pan and sauté until they begin to brown, 3–4 minutes.

Divide the green onions among individual plates. Top each serving with 3 tofu steaks and serve immediately.

Pyramid Servings

VEGETABLES	◖○○○○●
FRUITS	◖○○○○
CARBOHYDRATES	○○○○○○○○
PROTEIN & DAIRY	○○○○○●●
FATS	○○○○●

PER SERVING	
calories	265
kilojoules	1,109
protein	24 g
carbohydrate	17 g
total fat	14 g
saturated fat	2 g
monounsaturated fat	4 g
cholesterol	0 mg
sodium	391 mg
fiber	6 g

Yellow Lentils
with Spinach and Ginger

Rice and lentils are mainstays in southern India, where pungent spices give distinction to many dishes. If you can't find the yellow lentils, use yellow split peas. Serve as a hearty side dish or light main course.

SERVES 4

1 teaspoon white or black sesame seeds

1 tablespoon olive oil

1 shallot, minced

1 teaspoon ground ginger

½ teaspoon curry powder

½ teaspoon ground turmeric

1 cup (7 oz/220 g) yellow lentils, picked over, rinsed, and drained

1½ cups (12 fl oz/375 ml) vegetable stock (page 139), chicken stock (page 138), or broth

½ cup (4 fl oz/125 ml) light coconut milk

2 cups (4 oz/125 g) baby spinach leaves, stemmed and chopped, or 1 cup (4 oz/125 g) frozen chopped spinach, thawed

½ teaspoon salt

1 tablespoon chopped fresh cilantro (fresh coriander)

Toast only the white sesame seeds before using. Place the sesame seeds in a small, dry sauté or frying pan over medium heat. Cook briefly, shaking the pan often and watching carefully to prevent burning. Remove the seeds from the pan as soon as they begin to turn brown. Set aside.

In a large saucepan, heat the olive oil over medium heat. Add the shallot, ginger, curry powder, and turmeric and cook, stirring, until the spices are fragrant, about 1 minute.

Add the lentils, stock, and coconut milk. Raise the heat to medium-high and bring to a boil. Reduce the heat to low, cover partially, and simmer until the lentils are tender but still firm, about 12 minutes. The mixture should be brothy; add a little water if needed.

Stir in the spinach, cover, and simmer for about 3 minutes longer. The lentils should still hold their shape. Uncover and stir in the salt. Serve hot, garnished with the cilantro and toasted white or untoasted black sesame seeds.

Pyramid Servings

VEGETABLES	◀ ○ ○ ● ● ●
FRUITS	◀ ○ ○ ○ ○ ○
CARBOHYDRATES	○ ○ ○ ○ ○ ○ ○ ○
PROTEIN & DAIRY	○ ○ ○ ○ ○ ○ ●
FATS	○ ○ ○ ○ ●

PER SERVING	
calories	239
kilojoules	1,000
protein	14 g
carbohydrate	36 g
total fat	5 g
saturated fat	1 g
monounsaturated fat	3 g
cholesterol	0 mg
sodium	169 mg
fiber	9 g

Three-Bean Chili

SERVES 8

Traditional chili takes on a new look with the addition of colorful roasted bell peppers and black, cannellini, and Anasazi beans. Serve as a main dish with corn bread or crusty whole-grain bread.

Pyramid Servings

VEGETABLES	◀○○○●●
FRUITS	◀○○○○
CARBOHYDRATES	○○○○○○○○
PROTEIN & DAIRY	○○○○○●●
FATS	○○○○●

PER SERVING

calories	300
kilojoules	1,255
protein	16 g
carbohydrate	45 g
total fat	8 g
saturated fat	1 g
monounsaturated fat	4 g
cholesterol	5 mg
sodium	486 mg
fiber	16 g

In a large saucepan over high heat, combine the beans, water, bay leaf, and ½ teaspoon of the salt. Bring to a boil. Reduce the heat to low, cover partially, and simmer until the beans are tender but still firm, 60–70 minutes. Drain and discard the bay leaf.

When the beans are cooked, coarsely chop the roasted bell peppers and set aside. In a large saucepan, heat the oil over medium heat. Add the yellow onion and sauté until soft and lightly golden, about 6 minutes. Stir in the garlic, chili powder, oregano, cumin, red pepper flakes, and the remaining 1 teaspoon salt. Cook until fragrant, 1–2 minutes. Add the bell peppers, cooked beans, tomatoes, and cilantro and cook until the tomatoes are heated through, 5–6 minutes.

Ladle the chili into individual bowls and sprinkle with the cheese and green onions.

¾ cup (5 oz/155 g) *each* dried cannellini or red kidney beans, black beans, and Anasazi beans, picked over and rinsed, soaked overnight, and drained

4 cups (32 fl oz/1 l) water

1 bay leaf

1½ teaspoons salt

2 large green bell peppers (capsicums), roasted and seeded (page 165)

2 large red or yellow bell peppers (capsicums), roasted and seeded (page 165)

3 tablespoons olive oil or canola oil

1 yellow onion, chopped

4 cloves garlic, minced

1 tablespoon chili powder

1 tablespoon dried oregano

2 teaspoons ground cumin

½ teaspoon red pepper flakes

4 tomatoes, peeled and seeded (page 127), then diced

⅓ cup (½ oz/15 g) chopped fresh cilantro (fresh coriander)

6 tablespoons (1½ oz/45 g) shredded *queso asadero* or Monterey jack cheese

2 green (spring) onions, including tender green tops, thinly sliced

Caribbean Red Beans and Brown Rice

Brown rice pairs up with beans in this spicy Caribbean dish. Mix and match brown rice varieties to make your own blend, or purchase a packaged blend. If you can't find small red beans, use kidney beans.

SERVES 6

1½ cups (10½ oz/330 g) dried small red or kidney beans, picked over and rinsed, soaked overnight, and drained

6½ cups (52 fl oz/1.6 l) water

3 bay leaves

1¼ cups (9 oz/280 g) assorted brown rices, rinsed and drained

3 tablespoons olive oil or canola oil

1¼ teaspoons salt

1 yellow onion, chopped

½ green bell pepper (capsicum), seeded and chopped

1 celery stalk, chopped

4 cloves garlic, minced

½ teaspoon ground allspice

½ teaspoon ground cloves

½ teaspoon cayenne pepper

½ teaspoon freshly ground black pepper

1 cup (8 fl oz/250 ml) vegetable stock (page 139) or broth

1 tomato, cored and diced

2 tablespoons chopped fresh thyme

1 teaspoon hot-pepper sauce

3 tablespoons chopped fresh cilantro (fresh coriander)

In a large saucepan over high heat, combine the beans, 4 cups (32 fl oz/1 l) of the water, and the bay leaves. Bring to a boil. Reduce the heat to low, cover partially, and simmer until the beans are tender, 60–70 minutes. Drain and discard the bay leaves.

While the beans are cooking, combine the rices, 1 tablespoon of the oil, ½ teaspoon of the salt, and the remaining 2½ cups (20 fl oz/625 ml) water in a saucepan over medium-high heat. Cover and bring to a boil. Reduce the heat to low and simmer until the water is absorbed and the rice is tender, about 45 minutes. Set aside and keep warm.

In a large saucepan, heat the remaining 2 tablespoons oil over medium-high heat. Add the onion, bell pepper, and celery; sauté until the vegetables are softened, 6–8 minutes. Stir in the garlic and cook until softened, about 1 minute. Add the allspice, cloves, cayenne, the remaining ¾ teaspoon salt, and the black pepper. Cook for 1 minute. Stir in the cooked beans, the vegetable stock, tomato, thyme, and hot-pepper sauce. Cook until the vegetable mixture is heated through, 6–8 minutes.

Divide the rice among warmed individual bowls. Top each serving with beans and sprinkle with the cilantro.

Pyramid Servings

VEGETABLES	◕○○○○●
FRUITS	◕○○○○
CARBOHYDRATES	○○○○○●●
PROTEIN & DAIRY	○○○○○●●
FATS	○○○○●

PER SERVING	
calories	382
kilojoules	1,598
protein	14 g
carbohydrate	63 g
total fat	9 g
saturated fat	1 g
monounsaturated fat	5 g
cholesterol	0 mg
sodium	517 mg
fiber	11 g

Lentils with Wild Rice and Crispy Onions

This take on a traditional Middle Eastern side dish known as *koshari* combines spiced lentils with wild rice and a crown of crispy onion rings. As in an Egyptian version, tomato sauce adds complexity.

SERVES **10**

FOR THE TOMATO SAUCE

2 teaspoons olive oil

½ yellow onion, finely chopped

3 cloves garlic, minced

1½ cups (12 fl oz/375 ml) tomato sauce

3 tablespoons white vinegar

½ teaspoon red pepper flakes

¼ teaspoon salt

1¾ cups (14 fl oz/430 ml) water

⅔ cup (4 oz/125 g) wild rice

¾ teaspoon salt

2 tablespoons olive oil

½ yellow onion, finely chopped, plus 1 onion, thinly sliced

3 cloves garlic, minced

¾ teaspoon ground cumin

½ teaspoon ground cinnamon

2 cups (16 fl oz/500 ml) vegetable stock (page 139), chicken stock (page 138), or broth

1 cup (7 oz/220 g) brown or French green lentils, picked over, rinsed, and drained

Fresh cilantro (fresh coriander) or flat-leaf (Italian) parsley leaves for garnish

To make the tomato sauce, in a nonaluminum saucepan, heat the olive oil over medium heat. Add the onion and sauté until soft and lightly golden, about 6 minutes. Add the garlic and sauté for 1 minute longer; do not let the garlic brown. Stir in the tomato sauce, vinegar, red pepper flakes, and salt. When the mixture just begins to bubble, reduce the heat to low and simmer for 5 minutes. Remove from the heat and set aside.

In a saucepan, bring the water to a boil. Add the wild rice and ¼ teaspoon of the salt. Reduce the heat to low, cover, and simmer until the water is absorbed and the rice is tender, about 45 minutes.

In a saucepan, heat 1 tablespoon of the olive oil over medium heat. Add the chopped onion and sauté until soft and lightly golden, about 6 minutes. Add the garlic, cumin, and cinnamon and sauté for 1 minute longer; do not let the garlic brown. Add the stock, lentils, and the remaining ½ teaspoon salt and bring to a boil over high heat. Reduce the heat to low, cover partially, and simmer until the lentils are tender but still firm, about 30 minutes.

While the rice and lentils are cooking, heat the remaining 1 tablespoon olive oil in a nonstick frying pan over medium heat. Add the sliced onion and sauté until brown and crispy, about 30 minutes.

To serve, reheat the tomato sauce gently over medium heat. On a serving platter, spread the lentils in a layer; top with a layer of the rice. Pour the tomato sauce over the rice and top with the onion rings. Garnish with the cilantro.

Pyramid Servings

VEGETABLES	◖○○○○●
FRUITS	◖○○○○
CARBOHYDRATES	○○○○○○●
PROTEIN & DAIRY	○○○○○○●
FATS	○○○○○

PER SERVING	
calories	188
kilojoules	787
protein	9 g
carbohydrate	29 g
total fat	4 g
saturated fat	1 g
monounsaturated fat	0 g
cholesterol	0 mg
sodium	223 mg
fiber	8 g

Soybeans with Fennel, Thyme, and Oregano

SERVES 6

Cooking dried soybeans requires patience, but the long simmering time allows them to mingle with the richly flavored broth. Serve as a light starter or side dish.

Pyramid Servings

VEGETABLES ◀○○○○○
FRUITS ◀○○○○○
CARBOHYDRATES ○○○○○○○○
PROTEIN & DAIRY ○○○○○○●
FATS ○○○○○

PER SERVING

calories	93
kilojoules	389
protein	10 g
carbohydrate	7 g
total fat	3 g
saturated fat	1 g
monounsaturated fat	1 g
cholesterol	0 mg
sodium	246 mg
fiber	3 g

In a large saucepan over high heat, combine the soybeans, stock, fennel, onion, and garlic. Bring to a boil. Reduce the heat to low and skim off the foam that rises to the top. Cover partially and simmer until the soybeans are tender but still firm, about 2 hours. Check the liquid level every 30 minutes, adding water as needed to keep the beans fully covered.

When the beans are tender, add the tomato, thyme, oregano, salt, and pepper and cook until the tomato is softened, about 2 minutes. The soybeans will remain somewhat firm. Serve hot or warm.

1 cup (7 oz/220 g) dried soybeans, picked over and rinsed, soaked overnight, and drained

5 cups (40 fl oz/1.25 l) vegetable stock (page 139), chicken stock (page 138), or broth

1 small fennel bulb, trimmed and chopped

1 yellow onion, chopped

3 cloves garlic, minced

1 tomato, peeled and seeded (page 127), then diced

1 teaspoon chopped fresh thyme or ¼ teaspoon dried thyme

1 teaspoon chopped fresh oregano or ¼ teaspoon dried oregano

1 teaspoon salt

¼ teaspoon freshly ground pepper

Spicy Red Lentils

SERVES **6**

This Moroccan-style dish is quick to assemble—just chop some herbs and measure some spices. Serve it as a side dish with roasted meats or fish. In larger portions, it also makes a satisfying main course.

Pyramid Servings

VEGETABLES	◀○○○○○
FRUITS	◀○○○○○
CARBOHYDRATES	○○○○○○○○
PROTEIN & DAIRY	○○○○○●
FATS	○○○○●

PER SERVING

calories	172
kilojoules	720
protein	10 g
carbohydrate	24 g
total fat	5 g
saturated fat	1 g
monounsaturated fat	3 g
cholesterol	0 mg
sodium	212 mg
fiber	6 g

In a saucepan over high heat, combine the lentils, water, bay leaf, and ¼ teaspoon of the salt. Bring to a boil. Reduce the heat to low, cover partially, and simmer until the lentils are tender but still firm, 12–14 minutes. Drain and discard the bay leaf. Set aside.

In a small frying pan, heat the olive oil over medium heat. Add the chile and garlic and sauté until softened, about 1 minute. Add the cumin, ground coriander, and cinnamon and cook until fragrant, about 1 minute. Remove the pan from the heat.

In a large bowl, combine the lentils and the spice mixture. Toss gently to mix. Stir in the parsley, cilantro, and mint and season with the remaining ¼ teaspoon salt and the pepper. Stir in the vinegar and serve immediately.

1¼ cups (9 oz/280 g) dried red lentils, picked over, rinsed, and drained

3 cups (24 fl oz/750 ml) water

1 bay leaf

½ teaspoon salt

2 tablespoons olive oil

½ serrano chile, seeded and finely chopped

2 cloves garlic, minced

2 teaspoons ground cumin

½ teaspoon ground coriander

¼ teaspoon ground cinnamon

3 tablespoons chopped fresh flat-leaf (Italian) parsley

3 tablespoons chopped fresh cilantro (fresh coriander)

1½ tablespoons chopped fresh mint

½ teaspoon freshly ground pepper

2 tablespoons red wine vinegar

Edamame and Summer Bean Salad

Not your typical bean salad, this bright side dish made with fresh soybeans—known as edamame—is loaded with texture and flavor. Perfect for a picnic or barbecue, it's easy to make ahead.

SERVES 8

¾ lb (375 g) wax beans

2 cups (10 oz/315 g) shelled edamame

2 green (spring) onions

2 tomatoes, seeded and diced

1 tablespoon chopped fresh basil

1 tablespoon rice vinegar

1 tablespoon fresh lime juice

1 teaspoon honey

1 teaspoon Dijon mustard

2 teaspoons olive oil

½ teaspoon salt

¼ teaspoon freshly ground pepper

Trim the wax beans and cut crosswise into thirds. In a large pot fitted with a steamer basket, bring 1 inch (2.5 cm) water to a boil. Add the wax beans and edamame, cover, and steam until both are tender-crisp, about 5 minutes. Drain, rinse with cold water, and drain again.

Trim the green onions, then thinly slice on the diagonal, including the tender green tops.

In a large bowl, combine the steamed edamame and wax beans, green onions, tomatoes, and basil. Toss to mix evenly.

In a small bowl, combine the vinegar, lime juice, honey, and mustard. Whisk in the olive oil. Add the dressing to the vegetables and toss to coat. Season with the salt and pepper. Serve chilled or at room temperature.

Pyramid Servings

VEGETABLES	◀○○○○●
FRUITS	◀○○○○○
CARBOHYDRATES	○○○○○○○○
PROTEIN & DAIRY	○○○○○○●
FATS	○○○○○

PER SERVING	
calories	130
kilojoules	544
protein	9 g
carbohydrate	12 g
total fat	5 g
saturated fat	1 g
monounsaturated fat	2 g
cholesterol	0 mg
sodium	196 mg
fiber	4 g

Edamame

Many markets now offer Japanese-style soybeans in their pods from spring to fall. Rich in protein and a source of calcium and vitamins A and B, they make a fine appetizer or snack, or a colorful addition to soups and stir-fries. Drop whole pods into lightly salted boiling water, boil for 5 minutes, then drain, cool, and pop out the beans. Or find them in the pod or shelled in the frozen-vegetables case.

Classic Boston Baked Beans

The rich flavor of this hearty side dish comes from slow-roasted navy beans, onion, molasses, dry mustard, and a bit of smoky bacon. For a vegetarian version, replace the bacon with four drops of liquid smoke.

SERVES 12

2 cups (14 oz/440 g) dried small white (navy) beans, picked over and rinsed, soaked overnight, and drained

4 cups (32 fl oz/1 l) water

2 bay leaves

¾ teaspoon salt

1 yellow onion, chopped

½ cup (5½ oz/170 g) light molasses

1½ tablespoons dry mustard

3 strips thick-cut bacon, cut into ½-inch (12-mm) pieces

In a large, ovenproof pot with a tight-fitting lid or a Dutch oven, combine the beans, water, bay leaves, and ½ teaspoon of the salt over high heat. Bring to a boil. Reduce the heat to low, cover partially, and simmer until the beans have softened but are still firm, 65–75 minutes. Remove from the heat and discard the bay leaves. Do not drain the beans.

Preheat the oven to 350°F (180°C).

Stir the onion, molasses, mustard, bacon, and the remaining ¼ teaspoon salt into the beans. Cover and bake until the beans are tender and coated with a light syrup, 4½–5 hours. Check periodically to make sure the beans don't dry out, stirring and adding hot water as needed.

Pyramid Servings

VEGETABLES	◀○○○○○
FRUITS	◀○○○○○
CARBOHYDRATES	○○○○○○○○
PROTEIN & DAIRY	○○○○○●●
FATS	○○○○○

PER SERVING	
calories	200
kilojoules	837
protein	9 g
carbohydrate	33 g
total fat	4 g
saturated fat	1 g
monounsaturated fat	2 g
cholesterol	4 mg
sodium	197 mg
fiber	6 g

Fish & Shellfish

Seafoods, whether caught in the wild or farm-reared, are among the wisest main-course choices a cook can make.

216 Moroccan Fish Tagine

219 Mahimahi with Macadamia Nut Crust

220 Shrimp and Mango Curry

222 Mussels Marinière

224 Sea Bass en Papillote

225 Smoked Trout Spread

226 Salade Niçoise with Tapenade

229 Fresh Spring Rolls with Shrimp

231 Grouper with Tomato-Olive Sauce

232 Broiled Trout with Tomato and Red Onion Relish

234 Grilled Miso Salmon

235 Prawns Puttanesca

237 Thai Crab Cakes

238 Seared Salmon with Cilantro-Cucumber Salsa

240 Roasted Red Snapper

241 Swordfish Tacos with Lime and Cilantro

243 Pan-Braised Swordfish with Feta

244 Cornmeal-Crusted Sole with Chili Vinaigrette

Moroccan Fish Tagine

SERVES 4

A Moroccan tagine is a slow-simmered stew named after the conical pot in which it's cooked. Although this recipe calls for a saucepan, the flavors are authentic. Serve it over steamed couscous or bulgur.

Pyramid Servings

VEGETABLES	◀ ○ ○ ○ ○ ●
FRUITS	◀ ○ ○ ○ ○
CARBOHYDRATES	○ ○ ○ ○ ○ ○ ○ ○
PROTEIN & DAIRY	○ ○ ○ ○ ○ ● ●
FATS	○ ○ ○ ○ ●

PER SERVING	
calories	289
kilojoules	1,209
protein	38 g
carbohydrate	11 g
total fat	10 g
saturated fat	1 g
monounsaturated fat	3 g
cholesterol	52 mg
sodium	566 mg
fiber	3 g

In a large saucepan, heat the olive oil over medium heat. Add the onion and bell pepper and sauté until soft but not browned, about 8 minutes. Add the garlic and tomatoes and sauté until the tomatoes are tender, about 3 minutes. Stir in the cumin and paprika and simmer for 1 minute.

Carefully pour in the stock, raise the heat to high, and bring the mixture to a boil. Add the fish and mushrooms. When the mixture returns to a boil, reduce the heat to low. Simmer until the fish is opaque throughout, about 3 minutes.

Stir in the tahini, preserved lemon, parsley, cilantro, and salt. Ladle into warmed individual bowls and serve immediately.

1 tablespoon olive oil

1 yellow onion, chopped

1 yellow bell pepper (capsicum), seeded and diced

1 clove garlic, minced

2 tomatoes, peeled and seeded (page 127), then diced

1½ teaspoons ground cumin

½ teaspoon paprika

4 cups (32 fl oz/1 l) chicken stock (page 138), vegetable stock (page 139), or broth

1¼ lb (625 g) red snapper or seabass fillets cut into ¾-inch (2-cm) cubes

1 cup (3 oz/90 g) thinly sliced white mushrooms

2 tablespoons tahini

1 tablespoon finely chopped preserved lemon or grated lemon zest

1 tablespoon finely chopped fresh flat-leaf (Italian) parsley

1 tablespoon finely chopped fresh cilantro (fresh coriander)

½ teaspoon salt

Mahimahi with Macadamia Nut Crust

Baking these nut-crusted fillets in the upper third of the oven lets them brown nicely without the addition of oil. Serve with a side of Braised Kale with Cherry Tomatoes (page 54).

SERVES 4

¼ cup (½ oz/15 g) fresh whole-grain bread crumbs

3 tablespoons macadamia nuts, finely chopped

1 tablespoon finely chopped fresh flat-leaf (Italian) parsley

½ teaspoon grated lemon zest

½ teaspoon salt

¼ cup (2 fl oz/60 ml) nonfat milk

4 mahimahi fillets, each 5 oz (155 g) and about 1 inch (2.5 cm) thick

¼ teaspoon freshly ground pepper

Place a rack in the upper third of the oven and preheat to 450°F (230°C). Place a small wire rack in a shallow nonstick baking pan.

On a plate, stir together the bread crumbs, nuts, parsley, lemon zest, and ¼ teaspoon of the salt. Pour the milk into a shallow dish. Dip each fillet in the milk and then dredge in the nut mixture, coating completely and pressing lightly so the mixture adheres well.

Place the fillets on the rack in the baking pan, making sure that they do not touch. Sprinkle evenly with the remaining ¼ teaspoon salt and the pepper.

Bake until the fish is opaque throughout when tested with the tip of a knife and the crust is golden brown, 10–12 minutes. Transfer to warmed individual plates and serve immediately.

Pyramid Servings

VEGETABLES	◖○○○○○
FRUITS	◖○○○○○
CARBOHYDRATES	○○○○○○●
PROTEIN & DAIRY	○○○○○○●
FATS	○○○○○

PER SERVING	
calories	180
kilojoules	753
protein	28 g
carbohydrate	3 g
total fat	6 g
saturated fat	1 g
monounsaturated fat	4 g
cholesterol	104 mg
sodium	462 mg
fiber	1 g

Shrimp and Mango Curry

SERVES 4

This vibrant dish is enlivened by sweet bursts of mango. To make basil chiffonade, stack several leaves, roll them up lengthwise into a bundle, and slice thinly across. Serve with Brown Rice Pilaf (page 151).

Pyramid Servings

VEGETABLES	◀○○○○●
FRUITS	◀○○○○●
CARBOHYDRATES	○○○○○○○○
PROTEIN & DAIRY	○○○○○●●
FATS	○○○○●

PER SERVING

calories	395
kilojoules	1,653
protein	39 g
carbohydrate	26 g
total fat	15 g
saturated fat	2 g
monounsaturated fat	6 g
cholesterol	132 mg
sodium	353 mg
fiber	5 g

In a saucepan, heat 1 tablespoon of the olive oil over medium heat. Add the shallots, ginger, and garlic and sauté until fragrant, about 3 minutes. Add the tomato, curry powder, and coriander and simmer until the tomato begins to soften, about 1 minute.

Add the stock, coconut milk, and lemongrass. Raise the heat to high and bring to a boil, then reduce the heat to medium-low and simmer for 3 minutes to allow the flavors to blend. Remove from the heat.

In a nonstick sauté pan, heat the remaining 1 tablespoon olive oil over medium-high heat. Add the shrimp, sprinkle with the turmeric, and cook for about 3 minutes. Turn the shrimp and cook until pink and opaque throughout, about 2 minutes longer. Transfer to a bowl and keep warm.

Add the wine and deglaze the pan, stirring with a wooden spoon to scrape up any browned bits. Add the curry sauce to the pan, raise the heat to high, and bring to boil. Reduce the heat to medium, add the edamame, and cook until the edamame are tender-crisp, about 3 minutes. Return the shrimp to the pan and cook for 1 minute. Remove from the heat. Add the mango and salt and stir to combine. Discard the lemongrass.

Divide the curry among warmed individual plates and garnish with the basil.

2 tablespoons olive oil

1½ shallots, minced

2 tablespoons peeled and finely chopped fresh ginger

3 cloves garlic, minced

1 tomato, peeled and seeded (page 127), then diced

1½ teaspoons curry powder

¼ teaspoon ground coriander

1 cup (8 fl oz/250 ml) chicken stock (page 138), vegetable stock (page 139), or broth

½ cup (4 fl oz/125 ml) light coconut milk

1 stalk lemongrass, tender bottom 4 inches (10 cm) only, quartered lengthwise

1¼ lb (625 g) large shrimp (prawns), peeled and deveined

1 teaspoon ground turmeric

2 tablespoons dry white wine

1 cup (5 oz/155 g) shelled edamame

½ cup (3 oz/90 g) diced mango

½ teaspoon salt

2 tablespoons fresh basil chiffonade

Mussels Marinière

This classic French preparation of steamed mussels easily serves four as an appetizer. But with the addition of a crusty whole-grain baguette and a tossed salad, it makes a satisfying supper for two.

Pyramid Servings

VEGETABLES   ◀○○○○●
FRUITS   ◀○○○○○
CARBOHYDRATES ○○○○○○○○
PROTEIN & DAIRY ○○○○○●●
FATS   ○○○○○

PER SERVING	
calories	258
kilojoules	1,079
protein	28 g
carbohydrate	14 g
total fat	5 g
saturated fat	1 g
monounsaturated fat	1 g
cholesterol	64 mg
sodium	658 mg
fiber	0 g

Discard any mussels that do not close to the touch. In a large saucepan, combine the mussels, wine, shallots, and garlic. Bring to a boil over high heat. Reduce the heat to medium, cover, and cook, shaking the pan periodically, until all the mussels are opened, about 5 minutes. Remove the mussels from the pan with a slotted spoon and divide among individual shallow bowls. Discard any mussels that did not open.

Raise the heat to high and continue cooking the wine mixture to reduce slightly and deepen the flavors, 2–3 minutes. Pour the wine mixture over the mussels. Sprinkle with the parsley and serve.

1½ lb (750 g) mussels, scrubbed and debearded

1 cup (8 fl oz/250 ml) dry white wine

⅓ cup (1½ oz/45 g) chopped shallots or red onion

1 clove garlic, minced

3 tablespoons chopped fresh flat-leaf (Italian) parsley

Sea Bass en Papillote

SERVES 4

It's easy—and delicious—to cook fish fillets in packets of parchment paper, a technique called *en papillote* (pronounced en pap-e-YOTE). If you don't have parchment paper on hand, use aluminum foil.

Pyramid Servings

VEGETABLES	◀○○○○○
FRUITS	◀○○○○○
CARBOHYDRATES	○○○○○○○
PROTEIN & DAIRY	○○○○○●●
FATS	○○○○●

PER SERVING

calories	231
kilojoules	967
protein	28 g
carbohydrate	5 g
total fat	10 g
saturated fat	2 g
monounsaturated fat	6 g
cholesterol	58 mg
sodium	393 mg
fiber	2 g

Put the almonds in a food processor and process to the consistency of fine bread crumbs. Set aside.

Preheat the oven to 400°F (200°C). Cut four 15-inch (38-cm) squares of parchment (baking) paper. Fold 1 square in half to create a crease, then open up. Place 1 fillet next to the crease. Repeat with the remaining squares and fillets.

Top each fillet with one-fourth of the tomato, onion, almond meal, olive oil, wine, parsley, thyme, saffron, and salt and white pepper. Working with 1 square, fold the paper over the fish and vegetables, then fold the edges several times, crimping to seal the packet completely. Repeat to make 3 more packets. Place the packets on a baking sheet.

Bake until the paper is starting to brown, about 15 minutes. (If the fillets are thin, bake for 12 minutes.) Place the packets on plates. To serve, slit an X in each packet and fold open.

¼ cup (1½ oz/45 g) almonds

4 sea bass or halibut fillets, each 5 oz (155 g) and about 1 inch (2.5 cm) thick

1 small tomato, diced

¼ cup (1½ oz/45 g) minced yellow onion

1 tablespoon olive oil

4 teaspoons dry white wine

1 tablespoon chopped fresh flat-leaf (Italian) parsley

2 teaspoons chopped fresh thyme

½ teaspoon saffron threads, steeped in 2 tablespoons hot water

½ teaspoon *each* salt and freshly ground white pepper

Saffron

With its stunning golden hue and distinctive, earthy taste, saffron earns its place in the kitchen. Each slender saffron thread is plucked by hand from the center of a small crocus flower, making it one of the world's priciest spices. Only a tiny amount is needed, however, to give a dish evident color and character. For the best flavor, purchase saffron as threads, not powder, and steep them in hot water before using.

Smoked Trout Spread

An elegant party appetizer, this easy-to-prepare spread can be made up to a week in advance and kept tightly covered in the refrigerator. Serve it on whole-grain crackers or thin slices of plain or toasted baguette.

SERVES 12

¼ lb (125 g) smoked trout fillet, skinned and broken into pieces

½ cup (4 oz/125 g) 1-percent low-fat cottage cheese

¼ cup (1 oz/30 g) coarsely chopped red onion

2 teaspoons fresh lemon juice

1 teaspoon hot-pepper sauce

½ teaspoon Worcestershire sauce

1 celery stalk, diced

In a blender or food processor, combine the trout, cottage cheese, red onion, lemon juice, hot-pepper sauce, and Worcestershire. Process until smooth, stopping to scrape down the sides of the bowl as needed. Fold in the diced celery. Cover and refrigerate until just before serving. Makes 12 tablespoons (¾ cup/6 oz/185 g).

Pyramid Servings*

VEGETABLES	◀○○○○○
FRUITS	◀○○○○○
CARBOHYDRATES	○○○○○○○
PROTEIN & DAIRY	○○○○○○○
FATS	○○○○○

PER SERVING	
calories	26
kilojoules	109
protein	4 g
carbohydrate	1 g
total fat	1 g
saturated fat	0 g
monounsaturated fat	0 g
cholesterol	14 mg
sodium	234 mg
fiber	0 g

* Portion is not large enough to equal a serving in any category.

Trout

Like many kinds of fish and shellfish, trout are now being successfully farmed. The flavor and fat content of these captive fish may or may not be a match for those caught in the wild, but one fact remains: With their heart-healthy fish oils—trout have as much as some kinds of salmon—fish and shellfish are among a cook's best choices. Eating fish twice a week helps protect against heart disease.

Salade Niçoise with Tapenade

Named for Nice, its city of origin in southern France, this main-dish salad combines tuna—grilled fresh, not canned—with the traditional medley of fresh vegetables and seasonings, plus a few new flavors.

SERVES 4

Pyramid Servings

VEGETABLES	◖○○●●●
FRUITS	◖○○○○○
CARBOHYDRATES	○○○○○○○●
PROTEIN & DAIRY	○○○○○●●
FATS	○○○○●

PER SERVING

calories	399
kilojoules	1,669
protein	37 g
carbohydrate	24 g
total fat	16 g
saturated fat	2 g
monounsaturated fat	11 g
cholesterol	71 mg
sodium	575 mg
fiber	6 g

Place a rack in the lower third of the oven and preheat to 425°F (220°C). In a large baking pan, combine the potatoes, 1 tablespoon of the olive oil, the rosemary, ½ teaspoon of the salt, and the pepper. Stir the potatoes to coat evenly. Roast for 15 minutes. Stir the potatoes and sprinkle evenly with the onion. Continue roasting, shaking the pan every 10 minutes, until the potatoes are evenly browned and crusty and the onion is caramelized, about 20 minutes longer. Transfer to a large bowl and set aside.

While the potatoes are roasting, bring 1 inch (2.5 cm) water to a boil in a saucepan fitted with a steamer basket. Add the beans, cover, and steam until tender-crisp, about 5 minutes. Drain, rinse with cold water, and drain again. Set aside.

Prepare a hot fire in a charcoal grill or preheat a gas grill or broiler (grill). Away from the heat source, lightly brush the grill rack or broiler pan with olive oil. Position the cooking rack 4–6 inches (10–15 cm) from the heat source. Lightly brush the tuna fillets with olive oil and sprinkle both sides with the remaining ½ teaspoon salt. Arrange on the grill rack or broiler pan and grill or broil for 4 minutes. Turn carefully and cook on the other side until grill-marked and firm to the touch, about 4 minutes longer. (The cooking time will vary depending on the heat of the fire and desired rareness; watch carefully.) Transfer to a plate and keep warm.

In a large bowl, combine the olives, garlic, anchovies, capers, thyme, lemon juice, the remaining 2 tablespoons olive oil, the roasted potatoes, and the steamed beans. Toss gently until well combined. Divide among individual plates and place a tuna fillet on each plate. Garnish with the parsley.

1 lb (500 g) new potatoes, quartered

3 tablespoons extra-virgin olive oil, plus extra for brushing

1 teaspoon chopped fresh rosemary

1 teaspoon salt

¼ teaspoon freshly ground pepper

½ yellow onion, finely diced

½ lb (250 g) haricots verts or green beans, trimmed

4 tuna fillets, 5 oz (155 g) each

½ cup (2½ oz/75 g) Kalamata olives, pitted and chopped

1 clove garlic, minced

6 anchovy fillets, rinsed and chopped

1 tablespoon capers, rinsed and chopped

1 teaspoon chopped fresh thyme

1 tablespoon fresh lemon juice

2 tablespoons chopped fresh flat-leaf (Italian) parsley

Fresh Spring Rolls with Shrimp

Instead of being fried, like Chinese egg rolls, these appetizers are served fresh, letting the textures and flavors of the vegetable and shrimp filling shine through. Serve with the easy dipping sauce.

SERVES 4

2 cups (16 fl oz/500 ml) water

8 large shrimp (prawns), peeled and deveined

1 oz (30 g) cellophane noodles

1 cup (8 fl oz/250 ml) boiling water

½ cup (2½ oz/75 g) shredded carrot

¼ cup (1½ oz/45 g) peeled, seeded, and julienned cucumber

½ cup (1½ oz/45 g) thinly sliced napa cabbage

½ cup (1 oz/30 g) bean sprouts

2 tablespoons chopped fresh cilantro (fresh coriander)

4 rice-paper rounds, 8 inches (20 cm) in diameter

4 large fresh basil leaves, halved lengthwise

FOR THE SAUCE

2 tablespoons hoisin sauce

1 green (spring) onion, including tender green top, thinly sliced

1½ tablespoons fresh lime juice

1½ teaspoons fish sauce

1½ teaspoons unsalted natural peanut butter

¼ teaspoon red pepper flakes

Pinch of brown sugar

In a saucepan, bring the 2 cups water to a boil. Add the shrimp and immediately remove from the heat. Cover and "poach" until pink and opaque throughout, about 3 minutes. With a slotted spoon, transfer the shrimp to a bowl of ice water and let cool for 3 minutes. Drain and cut each shrimp in half lengthwise. Refrigerate until ready to use.

In a heatproof bowl, combine the noodles and boiling water and soak for 10 minutes. Drain and return the noodles to the bowl. Add the carrot, cucumber, cabbage, bean spouts, and cilantro. Toss gently to mix.

Place a double thickness of paper towels on a work surface. Fill a large shallow baking dish with water. Place 1 spring roll wrapper in the water and soak until pliable, about 30 seconds. Carefully transfer the wrapper to the paper towels and turn once to blot dry. Arrange ½ cup (3 oz/90 g) of the noodle mixture on the bottom half of the wrapper.

Fold the bottom edge toward the center and roll up the wrapper halfway, making sure to wrap tightly around the filling. Tuck 2 basil leaf halves along the inside crease of the half-rolled wrapper. Arrange 4 pieces of the shrimp, cut sides up, along the crease. Fold the right and left edges of the wrapper over the filling and finish rolling up. Repeat with the remaining wrappers, filling, basil, and shrimp. Transfer the rolls to a plate and cover with dampened paper towels.

To make the sauce, combine the hoisin sauce, green onion, lime juice, fish sauce, peanut butter, red pepper flakes, and brown sugar in a small bowl. Stir until well blended.

To serve, cut the rolls in half on the diagonal and place on small individual plates. Pool the sauce alongside each roll.

Pyramid Servings

VEGETABLES	◖○○○○●
FRUITS	◖○○○○
CARBOHYDRATES	○○○○○○●
PROTEIN & DAIRY	○○○○○○●
FATS	○○○○○

PER SERVING	
calories	99
kilojoules	414
protein	5 g
carbohydrate	17 g
total fat	2 g
saturated fat	0 g
monounsaturated fat	1 g
cholesterol	22 mg
sodium	256 mg
fiber	2 g

Grouper with Tomato-Olive Sauce

In the Mexican state of Veracruz, a local recipe calls for simmering fish in a rich sauce of garlic, tomatoes, capers, green olives, and chiles. This version uses grouper, but any firm white-fleshed fish will do.

SERVES 4

4 grouper fillets or steaks, each 5 oz (155 g) and about 1 inch (2.5 cm) thick

½ teaspoon salt

¼ teaspoon freshly ground pepper

1½ tablespoons extra-virgin olive oil

1 yellow onion, finely chopped

2 cloves garlic, minced

3 tomatoes, peeled and seeded (page 127), then diced

5 large pimiento-stuffed green olives, sliced

1 tablespoon capers, rinsed

1 jalapeño chile, seeded and cut into 1-inch (2.5-cm) julienne

2 tablespoons fresh lime juice

Sprinkle the grouper steaks on both sides with ¼ teaspoon of the salt and ⅛ teaspoon of the pepper. In a large, nonstick frying pan, heat 1½ teaspoons of the olive oil over medium-high heat. Add the fish to the pan and sear on both sides until lightly browned, about 2 minutes per side. Transfer to a plate and keep warm.

Reduce the heat to medium and add the remaining 1 tablespoon olive oil to the pan. Add the onion and sauté until soft and lightly golden, about 6 minutes. Add the garlic and sauté until softened, about 1 minute. Add the tomatoes, olives, capers, and jalapeño and simmer for 10 minutes to allow the flavors to blend. Stir in the remaining ¼ teaspoon salt and ⅛ teaspoon pepper. Return the fish to the pan, cover, and simmer until the fish is opaque throughout when tested with the tip of a knife, 6–8 minutes.

Transfer the grouper steaks to warmed individual plates. Stir the lime juice into the vegetables and pan juices and spoon some sauce over each steak. Serve immediately.

Pyramid Servings

VEGETABLES	◀○○○○○
FRUITS	◀○○○○○
CARBOHYDRATES	○○○○○○○○
PROTEIN & DAIRY	○○○○○●●
FATS	○○○○●

PER SERVING	
calories	241
kilojoules	1,008
protein	30 g
carbohydrate	13 g
total fat	8 g
saturated fat	1 g
monounsaturated fat	5 g
cholesterol	52 mg
sodium	596 mg
fiber	3 g

Broiled Trout with Tomato and Red Onion Relish

SERVES 4

Fresh trout has such a delicate, appealing flavor that it's well suited to preparations using a minimum of seasonings. The tangy relish here, made with roasted tomatoes, is the perfect complement.

Pyramid Servings

VEGETABLES	◀○○○●●
FRUITS	◀○○○○○
CARBOHYDRATES	○○○○○○○○
PROTEIN & DAIRY	○○○○○○●
FATS	○○○○○

PER SERVING

calories	259
kilojoules	1,084
protein	31 g
carbohydrate	10 g
total fat	10 g
saturated fat	3 g
monounsaturated fat	4 g
cholesterol	84 mg
sodium	359 mg
fiber	2 g

Preheat the broiler (grill). Position the rack 4 inches (10 cm) from the heat source.

Arrange the tomatoes cut side down on a baking sheet lined with aluminum foil or parchment (baking) paper. Broil (grill) until the skins wrinkle and begin to brown, about 5 minutes. Set aside and leave the broiler on.

In a frying pan, heat the olive oil over medium-high heat. Add the onion and sauté until soft and translucent, about 4 minutes. Add the vinegar and molasses and bring to boil. Reduce the heat to medium and simmer until slightly reduced, about 2 minutes. Add the broiled tomatoes, lemon zest, parsley, ¼ teaspoon of the salt, and the pepper. Stir to combine. Remove from the heat, set aside, and keep warm.

Lightly coat a broiler pan with olive oil cooking spray. Sprinkle the thyme and the remaining ¼ teaspoon salt over the fillets and place on the prepared pan. Broil (grill) until the fish is opaque throughout when tested with the tip of a knife, about 5 minutes. Transfer to warmed individual plates and serve topped with the warm tomato relish.

3 cups (18 oz/560 g) cherry tomatoes, halved

1 teaspoon olive oil

¼ cup (1 oz/30 g) chopped red onion

¼ cup (2 fl oz/60 ml) balsamic vinegar

1 teaspoon light molasses

1 tablespoon grated lemon zest

1 tablespoon chopped fresh flat-leaf (Italian) parsley

½ teaspoon salt

¼ teaspoon freshly ground pepper

1 teaspoon chopped fresh thyme

4 trout fillets, 5 oz (155 g) each

Grilled Miso Salmon

SERVES 4

A dab of creamy miso paste adds flavor to this easy dish. Mirin is a sweet rice cooking wine, available in some supermarkets and in most Asian markets. Try the marinade with grilled chicken or pork.

Pyramid Servings

VEGETABLES	◖○○○○○
FRUITS	◖○○○○○
CARBOHYDRATES	○○○○○○○○
PROTEIN & DAIRY	○○○○○●●
FATS	○○○○●

PER SERVING

calories	282
kilojoules	1,180
protein	29 g
carbohydrate	4 g
total fat	10 g
saturated fat	2 g
monounsaturated fat	3 g
cholesterol	78 mg
sodium	382 mg
fiber	<1 g

In a shallow baking dish, whisk together the mirin, chives, miso, soy sauce, tahini, and ginger. Add the fish to the marinade and turn to coat. Cover and marinate in the refrigerator for 1–2 hours, turning the fish occasionally.

Prepare a fire in a charcoal grill or place a grill pan over high heat. Remove the fish from the marinade and pat dry. Discard the marinade. When the grill or pan is very hot, place the fillets on it and cook, turning carefully with a spatula, until grill-marked, firm to the touch, and opaque in the center, about 4 minutes on each side.

Transfer the fillets to a serving platter. Garnish with the cilantro and sesame seeds and serve immediately.

½ cup (4 fl oz/125 ml) mirin

2 tablespoons minced fresh chives or green (spring) onion tops

1 tablespoon yellow miso

1 tablespoon low-sodium soy sauce

1 teaspoon tahini

1 teaspoon peeled and minced fresh ginger

4 salmon fillets, 5 oz (155 g) each, skinned

2 tablespoons chopped fresh cilantro (fresh coriander)

1 teaspoon sesame seeds, toasted (page 94)

Salmon

Once a seasonal delicacy, salmon is now sold widely year-round. Most of the available fish is farm-raised Atlantic salmon, although some markets occasionally offer wild Pacific varieties. Among these, chinook, or king, has the richest flavor; sockeye, the deepest color. Coho, or silver, is leaner than other salmon and has a more delicate taste. All salmon are high in healthful omega-3 fatty acids.

Prawns Puttanesca

Rich with Mediterranean flavors—olives, anchovies, capers—this sauce cooks in 5 minutes, retaining its freshness when tossed with shrimp. Serve with Broccoli Rabe with Toasted Garlic (page 70) and pasta.

SERVES 4

1 tablespoon olive oil

1¼ lb (625 g) large prawns (shrimp), peeled and deveined

½ teaspoon salt

½ teaspoon freshly ground black pepper

2 tablespoons dry white wine

4 tomatoes, peeled and seeded (page 127), then diced

¼ cup (2 oz/60 g) dry-packed sun-dried tomatoes, soaked in water to rehydrate, drained, and chopped

3 cloves garlic, minced

¼ cup (1½ oz/45 g) chopped pitted Niçoise olives

2 tablespoons capers, rinsed and chopped

6 anchovy fillets, rinsed and finely chopped

1 tablespoon grated lemon zest

1 tablespoon chopped fresh flat-leaf (Italian) parsley

1 tablespoon chopped fresh basil

½ teaspoon red pepper flakes (optional)

In a large, nonstick sauté or frying pan, heat the olive oil over medium-high heat. Add the shrimp, sprinkle with the salt and black pepper and cook for about 3 minutes. Turn the shrimp and cook until opaque and pink, about 2 minutes longer. Transfer to a bowl and keep warm.

Add the wine and deglaze pan, stirring with a wooden spoon to scrape up any browned bits. Add the fresh and sun-dried tomatoes and the garlic. Reduce the heat to medium and simmer until the tomatoes are tender, about 3 minutes.

Add all the remaining ingredients and cook for about 2 minutes longer to allow the flavors to blend. Return the shrimp to the pan and toss well to coat. Serve immediately.

Pyramid Servings

VEGETABLES	◀ ○ ○ ● ● ●
FRUITS	◀ ○ ○ ○ ○ ○
CARBOHYDRATES	○ ○ ○ ○ ○ ○ ○ ○
PROTEIN & DAIRY	○ ○ ○ ○ ○ ○ ●
FATS	○ ○ ○ ○ ○

PER SERVING	
calories	284
kilojoules	1,188
protein	31 g
carbohydrate	23 g
total fat	8 g
saturated fat	1 g
monounsaturated fat	4 g
cholesterol	132 mg
sodium	588 mg
fiber	4 g

Thai Crab Cakes

To make a tasty sauce, combine ¼ cup (2 oz/60 g) nonfat plain yogurt, 2 tablespoons *each* chopped fresh mint and basil, and a pinch *each* of salt and sugar in a food processor; process until smooth.

SERVES 4

½ cup (3½ oz/105 g) brown basmati rice, rinsed and drained

1½ cups (12 fl oz/375 ml) water

½ teaspoon salt

1 teaspoon sesame oil

½ red onion, chopped

1 clove garlic, minced

5 oz (155 g) fresh lump crab-meat, picked over to remove shell fragments

1 tablespoon fish sauce

½ teaspoon chile garlic sauce

2 tablespoons chopped fresh cilantro (fresh coriander)

1 egg, lightly beaten

3 tablespoons plain dried bread crumbs

1 tablespoon canola oil

Fresh cilantro (fresh coriander) sprigs for garnish

In a saucepan, combine the rice, water, and ¼ teaspoon of the salt. Cover and bring to a boil; stir once. Reduce the heat to low, re-cover, and simmer until the water is absorbed and the rice is tender, 45–50 minutes. Set aside.

In a small frying pan, heat the sesame oil over medium heat. Add the onion and sauté until soft and translucent, about 4 minutes. Stir in the garlic and sauté until softened, about 1 minute. Remove from the heat.

In a large bowl, combine the crabmeat, onion mixture, fish sauce, chile garlic sauce, cilantro, and the remaining ¼ teaspoon salt. Toss gently with a fork to combine. Stir in the cooked rice and toss gently to combine. Stir in the egg and mix until well blended.

Sprinkle the bread crumbs on a sheet of waxed paper or parchment (baking) paper. Divide the crab mixture into 4 portions and form each portion into a 3½-inch (9-cm) patty (or make 8 patties for appetizer portions). Dredge each patty in the bread crumbs.

In a large frying pan, heat the canola oil over medium-high heat. Add the patties to the pan and fry, turning once, until golden brown on both sides, about 5 minutes on each side. Top each with a cilantro sprig and serve immediately.

Pyramid Servings

VEGETABLES	◀ ○ ○ ○ ○ ○
FRUITS	◀ ○ ○ ○ ○ ○
CARBOHYDRATES	○ ○ ○ ○ ○ ○ ●
PROTEIN & DAIRY	○ ○ ○ ○ ○ ○ ●
FATS	○ ○ ○ ○ ●

PER SERVING	
calories	211
kilojoules	883
protein	13 g
carbohydrate	25 g
total fat	7 g
saturated fat	1 g
monounsaturated fat	3 g
cholesterol	80 mg
sodium	678 mg
fiber	2 g

Seared Salmon
with Cilantro-Cucumber Salsa

SERVES 4

Here, a summertime salsa contributes color, flavor, and texture to basic pan-seared salmon. You can make the salsa several hours in advance and refrigerate it until you are ready to serve.

Pyramid Servings

VEGETABLES	◀○○○○●
FRUITS	◀○○○○○
CARBOHYDRATES	○○○○○○○○
PROTEIN & DAIRY	○○○○○●●
FATS	○○○○●

PER SERVING

calories	243
kilojoules	1,017
protein	29 g
carbohydrate	6 g
total fat	11 g
saturated fat	2 g
monounsaturated fat	4 g
cholesterol	78 mg
sodium	654 mg
fiber	1 g

In a bowl, combine the cucumber, tomatoes, bell pepper, shallot, and chopped cilantro. Toss gently to mix. In a small bowl, whisk together the lime juice, 1 teaspoon of the canola oil, the honey, red pepper flakes, and ½ teaspoon of the salt. Pour the lime juice mixture over the cucumber mixture and toss gently to mix and coat evenly. Set aside.

Sprinkle the salmon fillets on both sides with the remaining ½ teaspoon salt and the black pepper. In a large, nonstick frying pan, heat the remaining ½ teaspoon canola oil over medium-high heat. Add the fish to the pan and cook, turning once, until opaque throughout when tested with the tip of a knife, 4–5 minutes on each side.

Transfer the salmon fillets to warmed individual plates and top each with one-fourth of the salsa. Garnish the plates with the cilantro sprigs and lime wedges. Serve immediately.

½ cucumber, peeled, halved lengthwise, seeded, halved lengthwise again, and thinly sliced crosswise

1 cup (6 oz/185 g) cherry tomatoes, quartered

½ yellow or orange bell pepper (capsicum), seeded and cut into 1-inch (2.5-cm) julienne

2 tablespoons chopped shallot or red onion

1 tablespoon chopped fresh cilantro (fresh coriander), plus sprigs for garnish

1 tablespoon fresh lime juice

1½ teaspoons canola oil

1 teaspoon honey

½ teaspoon red pepper flakes

1 teaspoon salt

4 salmon fillets, each 5 oz (155 g) and about 1 inch (2.5 cm) thick

¼ teaspoon freshly ground black pepper

Lime wedges for garnish

Roasted Red Snapper

SERVES 4

Dinner guests will be impressed with both the bright flavors and the look of this roasted whole fish. Yet it couldn't be simpler to prepare. Serve it with a salad and with crusty bread for soaking up the juices.

Pyramid Servings

VEGETABLES	◄○○○●●
FRUITS	◄○○○○○
CARBOHYDRATES	○○○○○○○○
PROTEIN & DAIRY	○○○○○●●
FATS	○○○○○

PER SERVING

calories	285
kilojoules	1,192
protein	37 g
carbohydrate	14 g
total fat	8 g
saturated fat	1 g
monounsaturated fat	5 g
cholesterol	63 mg
sodium	712 mg
fiber	2 g

In a shallow glass baking dish, combine the orange and lime juices, orange and lime zests, shallots, and 1 tablespoon of the oil.

Score the skin of the fish in a diamond pattern. Add the fish to the marinade and turn once to coat. Cover and refrigerate for 30 minutes, turning the fish occasionally.

Preheat the oven to 425°F (220°C). Lightly coat a shallow baking dish with cooking spray.

In a blender or small food processor, combine the garlic, basil, mint, thyme, the remaining 1 tablespoon oil, ½ teaspoon of the salt, and ¼ teaspoon of the pepper. Pulse to purée. In a small bowl, combine half of the herb paste with the leek. Toss gently to mix.

Sprinkle the leek mixture evenly over the bottom of the prepared baking dish. Top with the tomato slices, arranging them in a single layer. Sprinkle the tomatoes with the remaining ½ teaspoon salt and ¼ teaspoon pepper. Remove the fish from the marinade and pat dry. Discard the marinade. Rub the remaining herb paste over the fish, coating both sides. Place the fish on top of the tomatoes and cover the dish tightly with aluminum foil.

Roast the fish for 30 minutes, then uncover and roast until the fish is opaque throughout when tested with the tip of a knife, 10–12 minutes longer.

Lift the fish from the baking dish and place on a large platter. Divide the vegetables among 4 warmed individual plates. Peel the skin from the top of the fish, remove the top fillet, and divide it between 2 of the plates. Lift out the center fish bone and discard. Lift the second fillet and divide it between the remaining 2 plates. Serve immediately.

½ cup (4 fl oz/125 ml) fresh orange juice

½ cup (4 fl oz/125 ml) fresh lime juice

½ teaspoon grated orange zest

½ teaspoon grated lime zest

3 shallots or ½ red onion, chopped

2 tablespoons olive oil or canola oil

1 small whole red snapper, about 1½ lb (750 g), cleaned and scaled, head and tail left on

2 cloves garlic, coarsely chopped

2 tablespoons chopped fresh basil

2 tablespoons chopped fresh mint

1 tablespoon chopped fresh thyme

1 teaspoon salt

½ teaspoon coarsely ground pepper

1 small leek, including tender green top, halved lengthwise, and cut crosswise into 1½-inch (4-cm) pieces

2 large tomatoes, cut crosswise into slices ½ inch (12 mm) thick

Swordfish Tacos with Lime and Cilantro

For the tastiest tacos, be sure the swordfish is fresh, not frozen, and try to use freshly made corn tortillas. Other firm white-fleshed fish such as sea bass, cod, or snapper can replace the swordfish.

SERVES 6

¾ cup (3 oz/90 g) pitted black olives, chopped

2 tomatoes, seeded and diced, plus ½ cup (3 oz/90 g) chopped

3 green (spring) onions, thinly sliced

½ jalapeño chile, seeded and minced (optional)

4 tablespoons (2 fl oz/60 ml) fresh lime juice

1 teaspoon grated lime zest

1 tablespoon rice vinegar

3 tablespoons extra-virgin olive oil

4 tablespoons (⅓ oz/10 g) chopped fresh cilantro (fresh coriander)

½ teaspoon salt

¼ teaspoon pepper

1 small head romaine (cos) lettuce, thinly sliced (about 3 cups/6 oz/185 g)

1 cup (6 oz/185 g) coarsely grated radishes

½ roasted and seeded (page 165) red bell pepper (capsicum)

1 teaspoon chili powder

1 teaspoon ground cumin

12 small corn tortillas

1¾ lb (875 g) swordfish steaks or fillets, cut into 1-inch (2.5-cm) cubes

In a bowl, combine the olives, the diced tomatoes, green onions, jalapeño (if using), 2 tablespoons of the lime juice, the lime zest, the vinegar, 2 tablespoons of the olive oil, 2 tablespoons of the cilantro, the salt, and the pepper. Toss gently until all the ingredients are evenly distributed. Cover and refrigerate until ready to use. Place the romaine and radishes in separate bowls, cover, and refrigerate until ready to use.

Cut the roasted bell pepper half into chunks. In a blender or food processor, combine the roasted pepper, the ½ cup chopped tomato, ¼ teaspoon of the chili powder, ¼ teaspoon of the cumin, and the remaining 2 tablespoons lime juice. Pulse to purée. Stir in the remaining 2 tablespoons cilantro and set aside.

Preheat the oven to 300°F (150°C). Wrap the tortillas in aluminum foil and warm in the oven for about 10 minutes. Remove from the oven and keep warm.

Raise the oven temperature to 400°F (200°C). In a bowl, toss the swordfish cubes with the remaining 1 tablespoon olive oil, ¾ teaspoon chili powder, and ¾ teaspoon cumin. Arrange the fish in a single layer on a baking sheet and bake until the fish is opaque throughout when tested with the tip of a knife, about 5 minutes.

To serve, place 2 tortillas on each individual plate. Divide the tomato-olive mixture evenly among the tortillas and top with equal portions of the fish. Add some lettuce and radishes to each and drizzle with lime-cilantro sauce. Serve immediately.

Pyramid Servings

VEGETABLES	◀○○○●●
FRUITS	◀○○○○○
CARBOHYDRATES	○○○○○○●●
PROTEIN & DAIRY	○○○○○○●
FATS	○○○●●

PER SERVING	
calories	403
kilojoules	1,686
protein	33 g
carbohydrate	33 g
total fat	16 g
saturated fat	3 g
monounsaturated fat	9 g
cholesterol	55 mg
sodium	387 mg
fiber	5 g

Pan-Braised Swordfish with Feta

This Mediterranean-style swordfish dish goes from stove to table in less than 20 minutes. Serve it alongside steamed zucchini or Wilted Greens with Warm Balsamic Vinegar (page 34).

SERVES 4

4 swordfish steaks, each 5 oz (155 g) and ¾–1 inch (2–2.5 cm) thick

¾ teaspoon salt

¼ teaspoon freshly ground pepper

1½ teaspoons olive oil or canola oil

1 red onion, thinly sliced

2 cloves garlic, minced

1 cup (8 fl oz/250 ml) vegetable stock (page 139) or broth

½ cup (3 oz/90 g) golden raisins (sultanas)

2 tablespoons red wine vinegar

1 small lemon, thinly sliced

2 tablespoons crumbled feta cheese

1 tablespoon chopped fresh marjoram or oregano

1 tablespoon capers, rinsed

Sprinkle the swordfish steaks on both sides with ¼ teaspoon of the salt and ⅛ teaspoon of the pepper. In a large, nonstick frying pan, heat 1 teaspoon of the oil over medium-high heat. Add the fish to the pan and sear on both sides until lightly browned, about 2 minutes on each side. Transfer to a plate and keep warm.

Reduce the heat to medium and add the remaining ½ teaspoon oil to the pan. Add the onion and garlic and sauté for 1 minute. Stir in the stock, raisins, and vinegar. Return the swordfish to the pan and top with the lemon slices. Cover and simmer until the fish is opaque throughout when tested with the tip of a knife, 3–4 minutes.

Remove the lemon slices from the fish and set aside. Transfer the swordfish steaks to warmed individual plates. Stir the feta, the remaining ½ teaspoon salt and ⅛ teaspoon pepper, the marjoram, and the capers into the pan juices. Remove from the heat. Spoon some sauce over each swordfish steak and top with the reserved lemon slices. Serve immediately.

Pyramid Servings

VEGETABLES	◐ ○ ○ ○ ○ ○
FRUITS	◐ ○ ○ ○ ○ ●
CARBOHYDRATES	○ ○ ○ ○ ○ ○ ●
PROTEIN & DAIRY	○ ○ ○ ○ ○ ● ●
FATS	○ ○ ○ ○ ○

PER SERVING	
calories	277
kilojoules	1,159
protein	30 g
carbohydrate	19 g
total fat	9 g
saturated fat	3 g
monounsaturated fat	4 g
cholesterol	59 mg
sodium	700 mg
fiber	1 g

Cornmeal-Crusted Sole with Chili Vinaigrette

SERVES 4

Sole's delicate flavor is enhanced by a toasty cornmeal crust and a tangy vinaigrette. Serve with Caribbean Red Beans and Brown Rice (page 205) or Spicy Red Lentils (page 210).

Pyramid Servings

VEGETABLES ◀○○○○○
FRUITS ◀○○○○○
CARBOHYDRATES ○○○○○○○○
PROTEIN & DAIRY ○○○○○●●
FATS ○○○○●

PER SERVING

calories	275
kilojoules	1,151
protein	25 g
carbohydrate	13 g
total fat	12 g
saturated fat	2 g
monounsaturated fat	8 g
cholesterol	67 mg
sodium	551 mg
fiber	2 g

In a shallow bowl, stir together the flour, cornmeal, and ¼ teaspoon of the salt. Dredge the fillets in the flour mixture, coating completely, and shake off the excess. In a large, nonstick frying pan, heat 1 tablespoon of the olive oil over medium-high heat. Add the fish and cook, turning once, until the fish is just opaque throughout when tested with the tip of a knife and the crust is golden brown, about 3 minutes on each side. Transfer to individual plates and keep warm.

Add the wine and deglaze the pan, stirring with a wooden spoon to scrape up any browned bits. Cook to reduce by half. In a small bowl, combine the pan juices, lemon juice, stock, chili powder, mustard, cumin, and the remaining ½ teaspoon salt. Whisk in the remaining 2 tablespoons olive oil to make a thick vinaigrette.

To serve, drizzle the vinaigrette over the fillets and sprinkle with the cilantro and lemon zest. Serve immediately.

¼ cup (1½ oz/45 g) all-purpose (plain) flour

¼ cup (1½ oz/45 g) cornmeal, preferably stone-ground

¾ teaspoon salt

4 sole fillets, 5 oz (155 g) each

3 tablespoons extra-virgin olive oil

2 tablespoons dry white wine

1½ tablespoons fresh lemon juice

1½ tablespoons vegetable stock (page 139) or broth

¾ teaspoon chili powder

¼ teaspoon dry mustard

¼ teaspoon ground cumin

1 tablespoon chopped fresh cilantro (fresh coriander)

1 tablespoon grated lemon zest

Poultry & Meat

Poultry and meats can often step back from the center of the plate, taking on a supporting role.

249   Turkey Potpie with Baby Vegetables

250   Roasted Duck Breast with Lemongrass
        and Green Onion

252   Spicy Beef Kabobs

254   Braised Chicken with Mushrooms and Pearl Onions

255   Chicken Stir-Fry with Eggplant and Basil

257   Chicken and Portobello Baguette

259   Jamaican Barbecued Pork Tenderloin

260   Grilled Chicken Breasts with Roasted
        Yellow Tomato Sauce

261   Spinach Frittata

262   Roasted Rack of Lamb with Parsley Crust

264   Beef Stew with Fennel and Shallots

265   Pork Medallions with Five-Spice Powder

Chicken Stir-Fry with Eggplant and Basil, page 255

Turkey Potpie
with Baby Vegetables

This old-fashioned potpie has just a top crust, made with cornmeal and a hint of honey. The easy filling can be made a day ahead. Then mix the batter while the oven heats, and the pie is ready to assemble.

SERVES 8

10 baby carrots

1 cup (7 oz/220 g) pearl onions

1/3 lb (155 g) fresh white mushrooms

1¼ cups (8 oz/250 g) frozen artichoke hearts, thawed

¼ cup (2 fl oz/60 ml) plus 2 tablespoons olive oil

1 teaspoon dry mustard

¾ cup (4 oz/120 g) all-purpose (plain) flour

2½ cups (20 fl oz/625 ml) chicken stock (page 138) or broth

1 clove garlic, minced

2 lb (1 kg) skinless, boneless turkey breast, diced

1 cup (5 oz/155 g) shelled edamame or English peas

1 tomato, seeded and diced

1 tablespoon *each* fresh chopped dill and basil

¼ cup (2 oz/60 g) low-fat sour cream

1½ teaspoons salt

½ teaspoon freshly ground pepper

½ cup (2½ oz/75 g) cornmeal

1½ teaspoons baking powder

¾ cup (6 fl oz/180 ml) plain soy milk (soya milk)

1 tablespoon dark honey

Peel and halve the carrots, then thinly slice crosswise. Immerse the onions in a saucepan of boiling water for about 2 minutes, drain, and plunge in cold water. Cut off the root ends, slip off the skins, and then cut a shallow X in the root end of each onion. Brush the mushrooms clean, then thinly slice. Quarter the artichokes lengthwise. Set the prepared vegetables aside.

In a large, heavy, ovenproof saucepan or Dutch oven, heat the ¼ cup olive oil over low heat. Add the mustard and ¼ cup (1½ oz/45 g) of the flour and cook, whisking constantly, for 1–2 minutes.

Add the stock, still whisking constantly to avoid lumps, raise the heat to medium-high, and bring to a boil. Add the garlic, carrots, and onions. Reduce the heat to a gentle simmer and cook until the vegetables are softened, about 5 minutes. Add the turkey, mushrooms, artichoke hearts, edamame, tomato, dill, and basil. Cover and simmer until the turkey is opaque throughout, about 10 minutes. Whisk in the sour cream and season with 1 teaspoon of the salt and the pepper. Spoon the mixture into a 9-by-13-inch (23-by-33-cm) baking dish and set aside.

Preheat the oven to 425°F (220°C).

In a bowl, combine the cornmeal, the remaining ½ cup (2½ oz/75 g) flour, baking powder, and the remaining ½ teaspoon salt. In another bowl, whisk together the soy milk, the 2 tablepoons olive oil, and the honey. Add the dry ingredients, stirring just until moistened.

Pour the batter over the turkey mixture. Bake, uncovered, until lightly browned, about 40 minutes. Let stand for 10 minutes, then serve.

Pyramid Servings

VEGETABLES	◀○○○●●
FRUITS	◀○○○○○
CARBOHYDRATES	○○○○○○●
PROTEIN & DAIRY	○○○○●●
FATS	○○○○●

PER SERVING	
calories	384
kilojoules	1,607
protein	30 g
carbohydrate	34 g
total fat	14 g
saturated fat	3 g
monounsaturated fat	8 g
cholesterol	51 mg
sodium	657 mg
fiber	5 g

Roasted Duck Breast with Lemongrass and Green Onion

SERVES 4

Duck breast is remarkably lean once skinned, and more flavorful than chicken breast. Any breed of duck is fine in this dish, but if the breasts are large, bone and skin them, then cut 5-ounce (155-g) portions.

Pyramid Servings

VEGETABLES	◀○○○○○
FRUITS	◀○○○○○
CARBOHYDRATES	○○○○○○○○
PROTEIN & DAIRY	○○○○○●●
FATS	○○○○○

PER SERVING

calories	221
kilojoules	925
protein	30 g
carbohydrate	5 g
total fat	8 g
saturated fat	3 g
monounsaturated fat	2 g
cholesterol	109 mg
sodium	459 mg
fiber	1 g

In a blender or food processor, combine the lemongrass, green onions, garlic, ginger, and cilantro and process until finely chopped. Add the curry powder, cumin, turmeric, cinnamon, cardamom, pepper, fish sauce, and coconut milk and process to purée.

Place the duck breasts in a large lock-top plastic bag. Add the marinade to the bag and seal, pressing out the excess air. Put the bag in a large, shallow dish and marinate in the refrigerator for at least 2 hours and preferably overnight, turning the bag occasionally.

Preheat the oven to 400°F (200°C). Remove the duck breasts from the marinade and pat dry, reserving the marinade. Lightly coat a large, nonstick frying pan with an ovenproof handle with cooking spray. Place the pan over medium-high heat until hot. Add the duck breasts and cook, turning once, until lightly browned on both sides, about 4 minutes total. Pour off any accumulated fat from the pan and immediately transfer the pan to the oven. Roast the duck until fairly firm when pressed in the middle and slightly pink inside and an instant-read thermometer reads 160°F (71°C). Transfer the duck breasts to a cutting board, cover with a kitchen towel, and let rest for 10 minutes.

Meanwhile, place the pan over medium-high heat. Add the wine and deglaze the pan, using a wooden spoon to scrape up any browned bits. Add the tomato and cook until tender, about 5 minutes. Add the reserved marinade and the stock. Bring to a boil, then reduce the heat to low and simmer until the sauce thickens, about 2 minutes. Remove from the heat.

To serve, slice the duck breasts diagonally across the grain. Arrange on individual plates, fanning out the slices. Top the slices with the sauce and garnish with the mint.

2 stalks lemongrass, tender bottom 4 inches (10 cm) only, thinly sliced

2 green (spring) onions, trimmed

3 cloves garlic

2 tablespoons peeled and chopped fresh ginger

2 tablespoons chopped fresh cilantro (fresh coriander)

½ teaspoon curry powder

½ teaspoon ground cumin

½ teaspoon ground turmeric

½ teaspoon ground cinnamon

¼ teaspoon ground cardamom

¼ teaspoon freshly ground pepper

1 tablespoon fish sauce

1 cup (8 fl oz/250 ml) light coconut milk

4 skinless, boneless duck breast halves, 5 oz (155 g) each

2 tablespoons dry white wine

1 tomato, peeled and seeded (page 127), then diced

½ cup (4 fl oz/125 ml) chicken stock (page 138) or broth

1 tablespoon chopped fresh mint

Spicy Beef Kabobs

SERVES 8

This inventive dish combines lean ground beef, spices, and garlic with bulgur for a zesty kabob with a tangy sauce. For an appetizer, shape the mix into meatballs, sauté lightly, and serve with cocktail picks.

Pyramid Servings

VEGETABLES	◐○○○○○
FRUITS	◐○○○○
CARBOHYDRATES	○○○○○○●
PROTEIN & DAIRY	○○○○○●●
FATS	○○○○○

PER SERVING	
calories	301
kilojoules	1,259
protein	24 g
carbohydrate	22 g
total fat	13 g
saturated fat	4 g
monounsaturated fat	5 g
cholesterol	32 mg
sodium	458 mg
fiber	5 g

Place the onions in a blender or food processor and process to purée. Strain through a fine-mesh sieve into a 2-cup (16–fl oz/500-ml) measuring pitcher, pressing firmly with a rubber spatula or the back of a wooden spoon to extract all the juice. Discard the solids. Add the lemon juice and enough water to measure 1½ cups (12 fl oz/375 ml) liquid. In a large bowl, combine the onion juice mixture and the bulgur and soak for 10 minutes. Add the beef, pine nuts, garlic, 1 teaspoon of the salt, the cumin, cinnamon, cardamom, and pepper to the bulgur and stir to mix well.

Using a little less than ⅓ cup (1½ oz/45 g) for each kabob, form the beef mixture into 16 sausages, each about 4 inches (10 cm) long and ¾ inch (2 cm) in diameter. Thread onto the skewers. If the mixture is too crumbly, add water 1 tablespoon at a time, just until it holds together. Cover the prepared skewers and refrigerate until ready to cook.

Prepare a hot fire in a charcoal grill or preheat a gas grill or broiler (grill). Away from the heat source, lightly coat the grill rack or broiler pan with cooking spray. Position the cooking rack 4–6 inches (10–15 cm) from the heat source.

In a small bowl, whisk together the yogurt, tahini, lemon zest, mustard, and the remaining 1 teaspoon salt. Cover and refrigerate.

Place the kabobs on the grill rack or broiler pan. Grill or broil the kabobs, turning as needed, until evenly browned, about 8 minutes. Drizzle with the yogurt sauce and garnish with the cilantro.

2 yellow onions, coarsely chopped

2 tablespoons fresh lemon juice

2 cups (12 oz/375 g) fine-grind bulgur

1½ lb (750 g) very lean ground (minced) beef

¼ cup (1 oz/30 g) very finely chopped pine nuts

2 cloves garlic, minced

2 teaspoons salt

1 teaspoon ground cumin

½ teaspoon ground cinnamon

½ teaspoon ground cardamom

½ teaspoon freshly ground pepper

16 wooden skewers, soaked in water for 30 minutes, or metal skewers

2 cups (1 lb/500 g) nonfat plain yogurt

¼ cup (2½ oz/75 g) tahini

2 tablespoons grated lemon zest

2 teaspoons dry mustard

2 tablespoons chopped fresh cilantro (fresh coriander)

Braised Chicken with Mushrooms and Pearl Onions

SERVES 4

Use a deep, heavy pot with a tight-fitting lid for this dish. The alcohol cooks off as the chicken simmers. But if you'd rather not use wine, simply substitute additional stock and omit the balsamic vinegar.

Pyramid Servings

VEGETABLES	◁○○○○●
FRUITS	◁○○○○
CARBOHYDRATES	○○○○○○○○
PROTEIN & DAIRY	○○○○○●●
FATS	○○○○●

PER SERVING

calories	300
kilojoules	1,255
protein	34 g
carbohydrate	19 g
total fat	9 g
saturated fat	2 g
monounsaturated fat	5 g
cholesterol	92 mg
sodium	701 mg
fiber	3 g

In a shallow dish, stir together the flour, ½ teaspoon of the salt, and ¼ teaspoon of the pepper. Dredge the chicken pieces in the seasoned flour.

In a large, heavy saucepan or Dutch oven, heat the oil over medium-high heat. Add the chicken and cook, turning once, until browned on both sides, about 5 minutes total. Transfer to a platter. Add the shallot to the pan and sauté until softened, about 1 minute. Add the mushrooms and sauté until lightly browned, 3–4 minutes. Stir in the onions and sauté until they begin to pick up some brown color, 2–3 minutes.

Stir in the stock and wine and deglaze the pan, stirring with a wooden spoon to scrape up any browned bits. Return the chicken pieces to the pan, and bring to a boil. Cover, reduce the heat to low, and simmer, stirring occasionally, until the chicken and vegetables are tender, 45–50 minutes. Stir in the vinegar, the chopped thyme, and the remaining ½ teaspoon salt and ¼ teaspoon pepper.

To serve, divide the vegetables among warmed shallow individual bowls. Top each portion with 2 pieces of chicken, 1 light meat and 1 dark. Garnish with thyme sprigs. Serve immediately.

¼ cup (1½ oz/45 g) all-purpose (plain) flour

1 teaspoon salt

½ teaspoon freshly ground pepper

2 skinless, bone-in chicken breast halves, about ¾ lb (375 g) total weight, each cut in half crosswise

2 skinless, bone-in chicken thighs

2 chicken legs

1½ tablespoons olive oil or canola oil

1 shallot, chopped

1 lb (500 g) small white button mushrooms, brushed clean

½ lb (250 g) peeled pearl onions

¾ cup (6 fl oz/180 ml) vegetable stock (page 139), chicken stock (page 138), or broth

½ cup (4 fl oz/125 ml) port or dry red wine

2 tablespoons balsamic vinegar

2 tablespoons chopped fresh thyme, plus sprigs for garnish

Chicken Stir-Fry with Eggplant and Basil

This colorful main dish requires a fair amount of chopping, slicing, and dicing, but the cooking takes only minutes. Serve with Sichuan Broccoli and Cauliflower (page 42) and brown basmati rice.

SERVES 4

¼ cup (⅓ oz/10 g) coarsely chopped fresh basil

2 tablespoons chopped fresh mint

¾ cup (6 fl oz/180 ml) chicken stock (page 138) or broth

3 green (spring) onions, including tender green tops, 2 coarsely chopped and 1 thinly sliced

2 cloves garlic

1 tablespoon peeled and chopped fresh ginger

2 tablespoons extra-virgin olive oil

1 small eggplant (aubergine), with peel, diced (about 4 cups/13 oz/410 g)

1 yellow onion, coarsely chopped

1 red bell pepper (capsicum), seeded and cut into julienne

1 yellow bell pepper (capsicum), seeded and cut into julienne

1 lb (500 g) skinless, boneless chicken breasts, cut into strips ½ inch (12 mm) wide and 2 inches (5 cm) long

2 tablespoons low-sodium soy sauce

In a blender or food processor, combine the basil, mint, ¼ cup (2 fl oz/60 m) of the stock, the chopped green onions, garlic, and ginger. Pulse until the mixture is minced but not puréed. Set aside.

In a large, nonstick frying pan, heat 1 tablespoon of the olive oil over medium-high heat. Add the eggplant, yellow onion, and bell peppers and sauté until the vegetables are just tender, about 8 minutes. Transfer to a bowl and cover with a kitchen towel to keep warm.

Add the remaining 1 tablespoon olive oil to the pan and heat over medium-high heat. Add the basil mixture and sauté for about 1 minute, stirring constantly. Add the chicken strips and soy sauce and sauté until the chicken is almost opaque throughout, about 2 minutes. Add the remaining ½ cup (4 fl oz/120 ml) stock and bring to a boil. Return the eggplant mixture to the pan and stir until heated through, about 3 minutes. Transfer to a warmed serving dish and garnish with the sliced green onion. Serve immediately.

Pyramid Servings

VEGETABLES	◀○○●●●
FRUITS	◀○○○○○
CARBOHYDRATES	○○○○○○○○
PROTEIN & DAIRY	○○○○○○●
FATS	○○○○●

PER SERVING	
calories	248
kilojoules	1,167
protein	30 g
carbohydrate	13 g
total fat	8 g
saturated fat	1 g
monounsaturated fat	5 g
cholesterol	66 mg
sodium	408 mg
fiber	4 g

Chicken and Portobello Baguette

A purée of roasted red pepper and walnuts adds hearty flavors to this fine sandwich. If you're short on time, substitute ½ cup (4 oz/125 g) bottled roasted red peppers for freshly roasted ones.

SERVES 4

1 large red bell pepper (capsicum), roasted and seeded (page 165)

1 shallot, chopped

1½ tablespoons chopped walnuts

1½ tablespoons balsamic vinegar

1 teaspoon Dijon mustard

¼ teaspoon plus ⅛ teaspoon salt

¼ teaspoon plus ⅛ teaspoon freshly ground pepper

2 tablespoons extra-virgin olive oil

¾ lb (375 g) skinless, boneless chicken breasts

2 large portobello mushrooms, stemmed, brushed clean, and halved

1 whole-grain baguette, cut crosswise into 4 sections, each about 6 inches (15 cm) long

4 butter (Boston) lettuce leaves

1 tomato, thinly sliced

Chop the roasted bell pepper coarsely. In a blender or food processor, combine the roasted pepper, shallot, walnuts, 1 tablespoon of the vinegar, the mustard, ¼ teaspoon of the salt, and ¼ teaspoon of the pepper. Pulse a few times to purée and set aside.

In a large, nonstick frying pan, heat 1½ teaspoons of the olive oil over medium-high heat. Season the chicken breasts with the remaining ⅛ teaspoon salt and ⅛ teaspoon pepper. Add the chicken to the pan and cook, turning once, until lightly browned on both sides and no longer pink on the inside, 3–4 minutes on each side. Transfer to a cutting board and let cool. Thinly slice the chicken lengthwise into strips.

In the same frying pan, heat the remaining 1½ tablespoons olive oil over medium-high heat. Add the mushrooms and sauté, turning frequently, until well browned, 7–9 minutes. Remove from the heat and drizzle with the remaining 1½ teaspoons balsamic vinegar.

Using a serrated knife, split the baguette sections in half lengthwise. Spread about 1 tablespoon red pepper mixture on both halves of each baguette section. To assemble a sandwich, place 1 mushroom half on the bottom half of a baguette section. Top with one-fourth of the chicken, a lettuce leaf, and 1 or 2 tomato slices. Close the sandwich with the top half of the baguette section, and slice in half. Repeat to make 3 more sandwiches, then serve. (If making ahead, omit the red pepper mixture, wrap the sandwiches in plastic wrap, and refrigerate. Spread the red pepper mixture on the baguettes just prior to serving.)

Pyramid Servings

VEGETABLES	◀○○○●●
FRUITS	◀○○○○○
CARBOHYDRATES	○○○○○●●
PROTEIN & DAIRY	○○○○○○●
FATS	○○○●●

PER SERVING	
calories	400
kilojoules	1,674
protein	30 g
carbohydrate	44 g
total fat	13 g
saturated fat	2 g
monounsaturated fat	7 g
cholesterol	49 mg
sodium	692 mg
fiber	8 g

Jamaican Barbecued Pork Tenderloin

As lean as chicken breast, pork tenderloin has a milder, slightly sweet flavor. Here, it's coated with a jerk-style spice rub and grilled or broiled. Serve with Caribbean Red Beans and Brown Rice (page 205).

SERVES 4

2 teaspoons firmly packed brown sugar

1 teaspoon ground allspice

1 teaspoon ground cinnamon

½ teaspoon ground ginger

½ teaspoon onion powder

½ teaspoon garlic powder

¼ teaspoon cayenne pepper

⅛ teaspoon ground cloves

¾ teaspoon salt

½ teaspoon freshly ground black pepper

1 pork tenderloin, about 1 lb (500 g), trimmed of visible fat

2 teaspoons white vinegar

1½ teaspoons dark honey

1 teaspoon tomato paste

In a small bowl, combine the brown sugar, allspice, cinnamon, ginger, onion powder, garlic powder, cayenne, cloves, ½ teaspoon of the salt, and the black pepper. Rub the spice mixture over the pork and let stand for 15 minutes.

In another small bowl, combine the vinegar, honey, tomato paste, and the remaining ¼ teaspoon salt. Whisk to blend. Set aside.

Prepare a hot fire in a charcoal grill or preheat a gas grill or broiler (grill) to medium-high or 400°F (200°C). Away from the heat source, lightly coat the grill rack or broiler pan with cooking spray. Position the cooking rack 4–6 inches (10–15 cm) from the heat source.

Place the pork on the grill rack or broiler pan. Grill or broil at medium-high heat, turning several times, until browned on all sides, 3–4 minutes total. Remove to a cooler part of the grill or reduce the heat and continue cooking for 14–16 minutes. Baste with the glaze and continue cooking until the pork is slightly pink inside and an instant-read thermometer inserted into the thickest part reads 160°F (71°C), 3–4 minutes longer. Transfer to a cutting board and let rest for 5 minutes before slicing.

To serve, slice the pork tenderloin crosswise into 16 pieces and arrange on a warmed serving platter, or divide the slices among individual plates.

Pyramid Servings

VEGETABLES	◁○○○○○
FRUITS	◁○○○○○
CARBOHYDRATES	○○○○○○○○
PROTEIN & DAIRY	○○○○○●●
FATS	○○○○○

PER SERVING

calories	180
kilojoules	753
protein	24 g
carbohydrate	6 g
total fat	6 g
saturated fat	2 g
monounsaturated fat	3 g
cholesterol	75 mg
sodium	508 mg
fiber	1 g

Grilled Chicken Breasts with Roasted Yellow Tomato Sauce

SERVES 4

This recipe uses the grill or broiler both to cook the chicken and to make a smoky-flavored tomato sauce. Serve with Brussels Sprouts with Shallots and Lemon (page 66).

Pyramid Servings

VEGETABLES ◀○○○○●
FRUITS ◀○○○○○
CARBOHYDRATES ○○○○○○○○
PROTEIN & DAIRY ○○○○○●●
FATS ○○○○○

PER SERVING

calories	239
kilojoules	1,000
protein	35 g
carbohydrate	8 g
total fat	7 g
saturated fat	1 g
monounsaturated fat	4 g
cholesterol	82 mg
sodium	583 mg
fiber	2 g

Prepare a hot fire in a charcoal grill or preheat a gas grill or broiler (grill). Away from the heat source, lightly coat the grill rack or broiler pan with cooking spray. Position the cooking rack 4–6 inches (10–15 cm) from the heat source.

Arrange the tomatoes skin side down on the grill rack or skin side up on a broiler pan lined with aluminum foil. Grill or broil until the skins begin to blacken, about 5 minutes. Transfer to a bowl, cover with plastic wrap, and let steam until the skins loosen, about 10 minutes.

In a small frying pan, heat the olive oil over medium heat. Add the garlic and sauté until softened, about 1 minute. Remove from the heat and set aside.

Core and peel the tomatoes. In a blender or food processor, combine the tomatoes, the garlic with the oil, and the vinegar. Pulse until well blended. Stir in 1 tablespoon of the basil, ½ teaspoon of the salt, and ⅛ teaspoon of the pepper.

Sprinkle the chicken breasts with the remaining ¼ teaspoon salt and ⅛ teaspoon pepper. In a shallow dish, stir together the parsley, thyme, and the remaining 2 tablespoons basil. Dredge the chicken in the herb mixture, coating completely. Grill or broil the chicken, turning once, until browned on both sides and no longer pink on the inside, about 4 minutes on each side.

Transfer the chicken breasts to warmed individual plates. Spoon the tomato sauce on top, dividing evenly, and serve immediately.

4 yellow tomatoes, halved crosswise and seeded

1½ tablespoons extra-virgin olive oil

2 cloves garlic, minced

1 tablespoon balsamic vinegar

3 tablespoons chopped fresh basil

¾ teaspoon salt

¼ teaspoon freshly ground pepper

4 skinless, boneless chicken breast halves, about 5 oz (155 g) each

2 tablespoons chopped fresh flat-leaf (Italian) parsley

1 tablespoon chopped fresh thyme

Spinach Frittata

Since the ingredients in this recipe are ones you may well have on hand, this Italian-style omelet makes for an easy supper. Pair it with Braised Kale with Cherry Tomatoes (page 54).

SERVES 4

1 teaspoon olive oil

1 clove garlic, minced

3 cups (6 oz/185 g) baby spinach leaves

3 whole eggs, plus 4 egg whites

¾ teaspoon salt

¼ teaspoon freshly ground pepper

½ yellow onion, chopped

¼ cup (1 oz/30 g) minced red bell pepper (capsicum)

2 waxy red or white potatoes, about ¾ lb (375 g) total weight, peeled and shredded

2 tablespoons julienned fresh basil

¼ cup (1 oz/30 g) shredded part-skim mozzarella or provolone cheese

Preheat the broiler (grill). Position the rack 4 inches (10 cm) from the heat source.

In a large, nonstick frying pan with an flameproof handle, heat ½ teaspoon of the olive oil over medium heat. Add the garlic and sauté until softened, about 1 minute. Stir in the spinach and cook until it wilts, 1–2 minutes. Transfer to a bowl. Set the frying pan aside.

In a bowl, whisk together the whole eggs and egg whites. Stir in ¼ teaspoon of the salt and the pepper. Set aside.

Return the pan to medium heat and heat the remaining ½ teaspoon olive oil. Add the onion and sauté until soft and translucent, about 4 minutes. Stir in the remaining ½ teaspoon salt, the bell pepper, and the potatoes and cook until the potatoes begin to brown but are still tender-crisp, 2–3 minutes.

Spread the potatoes in an even layer in the pan. Spread the spinach evenly over the potatoes. Sprinkle with the basil. Pour in the beaten eggs and sprinkle evenly with the cheese. Cook until slightly set, about 2 minutes.

Carefully place the pan under the broiler and broil (grill) until the frittata is brown and puffy and completely set, about 3 minutes. Gently slide onto a warmed serving platter and cut into wedges. Serve immediately.

Pyramid Servings

VEGETABLES

FRUITS

CARBOHYDRATES

PROTEIN & DAIRY

FATS

PER SERVING	
calories	187
kilojoules	782
protein	14 g
carbohydrate	20 g
total fat	7 g
saturated fat	3 g
monounsaturated fat	3 g
cholesterol	166 mg
sodium	594 mg
fiber	4 g

Roasted Rack of Lamb with Parsley Crust

SERVES 4

For special occasions, a rack of lamb is an elegant main course that is simple to prepare. Serve it with Asparagus with Hazelnut Gremolata (page 50) and Two-Potato Gratin (page 64).

Pyramid Servings

VEGETABLES	◀○○○○○
FRUITS	◀○○○○○
CARBOHYDRATES	○○○○○○○○
PROTEIN & DAIRY	○○○○○●●
FATS	○○○○○

PER SERVING

calories	207
kilojoules	867
protein	28 g
carbohydrate	5 g
total fat	8 g
saturated fat	3 g
monounsaturated fat	3 g
cholesterol	86 mg
sodium	514 mg
fiber	1 g

Preheat the oven to 450°F (230°C).

Place the bread in a blender or food processor and pulse until it forms coarse crumbs. Add the parsley, thyme, and garlic; pulse to blend.

Season the racks of lamb with the salt and pepper. In a heavy ovenproof frying pan, heat the olive oil over medium-high heat. Add the lamb to the pan and cook, turning as needed, until browned on all sides, about 5 minutes. Remove the pan from the heat and brush the mustard over the rounded top and front of the racks (but not the underside of the bones.) Gently pat the bread crumb mixture into the mustard.

Roast until an instant-read thermometer inserted into the meat (but not touching the bone) reads 140°F (60°C) for medium-rare, 20–25 minutes. Transfer to a platter and let rest for 10 minutes.

To serve, cut the lamb between the ribs into separate bone-in chops and place on warmed individual plates.

1 slice (½ oz/15 g) whole-wheat (wholemeal) bread

2 tablespoons chopped fresh flat-leaf (Italian) parsley

1 tablespoon chopped fresh thyme

2 cloves garlic, minced

2 racks of lamb, frenched, about 1 lb (500 g) each, trimmed of visible fat

½ teaspoon salt

¼ teaspoon freshly ground pepper

½ teaspoon olive oil

1 tablespoon Dijon mustard

Beef Stew
with Fennel and Shallots

SERVES 6

The rich flavor of this stew gets a boost from portobello mushrooms and fresh fennel. For a hearty supper, serve it with Whole-Grain Buttermilk Biscuits (page 170). And keep in mind, the wine is optional.

Pyramid Servings

VEGETABLES	◀ ○ ○ ● ● ●
FRUITS	◀ ○ ○ ○ ○ ○
CARBOHYDRATES	○ ○ ○ ○ ○ ○ ○ ●
PROTEIN & DAIRY	○ ○ ○ ○ ○ ○ ●
FATS	○ ○ ○ ○ ○

PER SERVING	
calories	318
kilojoules	1,331
protein	21 g
carbohydrate	36 g
total fat	11 g
saturated fat	3 g
monounsaturated fat	6 g
cholesterol	47 mg
sodium	677 mg
fiber	6 g

Place the flour on a plate. Dredge the beef cubes in the flour. In a large, heavy saucepan, heat the oil over medium heat. Add the beef and cook, turning as needed, until browned on all sides, about 5 minutes. Remove the beef from the pan with a slotted spoon and set aside.

Add the fennel and shallots to the pan over medium heat and sauté until softened and lightly golden, 7–8 minutes. Add ½ teaspoon of the salt, ¼ teaspoon of the pepper, the thyme sprigs, and the bay leaf and sauté for 1 minute. Return the beef to the pan and add the vegetable stock and the wine, if using. Bring to a boil, then reduce the heat to low, cover, and simmer gently until the meat is tender, 40–45 minutes.

Add the carrots, potatoes, onions, and mushrooms. (The liquid will not cover the vegetables completely, but more liquid will accumulate as the mushrooms soften.) Simmer gently until the vegetables are tender, about 30 minutes longer. Discard the thyme sprigs and bay leaf. Stir in the parsley and the remaining 1 teaspoon salt and ½ teaspoon pepper.

Ladle into warmed individual bowls and serve immediately.

3 tablespoons all-purpose (plain) flour

1 lb (500 g) boneless lean beef stew meat, trimmed of visible fat and cut into 1½-inch (4-cm) cubes

2 tablespoons olive oil or canola oil

½ fennel bulb, trimmed and thinly sliced vertically (about 1 cup/3 oz/90 g)

3 large shallots, chopped

1½ teaspoons salt

¾ teaspoon pepper

2 fresh thyme sprigs

1 bay leaf

3 cups (24 fl oz/750 ml) vegetable stock (page 139) or broth

½ cup (4 fl oz/125 ml) red wine (optional)

4 large carrots, peeled and cut into 1-inch (2.5-cm) chunks

4 large red-skinned or white potatoes, peeled and cut into 1-inch (2.5-cm) chunks

18 small boiling onions, about 10 oz (315 g) total weight, halved crosswise

3 portobello mushrooms, brushed clean and cut into 1-inch (2.5-cm) chunks

⅓ cup (½ oz/15 g) finely chopped fresh flat-leaf (Italian) parsley

Pork Medallions with Five-Spice Powder

If your market doesn't carry five-spice powder, simply stir together ½ teaspoon *each* crushed fennel seed or star anise, freshly ground pepper, ground cloves, ground cinnamon, and ground ginger.

SERVES 4

FOR THE MARINADE

2 tablespoons low-sodium soy sauce

1 tablespoon green (spring) onion, including tender green top, minced

3 cloves garlic, minced

1 tablespoon olive oil

¾ teaspoon five-spice powder

1 lb (500 g) pork tenderloin, trimmed of visible fat

1 tablespoon olive oil

½ cup (4 fl oz/125 ml) water, plus 1–3 tablespoons as needed

¼ cup (2 fl oz/60 ml) dry white wine

⅓ cup (2 oz/60 g) chopped yellow onion

½ head green cabbage, thinly sliced (about 4 cups/12 oz/375 g)

1 tablespoon chopped fresh flat-leaf (Italian) parsley

To make the marinade, combine the soy sauce, green onion, garlic, olive oil, and five-spice powder in a shallow baking dish. Whisk to blend. Add the pork and turn once to coat. Cover and marinate in the refrigerator for at least 2 hours and preferably overnight, turning the pork occasionally.

Preheat the oven to 400°F (200°C).

Remove the pork from the marinade and pat dry. Discard the marinade. In a large, ovenproof frying pan, heat the olive oil over medium-high heat. Add the pork and cook, turning as needed, until lightly browned on all sides, about 5 minutes. Add the ½ cup water to the pan.

Transfer the hot pan to the oven and roast until the pork is slightly pink inside and an instant-read thermometer inserted into the center reads 160°F (71°C). Transfer the pork to a cutting board, cover with a kitchen towel, and let rest for 10 minutes.

Meanwhile, place the pan over medium-high heat. Add the wine and deglaze the pan, using a wooden spoon to scrape up any browned bits. Add the yellow onion and cook for about 1 minute. Add the cabbage and 1 tablespoon of the remaining water. Stir well, reduce the heat to medium, cover, and simmer until the cabbage is wilted, about 4 minutes. Add 1–2 tablespoons additional water, if needed.

Slice the pork tenderloin into 8 medallions. Divide the medallions and the wilted cabbage among individual plates and serve immediately.

Pyramid Servings

VEGETABLES	◖○○○○●
FRUITS	◖○○○○
CARBOHYDRATES	○○○○○○○○
PROTEIN & DAIRY	○○○○○●●
FATS	○○○○○

PER SERVING	
calories	235
kilojoules	987
protein	25 g
carbohydrate	6 g
total fat	11 g
saturated fat	2 g
monounsaturated fat	7 g
cholesterol	74 mg
sodium	203 mg
fiber	2 g

Desserts & Drinks

The very best sweets can be creamy, crunchy, juicy, and even chocolaty and still be good for you.

269   Warm Chocolate Soufflés

270   Lemon Custards with Fresh Blueberry Sauce

272   Date-Walnut Cake with Warm Honey Sauce

275   Summer Fruit Gratin

276   Caramelized Pear Bread Pudding

279   Almond and Apricot Biscotti

280   Red Plum Tart

282   Yogurt-Almond Ice Cream

284   Strawberry Balsamic Sorbet

285   Morning Mojito

286   Orange Dream

288   Frosty Almond Date Shake

289   Sweet Ginger Tisane

291   Watermelon-Cranberry Agua Fresca

Warm Chocolate Soufflés

Although these cakey soufflés are made with unsweetened cocoa instead of the usual rich chocolate, their flavor is just as intense. If you can't find fresh raspberries, sliced fresh strawberries will do nicely.

SERVES 6

½ cup (1½ oz/45 g) unsweetened cocoa powder

6 tablespoons (3 fl oz/90 ml) hot water

1 tablespoon unsalted butter

1 tablespoon canola oil

3 tablespoons all-purpose (plain) flour

1 tablespoon ground hazelnuts (filberts) or almonds

¼ teaspoon ground cinnamon

3 tablespoons firmly packed dark brown sugar

2 tablespoons honey

⅛ teaspoon salt

¾ cup (6 fl oz/180 ml) 1-percent low-fat milk

4 egg whites

3 tablespoons granulated sugar

1 teaspoon confectioners' (icing) sugar

1 cup (4 oz/125 g) raspberries

Preheat the oven to 375°F (190°C). Lightly coat six 1-cup (8–fl oz/250-ml) individual soufflé dishes or ramekins with cooking spray, or coat a 6-cup (48–fl oz/1.5-l) soufflé dish with the spray.

In a small bowl, combine the cocoa and hot water, stirring until smooth. Set aside.

In a small, heavy saucepan over medium heat, melt the butter. Add the canola oil and stir to combine. Add the flour, ground hazelnuts, and cinnamon and cook for 1 minute, stirring constantly with a whisk. Stir in the brown sugar, honey, and salt. Gradually add the milk and cook, stirring constantly, until thickened, about 3 minutes. Remove from the heat and stir into the cocoa mixture. Let cool slightly.

In a large spotlessly clean bowl, using an electric mixer on high speed, beat the egg whites until foamy. Add the granulated sugar, 1 tablespoon at a time, and beat until stiff peaks form. Using a rubber spatula, gently fold one-third of the egg whites into the cocoa mixture to lighten it. Then fold the remaining egg whites into the cocoa mixture, mixing only until no white streaks remain.

Gently scoop the cocoa–egg white mixture into the prepared dishes (or dish). Bake until the soufflé rises above the rim and is set in the center, 15–20 minutes for individual soufflés or 40–45 minutes for the large soufflé. Using a fine-mesh sieve, dust the top with the confectioners' sugar. Serve immediately, garnished with the raspberries.

Pyramid Servings

VEGETABLES	◖○○○○○
FRUITS	◖○○○○●
CARBOHYDRATES	○○○○○○○○
PROTEIN & DAIRY	○○○○○○●
FATS	○○○○○

PER SERVING	
calories	183
kilojoules	766
protein	6 g
carbohydrate	30 g
total fat	6 g
saturated fat	2 g
monounsaturated fat	3 g
cholesterol	7 mg
sodium	107 mg
fiber	4 g

Lemon Custards
with Fresh Blueberry Sauce

SERVES 4

Soy milk and tofu give these baked custards a melt-in-your-mouth, creamy texture. Keep the oven temperature low; soy milk is delicate and easily overcooked. The blueberry sauce is also good on pancakes.

Pyramid Servings

VEGETABLES	◖○○○○○
FRUITS	◖○○○●
CARBOHYDRATES	○○○○○○○○
PROTEIN & DAIRY	○○○○○○●
FATS	○○○○●

PER SERVING

calories	234
kilojoules	979
protein	11 g
carbohydrate	31 g
total fat	7 g
saturated fat	2 g
monounsaturated fat	3 g
cholesterol	159 mg
sodium	104 mg
fiber	1 g

Preheat the oven to 300°F (150°C). Lightly coat each of four ¾-cup (6–fl oz/180-ml) ramekins with ¼ teaspoon of the canola oil.

In a blender or food processor, combine the tofu and ½ cup (4 fl oz/125 ml) of the soy milk. Process until smooth, about 30 seconds.

In a bowl, whisk the eggs until well blended. Stir in the brown sugar, honey, lemon zest, vanilla extract, and lemon extract. Add the tofu mixture and the remaining 1 cup (8 fl oz/250 ml) soy milk. Whisk until well blended.

Divide the custard mixture evenly among the prepared ramekins. Arrange the ramekins in a large baking pan. Pour hot water into the pan to come halfway up the sides of the ramekins. Bake until the custards are set but the centers still jiggle slightly when the ramekins are gently shaken, about 50 minutes. Remove the ramekins from the water bath and let stand at room temperature until the custards are fully set, about 15 minutes. Cover and refrigerate until well chilled, at least 4 hours.

To make the blueberry sauce, combine the preserves and lemon juice; whisk until well blended in a small bowl. Stir in the blueberries.

To serve, loosen the edges of the custards with the tip of a knife and invert the ramekins onto individual plates. Top with the blueberry sauce.

1 teaspoon canola oil

½ cup (4 oz/125 g) silken or soft tofu

1½ cups (12 fl oz/375 ml) plain soy milk (soya milk)

3 eggs

2 tablespoons firmly packed light brown sugar

2 tablespoons honey

1 teaspoon lemon zest

½ teaspoon vanilla extract (essence)

FOR THE SAUCE

½ teaspoon lemon extract (essence)

¼ cup (2½ oz/75 g) all-fruit blueberry preserves

2 tablespoons fresh lemon juice

¾ cup (3 oz/90 g) blueberries

Date-Walnut Cake with Warm Honey Sauce

SERVES 8

This easy single-layer cake is moist and sweet. To make a sheet cake or two-layer cake for a birthday or special occasion, double the recipe. You can also use the sauce on frozen yogurt or pancakes.

Pyramid Servings

VEGETABLES	◀ ○○○○○
FRUITS	◀ ○○○●●
CARBOHYDRATES	○○○○○●●
PROTEIN & DAIRY	○○○○○○○
FATS	○○○○●

PER SERVING	
calories	300
kilojoules	1,255
protein	6 g
carbohydrate	48 g
total fat	10 g
saturated fat	1 g
monounsaturated fat	5 g
cholesterol	54 mg
sodium	154 mg
fiber	2 g

Preheat the oven to 350°F (180°C). Lightly coat a 9-inch (23-cm) round cake pan with cooking spray.

In a large bowl, combine the oats and boiling water. Stir to mix. Let stand until the water is absorbed, about 20 minutes. Stir in the brown sugar, honey, and canola oil. Add the eggs, one at a time, beating well after each addition. Stir in the vanilla.

In a small bowl, combine the flours, cinnamon, baking soda, nutmeg, and salt. Whisk to blend. Add the flour mixture to the oat mixture, alternating with the buttermilk, beginning and ending with the flour mixture. Gently fold in the dates and walnuts.

Pour the batter into the prepared pan and bake until the cake springs back when touched lightly in the center, 25–30 minutes. Place the pan on a wire rack to cool slightly. Transfer the cake to a serving plate.

To make the sauce, in a small, heavy saucepan over medium-low heat, combine the milk and nutmeg and bring to a simmer. Whisk in the honey, raise the heat to medium, and bring to a boil, stirring constantly. Continue cooking and stirring until the mixture thickens slightly, about 3 minutes.

Cut the cake into 8 wedges and serve warm or at room temperature. Drizzle with the warm honey sauce.

¾ cup (2½ oz/75 g) old-fashioned rolled oats

1 cup (8 fl oz/250 ml) boiling water

¼ cup (2 oz/60 g) firmly packed light brown sugar

¼ cup (3 oz/90 g) dark honey

¼ cup (2 fl oz/60 ml) canola oil

2 eggs

1 teaspoon vanilla extract (essence)

¾ cup (4 oz/125 g) all-purpose (plain) flour

½ cup (2 oz/60 g) whole-wheat (wholemeal) cake (soft-wheat) flour

1 teaspoon ground cinnamon

½ teaspoon baking soda (bicarbonate of soda)

¼ teaspoon ground nutmeg

⅛ teaspoon salt

⅓ cup (30 fl oz/80 ml) low-fat buttermilk

¼ cup (3 oz/90 g) chopped fresh Medjool dates or dried dates

1½ tablespoons chopped walnuts

FOR THE SAUCE

½ cup (4 fl oz/125 ml) 1-percent low-fat milk

¼ teaspoon ground nutmeg

¼ cup (3 oz/90 g) dark honey

Summer Fruit Gratin

Although this dessert uses a mix of summer stone fruits, it can be easily adapted. In early summer, combine raspberries and apricots; in the fall, try a combination of apples and cranberries.

SERVES 6

1 lb (500 g) cherries, pitted and halved

4 cups (1½ lb/750 g) peeled, pitted, and sliced mixed summer stone fruits such as nectarines, peaches, and apricots

1 tablespoon whole-wheat (wholemeal) flour

1 tablespoon turbinado sugar or firmly packed light brown sugar

FOR THE TOPPING

½ cup (1½ oz/45 g) old-fashioned rolled oats

¼ cup (1 oz/30 g) sliced (flaked) almonds

3 tablespoons whole-wheat (wholemeal) flour

2 tablespoons turbinado sugar or firmly packed light brown sugar

¼ teaspoon ground cinnamon

⅛ teaspoon ground nutmeg

⅛ teaspoon salt

2 tablespoons walnut oil or canola oil

1 tablespoon dark honey

Preheat the oven to 350°F (180°C). Lightly coat a 9-inch (23-cm) square baking dish with cooking spray.

In a bowl, combine the cherries and stone fruits. Sprinkle with the flour and turbinado sugar and toss gently to mix.

To make the topping, in another bowl, combine the oats, almonds, flour, turbinado sugar, cinnamon, nutmeg, and salt. Whisk to blend. Stir in the oil and honey and mix until well blended.

Spread the fruit mixture evenly in the prepared baking dish. Sprinkle the oat-almond mixture evenly over the fruit. Bake until the fruit is bubbling and the topping is lightly browned, 45–55 minutes. Serve warm or at room temperature.

Pyramid Servings

VEGETABLES	◖○○○○○
FRUITS	◖○○○●●
CARBOHYDRATES	○○○○○○●
PROTEIN & DAIRY	○○○○○○
FATS	○○○○●

PER SERVING	
calories	224
kilojoules	937
protein	4 g
carbohydrate	38 g
total fat	8 g
saturated fat	1 g
monounsaturated fat	3 g
cholesterol	0 mg
sodium	52 mg
fiber	5 g

Caramelized Pear Bread Pudding

SERVES 8

Raisins are often the fruit of choice in bread puddings, but in this classy version caramelized fresh pears are used both in and on top of the pudding. Serve it for dessert or feature it at breakfast or brunch.

Pyramid Servings

VEGETABLES	◀○○○○○
FRUITS	◀○○○○●
CARBOHYDRATES	○○○○○○○●
PROTEIN & DAIRY	○○○○○○●
FATS	○○○○●

PER SERVING

calories	255
kilojoules	1,067
protein	7 g
carbohydrate	43 g
total fat	8 g
saturated fat	2 g
monounsaturated fat	3 g
cholesterol	60 mg
sodium	175 mg
fiber	8 g

Preheat the oven to 350°F (180°C). Lightly coat a 9-inch (23-cm) square baking dish with cooking spray.

Arrange the bread cubes in a single layer on a baking sheet. Bake until lightly toasted, about 5 minutes. Set aside.

In a large, nonstick frying pan, melt 1½ teaspoons of the butter over medium heat until frothy. Stir in 1 tablespoon of the canola oil. Add half of the pear slices to the pan and sauté until evenly browned, about 10 minutes. Sprinkle a generous pinch of allspice onto the pears, then transfer them to a plate. Repeat with the remaining butter, oil, pears, and allspice.

Arrange half of the toasted bread cubes evenly in the bottom of the prepared baking dish. Top with half of the sautéed pears and then the remaining bread cubes.

In a large bowl, combine the milk, eggs, 2 tablespoons of the turbinado sugar, the honey, vanilla, cinnamon, and cloves. Whisk until well blended. Pour the milk mixture over the bread and cover with plastic wrap. Let stand for 20–30 minutes, pressing down gently every so often until the bread absorbs the milk mixture. Remove the plastic wrap and arrange the remaining pears on top. Sprinkle with the remaining 1 tablespoon turbinado sugar.

Bake until a knife inserted into the center of the pudding comes out clean, 45–55 minutes. Let cool for 10 minutes before serving.

12 oz (375 g) sturdy multigrain bread, cut into 1-inch (2.5-cm) cubes

1 tablespoon unsalted butter

2 tablespoons canola oil

3 large, firm yet ripe pears, peeled, halved, cored, and thinly sliced

2 pinches of allspice

2¾ cups (22 fl oz/680 ml) 1-percent low-fat milk

2 eggs, lightly beaten

3 tablespoons turbinado sugar or firmly packed light brown sugar

2 tablespoons dark honey

2 teaspoons vanilla extract (essence)

1 teaspoon ground cinnamon

⅛ teaspoon ground cloves

Almond and Apricot Biscotti

These classic twice-baked cookies get some extra flavor and crunch from whole-wheat flour. For variety, try making them with pecans or walnuts and raisins, dates, dried cherries, or dried blueberries.

MAKES 24 COOKIES

¾ cup (4 oz/125 g) whole-wheat (wholemeal) flour

¾ cup (4 oz/125 g) all-purpose (plain) flour

¼ cup (2 oz/60 g) firmly packed brown sugar

1 teaspoon baking powder

2 eggs, lightly beaten

¼ cup (2 fl oz/60 ml) 1-percent low-fat milk

2½ tablespoons canola oil

2 tablespoons dark honey

½ teaspoon almond extract (essence)

⅔ cup (4 oz/125 g) chopped dried apricots

¼ cup (1 oz/30 g) coarsely chopped almonds

Preheat the oven to 350°F (180°C).

In a large bowl, combine the flours, brown sugar, and baking powder. Whisk to blend. Add the eggs, milk, canola oil, honey, and almond extract. Stir with a wooden spoon until the dough just begins to come together. Add the chopped apricots and almonds. With floured hands, mix until the dough is well blended.

Place the dough on a long sheet of plastic wrap and shape by hand into a flattened log 12 inches (30 cm) long, 3 inches (7.5 cm) wide, and about 1 inch (2.5 cm) high. Lift the plastic wrap to invert the dough onto a nonstick baking sheet. Bake until lightly browned, 25–30 minutes. Transfer to another baking sheet to cool for 10 minutes. Leave the oven set at 350°F.

Place the cooled log on a cutting board. With a serrated knife, cut crosswise on the diagonal into 24 slices ½ inch (12 mm) wide. Arrange the slices, cut side down, on the baking sheet. Return to the oven and bake until crisp, 15–20 minutes. Transfer to a wire rack and let cool completely. Store in an airtight container.

Pyramid Servings

VEGETABLES	◀○○○○○
FRUITS	◀○○○○○
CARBOHYDRATES	○○○○○○○●
PROTEIN & DAIRY	○○○○○○○
FATS	○○○○○

PER 3 COOKIES

calories	79
kilojoules	331
protein	2 g
carbohydrate	12 g
total fat	3 g
saturated fat	0 g
monounsaturated fat	1 g
cholesterol	18 mg
sodium	37 mg
fiber	1 g

Red Plum Tart

SERVES 8

Fresh, ripe plums give this tart its intense, sweet flavor. Red-fleshed varieties such as Frontier or Elephant Heart look spectacular, but the dessert is also fine with Santa Rosa plums or with peaches or apricots.

Pyramid Servings

VEGETABLES	◖○○○○○
FRUITS	◖○○○○●
CARBOHYDRATES	○○○○○○○●
PROTEIN & DAIRY	○○○○○○○
FATS	○○○○●

PER SERVING	
calories	162
kilojoules	678
protein	2 g
carbohydrate	27 g
total fat	6 g
saturated fat	1 g
monounsaturated fat	1 g
cholesterol	4 mg
sodium	40 mg
fiber	2 g

Preheat the oven to 400°F (200°C).

To make the crust, in a food processor, combine the flours, oil, butter, granulated sugar, and salt. Pulse until the mixture resembles damp sand. Add the ice water a little at a time and pulse until the dough begins to form a rough mass. Gently shape the dough into a 4-inch (10-cm) disk on a sheet of heavy-duty plastic wrap. Cover with a second sheet. Roll out into a 10-inch (25-cm) round; the dough will be very thin. Place the dough round in the freezer for 5 minutes.

Remove the dough from the freezer. Peel off 1 plastic sheet and let the dough stand until it is pliable, about 1 minute.

Place an 8-inch (20-cm) round tart pan with a removable bottom on a nonstick baking sheet. Carefully fit the dough round into the tart pan. Trim the edges even with the rim and set aside. Reserve the scraps of dough.

In a food processor, combine the remaining scraps of dough, the turbinado sugar, and the wheat germ. Pulse to blend. Spread half of the mixture evenly in the tart shell.

Arrange the plum slices in the tart shell in a circular fashion, starting at the outer edge of the shell and working inward to form a second inner circle. The slices will overlap slightly.

In a small microwave-safe dish, microwave the preserves on high until melted, about 20 seconds. Brush the plums with the melted preserves. Sprinkle the remaining wheat germ mixture over the plums.

Bake until the fruit is tender and bubbling and the topping is lightly browned, 45–50 minutes. Let cool on a wire rack for 10 minutes, then cut into 8 wedges and serve.

FOR THE CRUST

⅔ cup (3 oz/90 g) whole-wheat (wholemeal) pastry (soft-wheat) flour

⅓ cup (2 oz/60 g) all-purpose (plain) flour

2 tablespoons walnut oil or canola oil

1 tablespoon unsalted butter

1 teaspoon granulated sugar

⅛ teaspoon salt

1 tablespoon ice-cold water

¼ cup (2 oz/60 g) turbinado or granulated sugar

1 tablespoon wheat germ

6 red-fleshed or other plums, about 1 lb (500 g) total weight, pitted and thinly sliced

2 tablespoons seedless all-fruit raspberry preserves

Yogurt-Almond Ice Cream

SERVES 6

This creamy dessert couldn't be easier to make. Instead of preparing a custard, all you need is chilled yogurt and vanilla soy milk. It's as simple as whisking the two together with honey, canola oil, and nuts.

Pyramid Servings

VEGETABLES	◀○○○○○
FRUITS	◀○○○○○
CARBOHYDRATES	○○○○○○○○
PROTEIN & DAIRY	○○○○○○●
FATS	○○○○●

PER SERVING

calories	164
kilojoules	686
protein	6 g
carbohydrate	25 g
total fat	5 g
saturated fat	0 g
monounsaturated fat	3 g
cholesterol	2 mg
sodium	63 mg
fiber	1 g

Place a bowl in the freezer to chill.

In a bowl, whisk together the yogurt, soy milk, honey, and canola oil until well blended. Pour the mixture into an ice-cream maker and freeze according to the manufacturer's instructions.

When the ice cream is firm, transfer to the chilled bowl and add the nuts. Stir gently to distribute evenly. Serve immediately or freeze until ready to serve.

2 cups (1 lb/500 g) nonfat plain yogurt, without gum additives or stabilizers

1 cup (8 fl oz/250 ml) low-fat vanilla soy milk (soya milk), chilled

⅓ cup (4 oz/125 g) honey

1 tablespoon canola oil

¼ cup (1 oz/30 g) coarsely chopped almonds

Strawberry Balsamic Sorbet

SERVES 4

Good-quality balsamic vinegar is the key to this frozen version of a classic Italian dish. Perfect served as dessert or as a between-course intermezzo, it's loaded with vitamin C.

Pyramid Servings

VEGETABLES ◀○○○○○
FRUITS ◀○○○●●
CARBOHYDRATES ○○○○○○○
PROTEIN & DAIRY ○○○○○○○
FATS ○○○○○

PER SERVING	
calories	98
kilojoules	410
protein	1 g
carbohydrate	24 g
total fat	<1 g
saturated fat	0 g
monounsaturated fat	0 g
cholesterol	0 mg
sodium	17 mg
fiber	1 g

In a small nonaluminum saucepan, bring the vinegar to a simmer over medium-low heat. Cook until reduced by half, about 5 minutes. Remove from the heat and let cool.

Place the halved strawberries in a blender or food processor. Process until very smooth. Pass the purée through a fine-mesh sieve placed over a bowl, pressing firmly on the solids with a rubber spatula or the back of a wooden spoon to extract all the juice. Discard the solids. Add the balsamic reduction and the honey to the purée and stir to combine. Cover and refrigerate until cold.

Freeze the strawberry mixture in an ice-cream maker according to the manufacturer's instructions. Store in the freezer until ready to serve or for up to 2 days. Spoon into individual bowls and garnish with the chopped strawberries.

¾ cup (6 fl oz/180 ml) balsamic vinegar

4 cups (1 lb/500 g) strawberries, hulled and halved, plus 4 berries, coarsely chopped

1 tablespoon dark honey

Balsamic Vinegar

At its best, balsamic vinegar is a costly condiment, made from wine grapes and aged in barrels, to be enjoyed drop by drop on vegetables, fruits, or ice cream. At its worst, it is an overly sweet, caramel-colored vinegar that can overwhelm a dish. Between the extremes are many midpriced Italian balsamics with subtle flavors. As a rule, the more expensive the better, but try a few brands to find one you like.

Morning Mojito

The mojito is the national drink of Cuba. It is based on a sweet syrup flavored with fresh lime juice and crushed fresh mint. This super-citrusy nonalcoholic version also includes orange and grapefruit juices.

SERVES 6

½ cup (6 oz/185 g) dark honey

½ cup (4 fl oz/125 ml) fresh lime juice

½ cup (½ oz/15 g) firmly packed fresh mint leaves

2 cups (16 fl oz/500 ml) fresh grapefruit juice, chilled

2 cups (16 fl oz/500 ml) fresh orange juice, chilled

2 teaspoons grated lime zest

1 lime, cut into 6 slices

In a small saucepan, combine the honey and lime juice. Bring to a boil over medium heat. Add the mint leaves and remove from the heat. Steep the honey mixture for 5 minutes, then pass the mixture through a fine-mesh sieve placed over a bowl, pressing down lightly on the leaves with the back of a wooden spoon. Refrigerate the syrup until cold.

In a large pitcher, combine the mint syrup, grapefruit and orange juices, and lime zest. Stir until the syrup is dissolved.

Pour into tall, chilled glasses and garnish each glass with a lime slice.

Pyramid Servings

VEGETABLES	◀○○○○○
FRUITS	◀○○●●●
CARBOHYDRATES	○○○○○○○○
PROTEIN & DAIRY	○○○○○○○
FATS	○○○○○

PER SERVING	
calories	163
kilojoules	682
protein	1 g
carbohydrate	42 g
total fat	0 g
saturated fat	0 g
monounsaturated fat	0 g
cholesterol	0 mg
sodium	4 mg
fiber	1 g

Citrus Zest

All citrus fruits are rich in vitamin C, but, surprisingly, the peel and spongy white layer beneath, called the albedo, contain about 75 percent of the fruits' healthful antioxidants. That's no reason to eat oranges like apples, peel and all. But it does add to the pleasure of using the tangy, aromatic zest in muffins, salad dressings, marinades for meats and fish, garnishes, and drinks.

Orange Dream

SERVES 4

Whip up this frothy cooler in seconds—it tastes like an old-fashioned Creamsicle. For best results, start with ice-cold soy milk, and use freshly squeezed orange juice. Creamy, custardlike silken tofu adds extra body.

Pyramid Servings

VEGETABLES	◀ ○ ○ ○ ○ ○
FRUITS	◀ ○ ○ ○ ○ ●
CARBOHYDRATES	○ ○ ○ ○ ○ ○ ○ ○
PROTEIN & DAIRY	○ ○ ○ ○ ○ ○ ●
FATS	○ ○ ○ ○ ○

PER SERVING

calories	105
kilojoules	439
protein	4 g
carbohydrate	20 g
total fat	1 g
saturated fat	<1 g
monounsaturated fat	<1 g
cholesterol	0 mg
sodium	56 mg
fiber	0 g

In a blender, combine the orange juice, soy milk, tofu, honey, orange zest, vanilla, and ice cubes. Blend until smooth and frothy, about 30 seconds.

Pour into tall, chilled glasses and garnish each glass with an orange segment.

1½ cups (12 fl oz/375 ml) fresh orange juice, chilled

1 cup (8 fl oz/250 ml) vanilla soy milk (soya milk), chilled

⅓ cup (3 oz/90 g) silken or soft tofu

1 tablespoon dark honey

1 teaspoon grated orange zest

½ teaspoon vanilla extract (essence)

5 ice cubes

4 peeled orange segments

Frosty Almond Date Shake

SERVES 4

This thick, creamy shake—great for a snack—is a breeze to make. Just be certain that the almond milk and yogurt are truly ice cold, and the banana is frozen. Peel and halve the banana before freezing.

Pyramid Servings

VEGETABLES	◀○○○○○
FRUITS	◀○○○○●
CARBOHYDRATES	○○○○○○○○
PROTEIN & DAIRY	○○○○○○●
FATS	○○○○○

PER SERVING

calories	141
kilojoules	590
protein	3 g
carbohydrate	31 g
total fat	2 g
saturated fat	<1 g
monounsaturated fat	1 g
cholesterol	0 mg
sodium	97 mg
fiber	2 g

Put the dates in a small bowl and sprinkle with the warm water. Let soak for 5 minutes to soften, then drain.

In a blender, combine the dates, almond milk, yogurt, banana, ice cubes, and the ⅛ teaspoon nutmeg. Blend until smooth and frothy, about 30 seconds.

Pour into tall, chilled glasses and garnish each with a dusting of nutmeg.

⅓ cup (2 oz/60 g) chopped pitted dates

2 tablespoons warm water

2 cups (16 fl oz/500 ml) vanilla almond milk, chilled

½ cup (4 oz/125 g) nonfat vanilla soy or dairy yogurt

1 very ripe banana, frozen

4 ice cubes

⅛ teaspoon ground nutmeg, plus extra for garnish

Almond Milk

Made from raw almonds that have been ground, soaked, and pressed, almond milk is a sweet, faintly nut-flavored alternative to low-fat or nonfat milk. Although it sounds new, it has been made since medieval times. It is usually richer than 1-percent low-fat milk, but its fat is largely the heart-healthy monounsaturated kind. It can replace milk or soy milk in most recipes.

Sweet Ginger Tisane

A tisane is a soothing drink made by steeping herbs, spices, fruits, or flowers in hot water. Here, ginger gives this welcome alternative to coffee or tea a pleasant spiciness.

SERVES 6

6 cups (48 fl oz/1.5 l) water

¼ cup (1 oz/30 g) peeled and chopped fresh ginger

⅓ cup (3 fl oz/80 ml) fresh lemon juice

½ cup (½ oz/15 g) firmly packed fresh mint leaves

6 tablespoons (4½ oz/140 g) dark honey

1 lemon, cut into 6 slices

In a large saucepan over high heat, combine the water, ginger, and lemon juice. Bring to a boil, then reduce the heat to low and simmer for 5 minutes. Remove from the heat, add the mint, and let steep for 5 minutes.

Pass the mixture through a fine-mesh sieve, placed over a pitcher, pressing down lightly on the ginger and mint. Discard the mint and ginger.

Stir the honey into the tisane. Serve hot or iced, garnished with a lemon slice.

Pyramid Servings

VEGETABLES	◖○○○○○
FRUITS	◖○○○○●
CARBOHYDRATES	○○○○○○○○
PROTEIN & DAIRY	○○○○○○○
FATS	○○○○○

PER SERVING	
calories	77
kilojoules	322
protein	<1 g
carbohydrate	20 g
total fat	0 g
saturated fat	0 g
monounsaturated fat	0 g
cholesterol	0 mg
sodium	8 mg
fiber	0 g

Fresh Ginger

Found year-round in super-markets, fresh ginger, or gingerroot, has a sweet, multilayered spiciness that surpasses the simple flavor of ground dried ginger. Its smooth skin must be peeled away, but peel gently—the flesh beneath is especially pungent, with a hotness unlike that of red or black pepper. Store unpeeled ginger in plastic in the refrigerator for up to 3 weeks or the freezer for up to a year.

Watermelon-Cranberry Agua Fresca

Aguas frescas are popular fresh-fruit drinks in Mexico. Although water is a standard ingredient, this undiluted version is a thirst-quenching refresher whether accompanying spicy foods or sipped in the sun.

SERVES **6**

2½ lb (1.25 kg) seedless watermelon, rind removed and diced (about 7 cups)

1 cup (8 fl oz/250 ml) fruit-sweetened cranberry juice (sometimes called cranberry nectar)

¼ cup (2 fl oz/60 ml) fresh lime juice

1 lime, cut into 6 slices

Place the melon in a blender or food processor. Process until smooth. Pass the purée through a fine-mesh sieve placed over a bowl to eliminate the pulp and clarify the juice. Pour the juice into a large pitcher. Add the cranberry and lime juices and stir to combine. Refrigerate until very cold.

Pour into tall, chilled glasses and garnish each with a fresh lime slice.

Pyramid Servings

VEGETABLES	◀○○○○○
FRUITS	◀○○○●●
CARBOHYDRATES	○○○○○○○○
PROTEIN & DAIRY	○○○○○○○
FATS	○○○○○

PER SERVING	
calories	94
kilojoules	393
protein	1 g
carbohydrate	22 g
total fat	0 g
saturated fat	0 g
monounsaturated fat	0 g
cholesterol	0 mg
sodium	1 mg
fiber	0 g

GLOSSARY

The ingredients used in this cookbook, many of which are described in this glossary, can be found in most well-stocked supermarkets or natural-foods stores. However, several items, especially exotic spices and condiments such as sumac and chipotle chiles, are easiest to find in Asian, Latin, Middle Eastern, or other specialty markets. Farmers' markets are a great source of uncommon fruits and vegetables.

ANCHOVIES These tiny fillets of sardine-like fish, preserved in salt and most often sold packed in oil, can add richness to a range of dishes from pastas to vinaigrettes. When used in small quantities, they have little impact on fat or sodium levels. Anchovy paste, sold in squeeze tubes, can be substituted in recipes in which the anchovies are minced, crushed, or blended.

ARTICHOKES The unopened flower heads of a thistle originally cultivated in the Mediterranean region, artichokes rank among the high-fiber vegetables. The edible part of a medium artichoke has almost 7 grams of fiber, about one-fourth of the suggested daily minimum.

ARUGULA Also known as rocket, arugula has small to mid-sized leaves and tender stems with a mild pungent flavor. It is common in gourmet salad mixes but is also delicious in pastas and sandwiches. Once a rarity, it's now sold widely (and easy to grow at home). Shop for arugula that's dark green, with no sign of wilting. Remove any thick stem ends. Store in a sealed plastic bag in the refrigerator; use within a day or two.

AVOCADOS Hass avocados have a pebbly skin that ripens from green to purple-black and firm, buttery flesh. Fuertes avocados remain green and have a lighter flavor. Choose hard avocados and let them ripen at room temperature. A ripe avocado dents easily when pressed at the stem end. Although avocados are high in fat, it's mostly the monounsaturated kind that helps lower cholesterol. They also contain beta-sitosterol, glutathione, and vitamin E, all of which have health benefits.

BARLEY Like wheat, oats, and rice, barley is a true grain—that is, the seed of a cultivated grass—eaten for at least 8,000 years. Barley contains small amounts gluten, a protein in wheat that when wet becomes elastic, permitting dough to rise. Barley breads are therefore more dense and dry. However, the grain abounds in soluble fiber, in particular a kind called beta-glucan that helps lower cholesterol. Pearl barley has had its tan bran removed and has been steamed and polished.

BLOOD ORANGES Native to Sicily, blood oranges have a peel and flesh that ranges in color from bright orange to deep red. Their juice is as sweet as that of navel and Valencia oranges, with a more intense flavor. Blood orange segments add spectacular color to salads and desserts. Once an exotic rarity, blood oranges are now becoming widely available during their winter harvest season.

BOK CHOY A cabbage-family, or cruciferous, green, bok choy has tender white stems and dark green leaves that are mild when cooked, commonly in stir-fries or soups. Baby bok choy is sweeter and more delicate and is often steamed or braised whole. Like other cruciferous vegetables, bok choy is rich in compounds that appear to help the body defend itself against cancerous cells.

BRAISING Meats and vegetables browned in a bit of oil, then simmered slowly with minimal liquid, develop superb flavor and texture. A braising pot should be heavy, to prevent scorching, with a tight lid, to retain moisture. Long, slow cooking tenderizes the connective tissue (collagen) in lean meats and the cellulose in fibrous vegetables.

BULGUR Whole wheat berries that have been parboiled, dried, and then crushed or ground into grains of various sizes, bulgur can be cooked briefly or simply soaked before being incorporated into a variety of dishes, from tabbouleh, the classic parsley salad, to baked goods and casseroles.

BUTTERMILK Cow's milk to which a yogurt-like culture has been added, buttermilk is a tangy, slightly thick dairy product that is especially good as a mildly acidic ingredient in baked goods such as waffles and pancakes. Most buttermilk available now is made from low-fat or nonfat milk, but check to verify that the product has 2 percent or less butterfat. "Old-fashioned" versions are typically made with whole milk.

CAPERS These young, olive-green flower buds of the Mediterranean caper bush are unpleasantly bitter when raw, and so are always pickled in salty vinegar or packed in salt for eating. They have a peppery flavor that comes from mustard oils in the buds. Rinse and blot dry brined capers before use. Soak salt-packed ones for several minutes, then rinse and dry. Both preparations are excellent in pasta sauces and with fish and meats. Caper berries, similar in appearance to green olives, are immature fruits of the same plant, pickled and served as a condiment.

CELLOPHANE NOODLES Also known as bean threads, these light noodles, made from the starch of green mung beans, are nearly transparent when cooked. Store them in airtight containers in a cool, dry place for up to 6 months. To prepare cellophane noodles for use, soak them in hot water or broth for 30 seconds, then drain thoroughly.

CHIFFONADE The culinary term for leafy fresh herbs or vegetables, such as basil, spinach, or lettuce, that have been cut into slender ribbons. To make a chiffonade, assemble the leaves to be cut into a neat stack, then fold or roll them lengthwise into a tight bundle. With a sharp kitchen knife, slice the stack crosswise into strips—thin for basil and other herbs, wider for large greens. Separate the ribbons before adding them to a dish. *See also* julienne.

CHILE PASTE A long-lived condiment easy to keep on hand, chile paste—made from hot red peppers mashed with salt and vinegar—can put a spicy Asian spin on basic dishes. It keeps indefinitely in the refrigerator.

CHILES Many markets now stock several kinds of fresh and dried chiles. Some, such as Anaheim, New Mexico, and poblano (called ancho when dried), are usually only mildly hot. Others, such as serranos and jalapeños, have been bred for hotness. Jalapeños smoked and then canned in a tomato sauce are sold as "chipotle chiles in adobo," used to give Mexican-style dishes a smoky hotness. They are best chopped finely or puréed. Freeze unused chipotles in an airtight container. With all chiles, the secret is to add them slowly and taste as you cook. For safety, wear rubber gloves or avoid touching your face until you've washed your hands and kitchen tools in hot, soapy water.

COCONUT, DRIED Sweetened varieties of dried coconut, available in supermarkets, are slightly moist and extremely sugary. Unsweetened versions, found in natural-foods stores and Asian markets, are drier and have a more pure coconut flavor. Both come shredded or flaked.

COCONUT MILK An indispensable ingredient in many Southeast Asian dishes, unsweetened coconut milk can be purchased in both full-fat and low-fat versions. The low-fat kind, usually labeled "lite coconut milk," contains one-third of the fat and fewer than half the calories of an equal amount of the regular. It's worth looking for; the fat in coconuts is even more highly saturated than butterfat.

COLLARD AND TURNIP GREENS Close relatives of cabbage and kale, with a hearty flavor, these greens are endowed with vitamin C, folate, beta-carotene, and especially calcium. Cooked collards and turnip greens have about 200 milligrams of calcium per cup; milk, 300.

COOKING SPRAYS Simply oils of various kinds mixed with a small amount of alcohol and lecithin (an emulsifier) in a pressurized can, cooking sprays are convenient for applying a thin coating of oil to pans and utensils. Canola oil spray is nearly flavorless, while olive oil versions have a mild olive taste. Use them lightly and always spray away from open flames or burners.

COUSCOUS Although it looks like a tiny grain, couscous is made from roughly milled kernels of durum wheat, or semolina. It is a staple in North African nations. Whole-wheat couscous, made from whole wheat berries, retains the brown bran and germ, making it more nutritious than the refined version. It cooks just as quickly.

CRYSTALLIZED GINGER Also known as candied ginger, crystallized ginger is sliced, peeled gingerroot that has been simmered in a sugar syrup and coated with coarse sugar. Sold in jars, it's handy for adding a note of sweet spiciness to both savory dishes and desserts.

DRIED CHERRIES Unlike raisins, which are simply grapes allowed to dry, dried cherries—typically made from a naturally tart variety—are sweetened with sugar, although they retain many of the fruit's nutrients.

EGGS Although they've been treated as a virtual emblem of cholesterol-rich foods, eggs can fit into a healthy eating plan. Because the main causes of high blood cholesterol are animal fats and hydrogenated oils, some recommendations allow up to four eggs a week, unless your cholesterol is high, in which case it's advisable to eat just two a week.

EGG WHITES, FOLDING Beaten egg whites lose volume if simply stirred in common fashion into a batter. To keep the final dish light and airy, incorporate the whites by a method called folding. Using a rubber spatula, gently scrape stiff, just-beaten egg whites into the bowl holding the batter or other mixture. Gently plunge the spatula into the mixture and, with a scooping motion, fold the bottom of the batter up and over the top. Repeat, rotating the bowl after each fold, until just a few pale streaks remain. If the mixture is thick, stir in one-fourth of the egg whites to lighten it, then gently fold in the rest.

ESCAROLE A member of the large family of edible greens that includes lettuce, radicchio, Belgian endive, and others, escarole grows in loose, pale heads of broad, somewhat frilly leaves. Its sweet but mildly bitter flavor is similar to endive's and can be served raw in a salad with other greens, or lightly cooked in soups or side dishes. Store in plastic in the refrigerator for up to 3 days.

FENNEL A fennel bulb is actually the white base of a tall, feathery-leaved plant in the carrot family. Its subtle licorice flavor makes it a pleasing addition to salads, stews, and other dishes. Shop for crisp, white bulbs with bright green tops; strip away outer layers that are tough or browned.

FIGS Look for Mission figs, which are purple when fresh and almost black when dried, or Calimyrna figs, which are golden in color and make fine snacks. Serve fresh figs promptly. Figs are higher in fiber than most fruits and are a tasty nondairy source of calcium.

FISH If you're a woman who is pregnant or nursing a baby or considering pregnancy, research suggests that you should eat no more than 12 ounces of fish a week, since many varieties contain small amounts of mercury. When the metal is consumed in a mother's meals, it poses a risk to unborn children and breast-feeding infants. Pregnant women and very young children should not eat shark, swordfish, king mackerel, or tilefish, four kinds of fish that naturally contain high amounts of this metal.

FISH SAUCE A dark, thin, salty liquid with a complex flavor, fish sauce, also known as *nam pla* (in Thailand) or *shottsuru* (in Japan), is an essential seasoning in many Thai and other Southeast Asian dishes and sauces. Left in its bottle, it keeps indefinitely in the refrigerator.

FLAXSEED The tiny reddish-brown seed of the flax plant, flaxseed—also known as linseed—is rich in omega-3 fatty acids, which appear to help lower heart disease risk. Flaxseed has a mild, nutty flavor that's good in baked goods and breakfast cereals. Because its oil spoils quickly, flaxseed should be stored airtight in the refrigerator or freezer and ground, if desired, just before use.

HARICOTS VERTS Also known as French green beans, *haricots verts* (pronounced AR-ee-coh vare) are a special variety of slender string beans harvested while very young so that they are stringless, seedless, and exceptionally tender. Small green beans are a fine substitute.

HOISIN SAUCE A common ingredient in Chinese dishes, hoisin sauce is a sweet and spicy, thick brown condiment made from soybeans, garlic, chiles, and spices. Refrigerated in a sealed jar or plastic container, it will keep indefinitely.

JULIENNE The culinary term for vegetables cut evenly into matchstick-shaped strips. Raw or lightly cooked vegetables are first thinly sliced lengthwise (about the thickness of a coin), then stacked and again thinly sliced in neat parallel rows, producing slender strips that are square in cross section. These can be lined up and cut to any length desired. *See also* chiffonade.

LEAN MEATS To cut back on fat, look for "select" grade red meats, which are less fatty than those labeled "prime" or "choice." The leanest cuts have fewer than 5 grams of fat per 3½ ounces (100 g). For comparison, 3½ ounces of skinless chicken breast meat has 1.2 grams of fat; chicken thigh meat, 3.9 grams. The leanest beef cuts (select grade, trimmed of visible fat) include top round (2.5 g), tip round (3.2 g), eye of round (3.6 g), sirloin, (3.7 g), and top loin (4.5 g). For extra-lean ground beef, ask to have one of these cuts specially ground by a butcher. The leanest pork cuts include the tenderloin (3.4 g), top loin chop (5.3 g), and ham (5.4 g). The leanest lamb cut is the leg (4.5 g).

LEMONGRASS A citrus-scented herb essential in the cuisine of Thailand, fresh lemongrass has a rigid, papery, pale green stalk about the shape of a green (spring) onion. Only the bulbous base is used, typically thinly sliced or chopped and added as a seasoning to soups, stir-fries, and teas. Lemongrass can also be purchased dried.

LENTILS Small legumes about the size and shape of split peas, lentils come in several varieties other than the common brown one. Relatively small varieties, such as French green lentils, or *lentilles du Puy*; black belugas, named for a type of caviar; and brown Spanish *pardinas* all hold their shape during cooking and are excellent in salads. Red and yellow lentils, typically used in Indian and Middle Eastern cooking, are usually

sold skinned; they cook faster and break apart more readily than other varieties and are best in purées and thick soups.

MASA HARINA Spanish for "dough flour," *masa harina* is a fine flour ground from corn kernels that have been boiled in water with a small amount of powdered lime, or calcium hydroxide (called *cal* in Spanish). The flour is used mainly to make Mexican specialties such as corn tortillas and tamales. Some Latin groceries carry refrigerated *masa* dough prepared specially for tamales.

MASCARPONE CHEESE A product of the Lombardy region in northern Italy, mascarpone cheese is a very soft, mild-flavored cow's-milk cheese with a smooth texture like that of sour cream or yogurt. Look for it in small tubs in the cheese or dairy case of well-stocked supermarkets, or in specialty-food shops. Sealed and refrigerated, it will last up to a week.

MUSHROOMS Beyond the common white and brown, or cremini, many varieties of mushroom are now under cultivation. Portobello mushrooms—hearty enough to stand in for beef—have exploded in popularity. Despite their Italianate name, portobellos are simply fully developed white or brown mushrooms, best used soon after purchase. Fresh enoki, oyster, shiitake, and straw mushrooms are also now widely available. Porcini, most often sold dried, have a strong, earthy flavor that adds depth and sophistication to pastas, gratins, risottos, and other dishes. (Milder fresh porcini are also available but are harder to find.) To rehydrate dried porcini, place the mushroom pieces in a bowl and add boiling water to cover. Let stand for 5 minutes, then pour the soaking liquid through a fine-mesh sieve into another bowl. In a colander, rinse the softened mushrooms. Use both the mushrooms and liquid to taste. While treasured mainly for their woodsy flavors, mushrooms are also an excellent source of niacin and a good source of riboflavin.

NAPA CABBAGE Also known as Chinese cabbage, napa cabbage has white ribs and pale yellow to pale green crinkly leaves formed in loose, oblong heads about the size of romaine (cos) lettuce heads. It is crisp and sweet, with a flavor that is milder than that of green and red cabbages. Use shredded napa cabbage in salads, soups, or side dishes.

NUTMEG Because the singular aroma and flavor of this spice come from volatile compounds that dissipate quickly, nutmeg that is freshly grated adds more to a dish than does the ground nutmeg sold in jars. Whole nutmeg is readily available in supermarket spice racks, and small, inexpensive graters designed specifically for nutmeg help produce the fine grains that look and taste best.

OLIVES Where supermarkets once offered only jumbo black and pimiento-stuffed green olives, they now shelve a widening array of domestic and imported olives. Commonly available are brine-cured Niçoise, Kalamata, and Greek black olives, as well as heavily seasoned Sicilian and other Italian-style green olives. Find more exotic varieties, such as French picholines and Spanish arbequinas, at specialty-food stores.

OYSTER SAUCE An essential seasoning in many Asian dishes, especially stir-fries, oyster sauce is a cooked and concentrated blend of oysters, brine, and soy sauce. Although salty, it adds a great deal of rich flavor in small quantities.

PARMESAN CHEESE Supermarkets now typically carry a variety of foreign and domestic Parmesan cheeses, but the version widely considered to have the most complex and appealing flavor is Parmigiano-Reggiano, an aged cow's-milk cheese named for the Italian provinces of Parma and Reggio Emilia. Although all Parmesans are quite salty, a small amount can add great depth of flavor to a dish, especially when the cheese is top quality, purchased in block form, and grated just before serving.

PARSLEY Mild curly-leaf parsley is the traditional favorite, but flavorful flat-leaf, or Italian, parsley is gaining in popularity. Renowned as a decorative garnish, parsley also deserves respect as a nutritious vegetable. One-fourth of a cup of chopped parsley has as much vitamin C as a whole cup of romaine lettuce. Parsley also contains calcium, potassium, and folate.

PEANUT BUTTER To avoid a quantity of unwanted sodium and artery-clogging fat, shop for "old-fashioned" or "natural" peanut butter made without added sugar, salt, or hydrogenated vegetable oil. Jars of these pure versions are often topped with a layer of separated peanut oil. Simply stir it in, then refrigerate.

PEARL ONIONS About the size of a grape or an olive, tiny white pearl onions are mild and sweet when cooked. Boiling onions, also mild and white skinned, are somewhat larger, typically around 1 inch (2.5 cm) across. To peel pearl or boiling onions, bring a saucepan half full of water to a boil, add the onions, and cook for 1–2 minutes, depending on their size. With a slotted spoon, transfer the onions to a large bowl partially filled with ice water. When the onions are cool, remove and squeeze each at its root end; the skin should slide off in one piece.

PINE NUTS Excellent raw or toasted, these small, ivory-colored nuts are the shelled seeds of several varieties of pine tree, treasured for their subtle flavor. Ground finely and blended with basil, olive oil, and garlic, they are a crucial ingredient in traditional Italian pesto. They are also delicious toasted and sprinkled whole or chopped on salads and side dishes, or baked into tarts and cookies.

PITA Also known as pocket bread, pita is a round Middle Eastern flat bread made from both white and whole-wheat (wholemeal) flours. Sliced crosswise, the rounds can be split open from the cut edge to form a pocket for salad greens, beans and meats, or other ingredients. Sliced into wedges and toasted in the oven, the bread makes an excellent appetizer or snack.

PLAINTAINS Like bananas, their softer and less starchy relatives, plantains sweeten and turn from green to yellow with dark spots as they ripen. To speed the process, place green plantains in a loosely closed paper bag at room temperature for up to several days.

PLUM TOMATOES With their dense flesh and scant juice, egg-shaped plum tomatoes, also known as Italian or Roma tomatoes, are ideal for pasta sauces and cooked dishes. For smooth sauces, peel and seed plum tomatoes before use (page 127); for best flavor, store all varieties at room temperature.

POSOLE The Spanish word for the large, specially treated corn kernels called hominy in English, *posole* can refer to both the grain and the Mexican and Southwestern stew in which it's key. Kernels of dried *posole* are soaked in water and powdered lime (calcium hydroxide) until their tough skins soften and slip off. The starchy white or yellow kernels are then rinsed and canned or used fresh. Cans of *posole* and hominy are sometimes labeled in both Spanish and English.

POTATOES Waxy round red and white potatoes (called new potatoes or creamers when small) are moist and firm and are the best choice for salads and soups. Starchy russet, long white, and purple-

and yellow-fleshed potatoes turn crumbly during cooking and are best mashed or baked. Potatoes contain potassium, vitamin C, and iron.

PRESERVED LEMONS An essential ingredient in many North African dishes, preserved lemons are prepared by submerging whole or quartered lemons in lemon juice and salt, often with spices added. After curing for weeks, the lemons soften and develop a distinctive flavor. Both the rind and pulp can be used; as with other strongly flavored ingredients, such as olives or anchovies, a little goes a long way. Look for preserved lemons in specialty-food shops.

QUESO ASADERO A commonly available Mexican-style melting cheese, *queso asadero* is slightly lower in fat than similar cheeses, such as Monterey jack.

RACK OF LAMB, FRENCHED The cut of lamb called a rack typically yields six to eight tiny but flavorful rib chops. For ease of serving and elegance of presentation after roasting, the rack should be frenched beforehand. This preparation, done by the butcher, involves trimming any meat and fat from between the ribs, leaving the rib-eye meat intact, then scraping the rib bones clean. Once roasted, the rack is cut into individual bone-in chops and served.

RICE PAPER ROUNDS Also known as spring roll wrappers or *banh trang,* these thin white sheets made of rice flour are a standard ingredient in Southeast Asian cooking. Soaked briefly, the dry rounds become flexible, translucent wrappers that can be topped with vegetables, noodles, and fish or meat, then rolled up to create fresh spring rolls.

SESAME OIL Plain sesame oil, pressed from untoasted seeds, is mild and nearly colorless. It is an excellent cooking oil, widely used in Asia and the Middle East. More widely available is roasted, or Asian, sesame oil. Made from toasted sesame seeds, it is pale to medium brown with a strong flavor and is best used with a light hand as a seasoning, not as a salad or cooking oil. Store roasted sesame oil in the refrigerator; use within 6 months.

SESAME SEEDS Raw sesame seeds are mild and faintly sweet, but when toasted they turn a golden color with a rich, nutty, and slightly bitter flavor. Black sesame seeds, with their dark hulls, or outer coverings, are widely used as a garnish in Japanese and Chinese cooking. (The seeds inside are a pale ivory color, with the usual crunch and mild flavor.) To toast sesame seeds, heat a small frying pan over medium-high heat, then add the seeds and toast, stirring, until the seeds are light brown and starting to crackle, 3–5 minutes. Always toast seeds just before using. Sesame seeds are rich in polyunsaturated oil, which can spoil over time; store untoasted seeds in an airtight container in the refrigerator for up to 6 months.

SHALLOTS Their tan, papery skins and pungent, layered flesh show that shallots are related to onions. They grow in loose clusters of small cloves, however, and have a distinctive flavor that some describe as midway between onion and garlic. Shallots are often used chopped or minced as a seasoning in sauces and vinaigrettes, but can be sliced and sautéed like yellow onions.

SHRIMP For years, seafood lovers were counseled to reduce their cholesterol intake by cutting back on shrimp (or prawns, as some sizes and varieties are known). Although shellfish vary, shrimp on average have twice as much cholesterol as dark-meat chicken. However, the chief cause of clogged arteries is the saturated fat in food, not the cholesterol. Eight large shrimp contain just 85 milligrams of cholesterol and less than 1 gram of fat, only a fraction of which is saturated. In other words, shrimp don't have to be banned from the kitchens of health-minded cooks.

SOBA NOODLES Delicious in soups or as a side dish, these tan-to-purplish Japanese noodles are made from wheat and buckwheat flours kneaded into a dough that is rolled thin and sliced or extruded into ribbons about the thickness of spaghetti. Soba noodles are widely available dried, but are sometimes available fresh in Asian groceries.

SOY MILK Made from cooked, mashed, and strained soybeans, soy milk has a flavor and texture much like ordinary milk but with a nutrition profile like that of the bean itself: respectable amounts of protein and unsaturated fat, along with compounds that appear to fight cardiovascular disease and cancer. It can be used cup for cup in place of milk in most recipes.

SOY SAUCE Known as shoyu in Japan, soy sauce is made from steamed soybeans and roasted wheat mixed with water, salt, and a yeastlike culture. After several months, the fermented mash is pressed and the sauce pasteurized. Some soy sauces, including wheat-free tamari, are thick, with a dark-chocolate color and intense flavor, while light soy sauces are thinner, paler, and often saltier. Standard soy sauces have as much as 920 milligrams of sodium per tablespoon. Reduced-sodium versions have 75 percent less sodium. Low-sodium varieties have no more than 140 milligrams of sodium per tablespoon.

SQUASH, SUMMER Prized for their mild flesh, thin skin, and edible seeds, summer squash are most tender and sweet when small. Crookneck, pattypan, and zucchini (courgettes) are popular examples, but more exotic varieties such as chayote (mirliton), ronde de Nice, and others have begun to appear in markets. Refrigerate in plastic for up to 5 days.

SQUASH, WINTER The sweet flavors, rich colors, and long shelf life of winter squash make them a welcome arrival in autumn. Acorn, butternut, delicata, kabocha, and sugar pumpkin squash all contain beta-carotene and vitamin C, as well as potassium and fiber.

SUN-DRIED TOMATOES Once an exotic Italian specialty, sun-dried tomatoes are now sold widely in a variety of forms. To avoid the extra helping of fat in oil-packed versions, shop for dry-packed tomatoes, available leather-dry in plastic bags or tubs, or slightly moist in antiseptic vacuum packs. To reconstitute sun-dried tomatoes before use, place them in a bowl and add boiling water to cover. Let stand until softened, about 5 minutes, then drain.

TAHINI Simply toasted and hulled sesame seeds ground to a smooth paste, tahini is a traditional seasoning in Middle Eastern dishes such as hummus and baba ghanoush. Like nut butters, it is flavorful but fatty and is best used in small amounts.

TAPENADE The southern French condiment called tapenade (tah-pen-AHD) is always made with chopped or crushed black or green olives. A classic version also includes garlic, capers, anchovies, lemon juice, and olive oil blended in a mortar and pestle or food processor.

TOMATILLOS Sometimes called Mexican green tomatoes, tomatillos are firmer and less juicy than tomatoes and grow to ripeness inside a pale-green papery sheath. Used both raw and cooked, they are an essential sweet-sour ingredient in many Mexican green sauces. Look for fresh or canned tomatillos in well-stocked supermarkets or Latin groceries.

TORTILLAS Corn tortillas are full of the flavor of yellow corn kernels and are more healthful than those made with white flour. Flour tortillas are typically made with hydrogenated shortening, which can raise blood cholesterol; corn tortillas have half the calories and no fat beyond what's naturally in the corn.

TURBINADO SUGAR Pale brown or blond with coarse, dry crystals, turbinado sugar is a partially purified form of raw sugar, manufactured from the residue left when sugar cane is processed into granulated white sugar and molasses. Preferred for some recipes for its mild molasses flavor, it can be used interchangeably with granulated sugar in most dishes.

VANILLA Many cooks keep two kinds of vanilla on hand: whole vanilla beans, the aromatic, coffee-colored seed pods of a tropical orchid, and pure vanilla extract (essence), a dark liquid made by steeping the beans in alcohol. The beans, mainly from Madagascar, are expensive but more flavorful than the extract. To use vanilla beans, slit them lengthwise with a small, sharp knife and scrape out the tiny dark seeds. Add the seeds to desserts, cookie and pastry doughs, and sauces.

WALNUT OIL Pressed from walnuts that have been lightly toasted, walnut oil has a pleasing flavor like that of the nuts themselves. It is best used as a flavor enhancer, not a principal ingredient, in salads and side dishes, especially those containing toasted walnuts. Because walnut oil spoils readily, it should be purchased in small quantities and stored in the refrigerator.

WATERCRESS A peppery-flavored, small-leaved green in the cabbage family, watercress is a native of Europe that thrives in soil flooded with flowing water. It is sold in bunches that include many thick, tough stems that should be trimmed off and discarded. The thin stems and leaves are delicious in salads and soups and as a garnish. To store, fill a large jar partway with water, immerse the watercress stems in the jar, and cover the tops with a plastic bag. The greens will stay fresh for up to 5 days. Like all the other cruciferous vegetables, watercress contains compounds that may help prevent cancer.

WHEAT GERM Renowned as a healthy food, wheat germ is the grain's unsprouted green bud, or embryo, which is lost, along with the fiber-rich bran, during processing. It contains a big portion of the wheat seed's proteins, minerals, and vitamins, including vitamin E. Raw or toasted (both kinds are available), the germ has a crunchy texture and nutty flavor that's delicious in breads and cereals. Because of its oil, which can spoil, wheat germ should be bought in small quantities and stored in an airtight container in the refrigerator.

WHIPPED CREAM CHEESE Available in most supermarkets alongside regular cream cheese, this lighter version has the same ingredients but approximately two-thirds of the fat, cholesterol, and sodium per tablespoon.

WILD RICE Not a true rice variety, this flavorful grain is the seed of a type of native American grass harvested by hand in shallow lakes near the central border of the United States and Canada. Its grains are longer than those of long-grain rice and are darker, chewier, and more strongly flavored than brown rice. Wild rice is best when blended with milder grains.

YOGURT CHEESE Simply yogurt drained of its liquid whey, thick and creamy yogurt cheese is a handy homemade ingredient that can replace whipped cream, crème fraîche, and sour cream in many recipes. A few hours in cheesecloth (muslin) or a coffee filter renders this cheese from yogurt; use nonfat or low-fat versions, and be sure to start with yogurt made without gelatin, gums, or other thickeners, or it will not drain.

GENERAL INDEX

A
Activity, physical, 15
Aging, 14
Almonds
   milk, 288
   protein in, 20
Anchovies, 292
Antioxidants
   in fruits and vegetables, 11, 14, 285
   in whole grains, 16
Apples, 95
Artichokes, 292
Arugula, 292
Avocados, 20, 21, 292

B
Barley, 17, 292
Beans
   canned vs. dried, 198
   edamame, 211
   fiber in, 17
   haricots verts, 294
   protein in, 18
Beef, 18, 294
Bell peppers, roasting, 165
Beta-carotene, 14, 293, 297
Beta-glucan, 292
Beta-sitosterol, 14, 20, 292
Beverages, healthier, 23
Blood oranges, 292
Blood pressure, 18, 19
Blood sugar, 17
Bok choy, 292
Braising, 292
Broccoli, 14
Broth, canned, 139
Buckwheat, 158
Bulgur, 16, 292
Butter, 23
Buttermilk, 292

C
Cabbage, napa, 295
Calcium, 14, 18, 211, 293, 295
Calories
   empty, 12
   excess, 11
   goal for, 11
   physical activity and, 15
Cancer, 11, 14, 15, 16, 23, 292, 297
Canola oil, 20, 21, 23, 293
Capers, 292
Carbohydrates
   daily servings goals for, 11, 17
   kinds of, 16
   sources of, 16
Cauliflower, 14
Celery root, 66
Cellophane noodles, 292
Changes, healthy, 23
Cheese
   cream, whipped, 297
   mascarpone, 294
   Parmesan, 295
   queso asadero, 296
   yogurt, 297
Cherries, dried, 293
Chicken, 18, 294
Chickpeas, 198
Chiffonade, 293
Chile paste, 293
Chiles, 293
Chinese cabbage, 295
Cholesterol
   in eggs, 293
   LDL vs. HDL, 20, 21
   lowering, 14, 18, 20
   in shrimp, 296
Citrus fruits, 285
Coconut
   dried, 293
   milk, 293
Collard greens, 293
Cooking sprays, 293
Corn
   masa harina, 294
   oil, 21
   posole, 295
   tortillas, 297
Couscous, 293
Cream cheese, whipped, 297

D
Daily servings goals, 11, 12
Dairy products. *See also* Milk
   fats in, 20, 21
   protein in, 18, 19
Diabetes, 11, 17

E
Edamame, 211
Eggs
   cholesterol and, 293
   folding whites of, 293
Escarole, 293
Exercise, 15

F
Fats
   beneficial, 11, 20, 21
   daily servings goals for, 11, 20, 21
   harmful, 20, 21
   monounsaturated, 21
   polyunsaturated, 21
   saturated, 20, 21
   trans, 20, 21
Fennel, 293
Fiber
   benefits of, 17
   recommended amount of, 17
   sources of, 11, 14, 16, 17, 23, 95, 292, 294, 297
   types of, 17
Figs, 293–94
Fish
   anchovies, 292
   mercury in, 294
   omega-3 fatty acids in, 18, 21, 23, 234
   protein in, 18
   salmon, 234
   servings of, per week, 18, 23
   trout, 225
Fish sauce, 294
Flavonoids, 14
Flaxseed, 21, 294
Flour, whole-wheat, 176
Folate (folic acid), 18, 20, 293, 295
Food groups. *See* Mayo Clinic Healthy Weight Pyramid
Fruits. *See also individual fruits*
   benefits of, 11, 14, 23
   daily servings goals for, 11, 15, 23, 24
   for desserts, 23
   fiber in, 17

G
Ginger
   crystallized, 293
   fresh, 289
Glucose, 17
Glutathione, 292
Grains
   fiber in, 17
   whole vs. refined, 16
Grapes, 14

H
Ham, 294
Haricots verts, 294
Healthy Weight Pyramid. *See* Mayo Clinic Healthy Weight Pyramid
Heart disease
   blood pressure and, 19
   cholesterol and, 20, 21
   lowering risk of, 11, 14, 15, 95
   omega-3 fatty acids and, 18, 23
Herbs, 190
Hoisin sauce, 294
Hominy, 295
Hydrogenated oils, 21

I
Inactivity, 15
Iron, 199, 296

I
Julienne, 294
Juices, fruit, 14, 23

K

Kale, 54
Kidney stones, 18

L

Lamb, 18, 294, 296
Legumes, 18
Lemongrass, 294
Lemons, preserved, 296
Lentils, 18, 294
Lutein, 14
Lycopene, 14

M

Magnesium, 14
Margarine, 20, 23
Masa harina, 294
Mascarpone cheese, 294
Mayo Clinic Healthy Weight Pyramid
    benefits of, 11
    components of, 10
    daily servings goals in, 11, 12
    using, in menu planning, 24
Meats
    fats in, 20, 21, 294
    protein in, 18
    substitutes for, 18
Melons, 83
Menus
    planning, 24
    sample, 25–27
Mercury, 294
Milk
    almond, 288
    butter-, 292
    decreasing fat in, 23
    nutritional value of, 18
    soy, 296
Minerals, 14
Miso, 126
Mushrooms, 294–95

N

Napa cabbage, 295
Niacin, 20, 295
Noodles
    cellophane, 292
    soba, 296
Nutmeg, 295
Nutritional analysis, 13
Nuts
    fats in, 20, 21
    nutritional value of, 20
    toasting, 94

O

Oats, 17, 171
Oils, choosing, 20, 21, 23. *See also individual oils*
Olives
    oil, 20, 21, 23, 66, 293
    varieties of, 295

Omega-3 fatty acids, 18, 21, 23, 234, 294
Onions, 295
Oranges, 14, 292
Oyster sauce, 295

P

Parmesan cheese, 295
Parsley, 295
Pasta, 16. *See also* Noodles
Peanut butter, 20, 295
Peas, 18
Pectin, 95
Phytochemicals, 14
Pine nuts, 295
Pita, 295
Plantains, 295
Pocket bread, 295
Pork, 18, 294
Portion size, 13
Posole, 295
Potassium, 14, 295, 296, 297
Potatoes, 16, 295–96
Processed foods, 16, 19, 20
Protein
    daily servings goals for, 11, 19
    importance of, 18
    incomplete, 18
    sources of, 18

Q

Queso asadero, 296
Quiz, 22

R

Radicchio, 48
Resveratrol, 14
Riboflavin, 295
Rice, 16, 151
Rice paper rounds, 296
Rocket, 292
Roughage, 17

S

Saffron, 224
Salmon, 234
Salt, 19
Selenium, 20
Sesame oil, 296
Sesame seeds, 94, 296
Shallots, 296
Shellfish, 18
Shoyu, 296
Shrimp, 296
Soba noodles, 296
Sodium, 19, 296
Soybeans, 18, 21, 211
Soy milk, 296
Soy oil, 21
Soy sauce, 296
Spring roll wrappers, 296
Squash
    summer, 296

winter, 297
Starch, 16
Stock, 139
Strokes, 15, 18, 19, 21
Sugar, 16, 297
Sumac, 115
Sweet potatoes, 16
Sweets
    calories in, 12
    fruits replacing, 11, 12
Swiss chard, 37

T

Tahini, 297
Tapenade, 297
Thiamin, 20
Tofu, 21, 198
Tomatillos, 297
Tomatoes
    lycopene in, 14
    peeling and seeding, 127
    plum, 295
    sun-dried, 297
Tortillas, 297
Trans fats, 20, 21
Triglycerides, 18
Trout, 225
Turbinado sugar, 297
Turkey, 18
Turnip greens, 293

V

Vanilla, 297
Vegetables. *See also individual vegetables*
    benefits of, 11, 14
    cruciferous, 14, 292
    daily servings goals for, 11, 15, 23, 24
    fiber in, 17
Vegetarian meals, 18, 24
Vinegar, balsamic, 284
Vitamins
    A, 211
    B, 18, 151, 199, 211
    C, 14, 54, 285, 293, 295, 296, 297
    D, 18
    E, 16, 20, 292, 297

W

Walking, 15
Walnuts and walnut oil, 21, 297
Watercress, 297
Wheat germ, 297
Wild rice, 297

Y

Yogurt
    cheese, 297
    protein and calcium in, 18

Z

Zeaxanthin, 14
Zest, 285

RECIPE INDEX

A

Agua Fresca, Watermelon-Cranberry, 291
Almonds and almond milk
    Almond and Apricot Biscotti, 279
    Ambrosia with Coconut and Toasted
        Almonds, 90
    Baked Apples with Cherries and
        Almonds, 96
    Frosty Almond Date Shake, 288
    Muesli Breakfast Bars, 168
    Summer Fruit Gratin, 275
    Yogurt-Almond Ice Cream, 282
Ambrosia with Coconut and Toasted
    Almonds, 90
Apples
    Ambrosia with Coconut and Toasted
        Almonds, 90
    Apple and Sweet Onion Marmalade, 95
    Baked Apples with Cherries and
        Almonds, 96
    Muesli Breakfast Bars, 168
Apricots
    Almond and Apricot Biscotti, 279
    Apricot Coulis, 82
    Brown Rice Pilaf, 151
    Summer Fruit Gratin, 275
Artichokes alla Romana, 55
Asparagus with Hazelnut Gremolata, 50
Avocado
    Avocado Salad with Ginger-Miso
        Dressing, 114
    Avocado-Tomatillo Salsa, 154
    Mesclun Salad with Radishes,
        Avocado, and Blood Oranges, 106

B

Bananas
    Ambrosia with Coconut and Toasted
        Almonds, 90
    Banana-Oatmeal Hotcakes with Spiced
        Maple Syrup, 167
    Frosty Almond Date Shake, 288
    Sautéed Bananas with Caramel Sauce,
        79
    Tropical Fruits with Mint and Spices,
        80
Barley and Roasted Tomato Risotto, 159
Beans. *See also* Chickpeas; Soybeans
    Black Bean Burgers with Chipotle
        Ketchup, 194
    Black-Eyed Pea and Sweet Corn Salsa,
        183
    Cannellini Beans with Wilted Greens,
        193
    Caribbean Red Beans and Brown Rice,
        205
    Classic Boston Baked Beans, 213

    Fava Beans with Garlic, 186
    Green Beans with Red Pepper and
        Garlic, 33
    Grilled Flank Steak Salad with Roasted
        Corn Vinaigrette, 117
    Lima Bean Ragout with Tomatoes and
        Thyme, 190
    Red Bean Chilaquiles, 185
    Salade Niçoise with Tapenade, 226
    Stewed Flageolets in Lemon Broth, 196
    Three-Bean Chili, 204
    Tuscan White Bean Stew, 125
Beef
    Beef Stew with Fennel and Shallots, 264
    Grilled Flank Steak Salad with Roasted
        Corn Vinaigrette, 117
    Spicy Beef Kabobs, 252
Beets and Carrots, Baby, with Dill, 30
Bell peppers
    Creamy Polenta with Roasted Red
        Pepper Coulis, 165
    Fattoush, 115
    Green Beans with Red Pepper and
        Garlic, 33
    Ratatouille with Roasted Tomato
        Vinaigrette, 109
    Spaghetti with Summer Squash and
        Peppers, 147
    Three-Bean Chili, 204
Berries. *See also individual berries*
    Mixed Fresh Berries with Ginger Sauce, 75
    Nutty Berry Granola, 177
Biscotti, Almond and Apricot, 279
Biscuits, Whole-Grain Buttermilk, 170
Black-Eyed Pea and Sweet Corn Salsa, 183
Blueberries
    Blueberry Syrup, 174
    Fresh Blueberry Sauce, 270
    Nutty Berry Granola, 177
    Tropical Fruits with Mint and Spices, 80
Bok choy
    Chicken Adobo Soup with Bok Choy, 132
    Tofu Hoisin with Baby Bok Choy, 199
Bread. *See also* Pita bread; Sandwiches
    Caramelized Pear Bread Pudding, 276
    Croutons, 125
    Double-Corn Spoon Bread, 162
    Fresh Tomato Soup with Crispy Herb
        Toasts, 127
    Irish Brown Bread, 176
    Three-Grain Raspberry Muffins, 173
    Whole-Grain Buttermilk Biscuits, 170
Broccoli and Cauliflower, Sichuan, 42
Broccoli Rabe with Toasted Garlic, 70
Brussels Sprouts with Shallots and Lemon,
    66
Buckwheat Pilaf, Savory, with Toasted
    Spices, 158
Bulgur
    Bulgur and Chickpeas with Preserved-
        Lemon Vinaigrette, 156
    Spicy Beef Kabobs, 252

    Tabbouleh, 143
Burgers, Black Bean, with Chipotle
    Ketchup, 194

C

Cabbage
    Chicken Salad with Thai Flavors, 108
    Pork Medallions with Five-Spice Powder,
        265
    Warm Coleslaw with Honey Dressing, 102
Cakes
    Date-Walnut Cake with Warm Honey
        Sauce, 272
    Pumpkin-Hazelnut Tea Cake, 179
Cantaloupe. *See* Melons
Caramel Sauce, 79
Caribbean Red Beans and Brown Rice, 205
Carrots
    Baby Beets and Carrots with Dill, 30
    Curried Carrot Soup, 133
Cauliflower and Broccoli, Sichuan, 42
Celery Root, Braised, 67
Cherries
    Baked Apples with Cherries and
        Almonds, 96
    Summer Fruit Gratin, 275
Chicken
    Braised Chicken with Mushrooms and
        Pearl Onions, 254
    Chicken Adobo Soup with Bok Choy, 132
    Chicken and Portobello Baguette, 257
    Chicken Salad with Thai Flavors, 108
    Chicken Stir-Fry with Eggplant and
        Basil, 255
    Easy Chicken Stock, 138
    Gingery Chicken Noodle Soup, 130
    Grilled Chicken Breasts with Roasted
        Yellow Tomato Sauce, 260
Chickpeas
    Bulgur and Chickpeas with Preserved-
        Lemon Vinaigrette, 156
    Chickpea Hummus, 198
    Chickpea Polenta with Olives, 188
Chilaquiles, Red Bean, 185
Chiles
    Chipotle Ketchup, 194
    Corn Chowder with Roasted Poblanos, 122
Chili, Three-Bean, 204
Chipotle Ketchup, 194
Chive Cream, 129
Chocolate Soufflés, Warm, 269
Chutney, Pear and Toasted Pecan, 94
Cilantro-Cucumber Salsa, 238
Citrus Syrup, 76
Coconut, Ambrosia with Toasted Almonds
    and, 90
Coleslaw, Warm, with Honey Dressing, 102
Corn
    Black-Eyed Pea and Sweet Corn Salsa, 183
    Corn Chowder with Roasted Poblanos, 122
    Corn Tamales with Avocado-Tomatillo
        Salsa, 154

Double-Corn Spoon Bread, 162
Posole with Fresh Corn Gorditas, 135
Roasted Corn Vinaigrette, 117
Cornmeal
    Cornmeal-Crusted Sole with Chili
        Vinaigrette, 244
    Creamy Polenta with Roasted Red
        Pepper Coulis, 165
    Double-Corn Spoon Bread, 162
    Three-Grain Raspberry Muffins, 173
Couscous
    Chicken Adobo Soup with Bok Choy, 132
    Curried Vegetable Couscous, 164
Crab Cakes, Thai, 237
Cranberries
    Cranberry-Walnut Oatmeal, 171
    Nutty Berry Granola, 177
    Watermelon-Cranberry Agua Fresca, 291
Croutons, 125
Cucumbers
    Cilantro-Cucumber Salsa, 238
    Fattoush, 115
    Tabbouleh, 143
Custards, Lemon, with Fresh Blueberry
    Sauce, 270

D
Dates
    Date-Walnut Cake with Warm Honey
        Sauce, 272
    Frosty Almond Date Shake, 288
Drinks
    Frosty Almond Date Shake, 288
    Morning Mojito, 285
    Orange Dream, 286
    Sweet Ginger Tisane, 289
    Watermelon-Cranberry Agua Fresca, 291
Duck Breast, Roasted, with Lemongrass and
    Green Onion, 250

E
Edamame. See Soybeans
Eggplant
    Chicken Stir-Fry with Eggplant and
        Basil, 255
    Eggplant with Toasted Spices, 36
    Greek Salad, 111
    Ratatouille with Roasted Tomato
        Vinaigrette, 109
Eggs
    Lemon Custards with Fresh Blueberry
        Sauce, 270
    Spinach Frittata, 261
    Warm Chocolate Soufflés, 269

F
Farfalle with Fresh Tomato Sauce, 144
Fattoush, 115
Fennel
    Beef Stew with Fennel and Shallots, 264
    Fennel and Leeks with Roasted Onion
        Vinaigrette, 118

Soybeans with Fennel, Thyme, and
    Oregano, 208
Figs, Fresh, with Walnuts and Mascarpone,
    92
Fish. See also Salmon; Trout
    Cornmeal-Crusted Sole with Chili
        Vinaigrette, 244
    Grouper with Tomato-Olive Sauce, 231
    Mahimahi with Macadamia Nut Crust,
        219
    Moroccan Fish Tagine, 216
    Pan-Braised Swordfish with Feta, 243
    Roasted Red Snapper, 240
    Salade Niçoise with Tapenade, 226
    Sea Bass en Papillote, 224
    Swordfish Tacos with Lime and Cilantro,
        241
Fool, Melon, 85
French Green Lentil Salad, 191
Frittata, Spinach, 261
Fruits. See also individual fruits
    Ambrosia with Coconut and Toasted
        Almonds, 90
    Summer Fruit Gratin, 275
    Tropical Fruits with Mint and Spices, 80

G
Ginger
    Ginger-Miso Dressing, 114
    Ginger Sauce, 75
    Sweet Ginger Tisane, 289
Granola, Nutty Berry, 177
Greek Salad, 111
Greens. See also individual greens
    Cannellini Beans with Wilted Greens, 193
    Mesclun Salad with Radishes, Avocado,
        and Blood Oranges, 106
    Seared Scallops with New Potatoes and
        Field Greens, 100
    Wilted Greens with Warm Balsamic
        Vinegar, 34
Grouper with Tomato-Olive Sauce, 231

H
Honeydew melons. See Melons
Hummus, Chickpea, 198

I
Ice Cream, Yogurt-Almond, 282
Irish Brown Bread, 176

J
Jamaican Barbecued Pork Tenderloin, 259

K
Kabobs, Spicy Beef, 252
Kale, Braised, with Cherry Tomatoes, 54
Ketchup, Chipotle, 194

L
Lamb, Roasted Rack of, with Parsley Crust,
    262

Lasagne, Spinach, with Sun-Dried Tomato
    Sauce, 153
Leeks
    Fennel and Leeks with Roasted Onion
        Vinaigrette, 118
    Steamed Summer Squash with Warm
        Leek Vinaigrette, 63
Lemons
    Lemon Custards with Fresh Blueberry
        Sauce, 270
    Preserved-Lemon Vinaigrette, 156
    Sweet Ginger Tisane, 289
Lentils
    French Green Lentil Salad, 191
    Lentils with Wild Rice and Crispy
        Onions, 207
    Spicy Red Lentils, 210
    Yellow Lentils with Spinach and Ginger,
        203
Linguine with Mushrooms, 150

M
Mahimahi with Macadamia Nut Crust, 219
Mangoes
    Shrimp and Mango Curry, 220
    Tropical Fruits with Mint and Spices, 80
Marmalade, Apple and Sweet Onion, 95
Melons
    Casaba Melon with Sweet Curry Cream,
        83
    Melon Fool, 85
    Tropical Fruits with Mint and Spices, 80
    Watermelon-Cranberry Agua Fresca,
        291
Mesclun Salad with Radishes, Avocado, and
    Blood Oranges, 106
Miso Soup with Watercress and Shiitakes, 126
Morning Mojito, 285
Moroccan Fish Tagine, 216
Muesli Breakfast Bars, 168
Muffins, Three-Grain Raspberry, 173
Mushrooms
    Beef Stew with Fennel and Shallots, 264
    Braised Chicken with Mushrooms and
        Pearl Onions, 254
    Chicken and Portobello Baguette, 257
    Grilled Portobello Mushrooms with
        Thyme and Garlic, 40
    Linguine with Mushrooms, 150
    Miso Soup with Watercress and
        Shiitakes, 126
    Quinoa Risotto with Arugula and
        Parmesan, 148
    Spinach Lasagne with Sun-Dried Tomato
        Sauce, 153
Mussels Marinière, 222

N
Nectarines
    Peach-Nectarine Salsa, 86
    Summer Fruit Gratin, 275
Noodles. See Pasta and noodles

O

Oats
  Banana-Oatmeal Hotcakes with Spiced
    Maple Syrup, 167
  Cranberry-Walnut Oatmeal, 171
  Date-Walnut Cake with Warm Honey
    Sauce, 272
  Muesli Breakfast Bars, 168
  Nutty Berry Granola, 177
  Three-Grain Raspberry Muffins, 173
Olives
  Chickpea Polenta with Olives, 188
  Pita Wedges with Green Olive Tapenade,
    52
  Prawns Puttanesca, 235
  Salade Niçoise with Tapenade, 226
Onions
  Apple and Sweet Onion Marmalade, 95
  Braised Chicken with Mushrooms and
    Pearl Onions, 254
  Lentils with Wild Rice and Crispy
    Onions, 207
  Pan-Braised Onions with Rosemary, 69
  Roasted Onion Vinaigrette, 118
  Tomato and Red Onion Relish, 232
Oranges
  Ambrosia with Coconut and Toasted
    Almonds, 90
  Ginger Sauce, 75
  Mesclun Salad with Radishes, Avocado,
    and Blood Oranges, 106
  Morning Mojito, 285
  Orange Dream, 286
  Orange Slices with Citrus Syrup, 76
  Tropical Fruits with Mint and Spices, 80
Orzo with Cherry Tomatoes, Capers, and
  Lemon, 161

P

Pancakes
  Banana-Oatmeal Hotcakes with Spiced
    Maple Syrup, 167
Pasta and noodles. See also Couscous
  Farfalle with Fresh Tomato Sauce, 144
  Gingery Chicken Noodle Soup, 130
  Linguine with Mushrooms, 150
  Orzo with Cherry Tomatoes, Capers, and
    Lemon, 161
  Spaghetti with Summer Squash and
    Peppers, 147
  Spinach Lasagne with Sun-Dried Tomato
    Sauce, 153
Peaches
  Peach Coulis, 82
  Peach-Nectarine Salsa, 86
  Summer Fruit Gratin, 275
Pears
  Caramelized Pear Bread Pudding, 276
  Grilled Pear and Watercress Salad, 105
  Pear and Toasted Pecan Chutney, 94
Peas
  Garden Peas with Fresh Mint, 57

Split Pea Soup, 129
Sugar Snap Peas with Fresh Marjoram,
  61
Pecans
  Muesli Breakfast Bars, 168
  Pear and Toasted Pecan Chutney, 94
Pineapple
  Ambrosia with Coconut and Toasted
    Almonds, 90
  Grilled Pineapple, 89
Pita bread
  Fattoush, 115
  Pita Wedges with Green Olive Tapenade,
    52
Plantain and Butternut Squash Mash, 45
Plum Tart, Red, 280
Polenta
  Chickpea Polenta with Olives, 188
  Creamy Polenta with Roasted Red
    Pepper Coulis, 165
Pork
  Jamaican Barbecued Pork Tenderloin,
    259
  Pork Medallions with Five-Spice Powder,
    265
  Posole with Fresh Corn Gorditas, 135
Posole with Fresh Corn Gorditas, 135
Potatoes
  Corn Chowder with Roasted Poblanos,
    122
  Salade Niçoise with Tapenade, 226
  Seared Scallops with New Potatoes and
    Field Greens, 100
  Spinach Frittata, 261
  Two-Potato Gratin, 64
  Warm Potato Salad, 39
Potpie, Turkey, with Baby Vegetables, 249
Prawns. See Shrimp and prawns
Pudding, Caramelized Pear Bread, 276
Pumpkin-Hazelnut Tea Cake, 179

Q

Quinoa Risotto with Arugula and
  Parmesan, 148

R

Radicchio, Grilled, 48
Radishes, Mesclun Salad with Avocado,
  Blood Oranges, and, 106
Raspberries
  Mixed Fresh Berries with Ginger Sauce,
    75
  Raspberry Coulis, 82
  Three-Grain Raspberry Muffins, 173
  Tropical Fruits with Mint and Spices, 80
  Warm Chocolate Soufflés, 269
Ratatouille, with Roasted Tomato
  Vinaigrette, 109
Red snapper
  Moroccan Fish Tagine, 216
  Roasted Red Snapper, 240
Relish, Tomato and Red Onion, 232

Rice
  Brown Rice Pilaf, 151
  Caribbean Red Beans and Brown Rice, 205
  Chicken Adobo Soup with Bok Choy, 132
  Thai Crab Cakes, 237

S

Salads
  Avocado Salad with Ginger-Miso
    Dressing, 114
  Bulgur and Chickpeas with Preserved-
    Lemon Vinaigrette, 156
  Chicken Salad with Thai Flavors, 108
  Edamame and Summer Bean Salad, 211
  Fattoush, 115
  Fennel and Leeks with Roasted Onion
    Vinaigrette, 118
  French Green Lentil Salad, 191
  Greek Salad, 111
  Grilled Flank Steak Salad with Roasted
    Corn Vinaigrette, 117
  Grilled Pear and Watercress Salad, 105
  Mesclun Salad with Radishes, Avocado,
    and Blood Oranges, 106
  Ratatouille with Roasted Tomato
    Vinaigrette, 109
  Salade Niçoise with Tapenade, 226
  Seared Scallops with New Potatoes and
    Field Greens, 100
  Tabbouleh, 143
  Warm Coleslaw with Honey Dressing, 102
  Warm Potato Salad, 39
  Yellow Pear and Cherry Tomato Salad, 112
Salmon
  Grilled Miso Salmon, 234
  Seared Salmon with Cilantro-Cucumber
    Salsa, 238
Salsas
  Avocado-Tomatillo Salsa, 154
  Black-Eyed Pea and Sweet Corn Salsa, 183
  Cilantro-Cucumber Salsa, 238
  Peach-Nectarine Salsa, 86
Sandwiches
  Black Bean Burgers with Chipotle
    Ketchup, 194
  Chicken and Portobello Baguette, 257
Sauces
  Apricot Coulis, 82
  Caramel Sauce, 79
  Chive Cream, 129
  Fresh Blueberry Sauce, 270
  Fresh Tomato Sauce, 144
  Ginger Sauce, 75
  Peach Coulis, 82
  Raspberry Coulis, 82
  Roasted Red Pepper Coulis, 165
  Roasted Yellow Tomato Sauce, 260
  Sun-Dried Tomato Sauce, 153
  Sweet Curry Cream, 83
  Tomato Sauce, 207
  Warm Honey Sauce, 272
Scallops, Seared, with New Potatoes and

Field Greens, 100
Sea bass
    Moroccan Fish Tagine, 216
    Sea Bass en Papillote, 224
Sesame-Crusted Tofu, 201
Shake, Frosty Almond Date, 288
Shrimp and prawns
    Fresh Spring Rolls with Shrimp, 229
    Prawns Puttanesca, 235
    Shrimp and Mango Curry, 220
Sichuan Broccoli and Cauliflower, 42
Sole, Cornmeal-Crusted, with Chili
    Vinaigrette, 244
Sorbet, Strawberry Balsamic, 284
Soufflés, Warm Chocolate, 269
Soups
    Chicken Adobo Soup with Bok Choy, 132
    Corn Chowder with Roasted Poblanos,
      122
    Curried Carrot Soup, 133
    Fresh Tomato Soup with Crispy Herb
      Toasts, 127
    Gingery Chicken Noodle Soup, 130
    Miso Soup with Watercress and
      Shiitakes, 126
    Posole with Fresh Corn Gorditas, 135
    Split Pea Soup, 129
    Summer Vegetable Soup, 136
Soybeans
    Edamame and Summer Bean Salad, 211
    Gingery Chicken Noodle Soup, 130
    Shrimp and Mango Curry, 220
    Soybeans with Fennel, Thyme, and
      Oregano, 208
Spaghetti with Summer Squash and
    Peppers, 147
Spinach
    Chicken Salad with Thai Flavors, 108
    Greek Salad, 111
    Spinach Frittata, 261
    Spinach Lasagne with Sun-Dried Tomato
      Sauce, 153
    Yellow Lentils with Spinach and Ginger,
      203
Spoon Bread, Double-Corn, 162
Spreads
    Chickpea Hummus, 198
    Smoked Trout Spread, 225
Spring Rolls, Fresh, with Shrimp, 229
Squash
    Baked Acorn Squash with Pine Nuts and
      Garlic, 58
    Butternut Squash and Plantain Mash, 45
    Ratatouille with Roasted Tomato
      Vinaigrette, 109
    Spaghetti with Summer Squash and
      Peppers, 147
    Steamed Summer Squash with Warm
      Leek Vinaigrette, 63
    Summer Vegetable Soup, 136
Stews
    Beef Stew with Fennel and Shallots, 264

Moroccan Fish Tagine, 216
Tuscan White Bean Stew, 125
Stocks
    Easy Chicken Stock, 138
    Easy Vegetable Stock, 139
Strawberries
    Mixed Fresh Berries with Ginger Sauce, 75
    Strawberry Balsamic Sorbet, 284
Summer Fruit Gratin, 275
Summer Vegetable Soup, 136
Sweet potatoes
    Roasted Root Vegetables with Cumin
      and Coriander, 47
    Sweet-Potato Waffles with Blueberry
      Syrup, 174
    Two-Potato Gratin, 64
Swiss Chard, Creamed, 37
Swordfish
    Pan-Braised Swordfish with Feta, 243
    Swordfish Tacos with Lime and Cilantro,
      241
Syrups
    Blueberry Syrup, 174
    Citrus Syrup, 76
    Spiced Maple Syrup, 167

T
Tabbouleh, 143
Tacos, Swordfish, with Lime and Cilantro,
    241
Tagine, Moroccan Fish, 216
Tamales, Corn, with Avocado-Tomatillo
    Salsa, 154
Tapenade
    Pita Wedges with Green Olive Tapenade,
      52
    Salade Niçoise with Tapenade, 226
Tart, Red Plum, 280
Thai Crab Cakes, 237
Tisane, Sweet Ginger, 289
Tofu
    Ginger-Miso Dressing, 114
    Lemon Custards with Fresh Blueberry
      Sauce, 270
    Miso Soup with Watercress and
      Shiitakes, 126
    Orange Dream, 286
    Seared Scallops with New Potatoes and
      Field Greens, 100
    Sesame-Crusted Tofu, 201
    Tofu Hoisin with Baby Bok Choy, 199
Tomatillo-Avocado Salsa, 154
Tomatoes
    Barley and Roasted Tomato Risotto, 159
    Braised Kale with Cherry Tomatoes, 54
    Chipotle Ketchup, 194
    Cilantro-Cucumber Salsa, 238
    Eggplant with Toasted Spices, 36
    Fattoush, 115
    Fresh Tomato Sauce, 144
    Fresh Tomato Soup with Crispy Herb
      Toasts, 127

Grilled Flank Steak Salad with Roasted
    Corn Vinaigrette, 117
Grouper with Tomato-Olive Sauce, 231
Lima Bean Ragout with Tomatoes and
    Thyme, 190
Miso Soup with Watercress and
    Shiitakes, 126
Orzo with Cherry Tomatoes, Capers, and
    Lemon, 161
Prawns Puttanesca, 235
Ratatouille with Roasted Tomato
    Vinaigrette, 109
Red Bean Chilaquiles, 185
Roasted Yellow Tomato Sauce, 260
Summer Vegetable Soup, 136
Sun-Dried Tomato Sauce, 153
Tabbouleh, 143
Three-Bean Chili, 204
Tomato and Red Onion Relish, 232
Tomato Sauce, 207
Yellow Pear and Cherry Tomato Salad, 112
Tortillas
    Red Bean Chilaquiles, 185
    Swordfish Tacos with Lime and Cilantro,
      241
Trout
    Broiled Trout with Tomato and Red
      Onion Relish, 232
    Smoked Trout Spread, 225
Turkey Potpie with Baby Vegetables, 249
Tuscan White Bean Stew, 125

V
Vegetables. *See also individual vegetables*
    Curried Vegetable Couscous, 164
    Easy Vegetable Stock, 139
    Ratatouille with Roasted Tomato
      Vinaigrette, 109
    Roasted Root Vegetables with Cumin
      and Coriander, 47
    Summer Vegetable Soup, 136
    Turkey Potpie with Baby Vegetables, 249

W
Waffles, Sweet-Potato, with Blueberry
    Syrup, 174
Watercress
    Grilled Pear and Watercress Salad, 105
    Miso Soup with Watercress and
      Shiitakes, 126
Watermelon-Cranberry Agua Fresca, 291
Wild Rice, Lentils with Crispy Onions and,
    207

Y
Yogurt
    Melon Fool, 85
    Sweet Curry Cream, 83
    Yogurt-Almond Ice Cream, 282

Z
Zucchini. *See* Squash

THE NEW MAYO CLINIC COOKBOOK
Conceived and produced by
WELDON OWEN INC.
415 Jackson Street, San Francisco, CA 94111
Telephone: 415-291-0100 Fax: 415-291-8841
and
MAYO CLINIC HEALTH INFORMATION
200 First Street, SW
Rochester, MN 55905

WELDON OWEN INC.
Group Publisher, Bonnier Publishing Group: John Owen
CEO, President: Terry Newell
Senior VP, International Sales: Stuart Laurence
VP, Sales and New Business Development: Amy Kaneko
Managing Editor: Sheridan Warrick
Designer and Photography Director: Julia Flagg
Contributing Writer: Peter Jaret
Copy Editors: Carrie Bradley, Sharon Silva
Production Director: Chris Hemesath
Production Manager: Michelle Duggan
Color Manager: Teri Bell
Proofreader: Desne Ahlers
Indexer: Ken DellaPenta
Food Stylist: Dan Becker
Prop Stylist: Leigh Noë

MAYO CLINIC
Co-editors: Donald Hensrud, M.D.; Jennifer Nelson, R.D.
Editor in Chief, Books and Newsletters: Christopher Frye
Contributing Editor: Nicole Spelhaug
Product Marketing Manager: Rebecca Roberts

A WELDON OWEN PRODUCTION
Copyright © 2004 Weldon Owen Inc.
Editorial Content Copyright © 2004 Mayo Foundation
for Medical Education and Research

This edition first printed in 2009.

10 9 8 7 6 5 4

ISBN 10: 1-74089-972-5
ISBN 13: 978-1-74089-972-7

Printed in China by 1010 Printing International LTD.

ACKNOWLEDGMENTS
Special thanks to Kyrie Forbes, Joan Olson,
Guarina Lopez, Jessica Giblin, and Catherine Jacobes
for their creative contribution and valuable assistance.

A NOTE ON WEIGHTS AND MEASURES
All recipes include customary U.S. and metric measurements. Metric conversions are based on
a standard developed for this book and have been rounded off. Actual weights may vary.